MCSE

TESTPREP

TCP/IP

Que

MCSE TestPrep: TCP/IP

For Spencer

Emmett Dulaney

Published by:
Que Publishing
201 West 103rd Street
Indianapolis, IN 46290 USA

International Standard Book Number: 1-56205-843-6

Library of Congress Catalog Card Number: 98-84018

01 00 99 98   4 3 2 1

Interpretation of the printing code: the rightmost double-digit number is the year of the book's printing; the rightmost single-digit, the number of the book's printing. For example, a printing code of 98-1 shows that the first printing of the book occurred in 1998.

Composed in AGaramond and MCPdigital by Macmillan Computer Publishing

Printed in the United States of America

President *Richard K. Swadley*

Publisher *Don Fowley*

Associate Publisher *David Dwyer*

Executive Editor *John Kane*

Managing Editor *Sarah Kearns*

Indexing Manager *Ginny Bess*

Acquisitions Editor
Steve Weiss

Development Editor
Howard Jones

Project Editor
Kate Shoup Welsh

Copy Editor
June Waldman

Indexer
Sandy Henselmeier

Technical Reviewer
Rob Scrimger
Dinesh Vadhia

Editorial Coordinator
Mandie Rowell

Resource Coordinator
Deborah Frisby

Editorial Assistants
Stacey Beheler
Jen Chisholm

Cover Designer
Jay Corpus

Book Designer
Glenn Larsen

Copy Writer
David Reichwein

Production Team Supervisor
Vic Peterson

Production
Laura A. Knox
Angela Perry
Megan Wade

About the Author

Emmett Dulaney is the "Certification Corner" columnist for *NT Systems Magazine*. An MCP, MCSE, CNE, and LAN Server Engineer, Emmett also is an instructor for DataTech, and is the author of the upcoming *MCSE Training Guide: IIS 4.0*, from New Riders Publishing. He can be reached at edulaney@iquest.net.

Acknowledgments

I would like to thank Steve Weiss for his devotion to this project, Rob Scrimger for his helpful knowledge, and Howard Jones for his insight.

Contents at a Glance

Table of Contents

Tell Us What You Think!

As a reader, you are the most important critic on and commentator of our books. We value your opinion and want to know what we're doing right, what we could do better, what areas you'd like to see us publish in, and any other words of wisdom you're willing to pass our way. You can help us make strong books that meet your needs and give you the computer guidance you require.

Do you have access to the World Wide Web? Then check out our site at http://www.mcp.com.

> **If you have a technical question about this book, call the technical support line at 317-581-3833 or send email to** support@mcp.com.

As the executive editor of the group that created this book, I welcome your comments. You can fax, email, or write me directly to let me know what you did or didn't like about this book—as well as what we can do to make our books stronger. Here's the information:

Fax: 317-581-4663

Email: jkane@mcp.com

Mail: John Kane
          Executive Editor
          Macmillan Computer Publishing
          201 W. 103rd Street
          Indianapolis, IN 46290

Introduction

The *MCSE TestPrep* series is written as a study aid for people preparing for Microsoft certification exams. The series is intended to help reinforce and clarify information with which the student is already familiar. This series is not intended to be a single source for student preparation, but rather a review of information and a set of practice tests to help increase the likelihood of success when taking the actual exam.

Who Should Read This Book

The TCP/IP book in the *MCSE TestPrep* series is intended specifically for students preparing for Microsoft's *Internetworking with Microsoft TCP/IP on Microsoft Windows NT 4.0* (70–59) exam, which is one of the electives in the MCSE program.

How This Book Helps You

In addition to presenting a summary of information relevant to each of the exam objectives, this book provides a wealth of review questions similar to those you will encounter in the actual exam. This book is designed to help you make the most of your study time by presenting concise summaries of information that you need to understand to succeed on the exam. The practice problems at the end of each objective help reinforce what you have learned. Each answer is explained in detail in the answers and explanations section following the practice problems. Also, key words are noted for that section. The practice exam at the conclusion of some chapters will help you determine whether you have mastered the facts. In addition, the book contains four full-length practice exams.

How to Use This Book

When you feel like you're fairly well prepared for the exam, use this book as a test of your knowledge. After you have taken the practice tests and feel confident in the material on which you were tested, you are ready to schedule your exam. Use this book for a final quick review just before taking the test to make sure that all the important concepts are set in your mind.

What the TCP/IP Exam (70–59) Covers

The *Internetworking with Microsoft TCP/IP on Microsoft Windows NT 4.0* certification exam measures your ability to implement, administer, and troubleshoot computer systems running TCP/IP. It focuses on determining your skill level in five major categories:

- Planning
- Installation and Configuration
- Connectivity
- Monitoring and Optimization
- Troubleshooting

The *Internetworking with Microsoft TCP/IP on Microsoft Windows NT 4.0* certification exam uses these categories to measure your ability. Before taking this exam, you should be proficient in the job skills discussed in the following sections.

Planning

The Planning section is designed to ensure that you understand the hardware requirements of TCP/IP as well as the capabilities and limitations of the protocol. The knowledge needed here also requires understanding of general networking concepts.

Objective for Planning

- Given a scenario, identify valid network configurations.

Installation and Configuration

The Installation and Configuration part of the TCP/IP exam is the meat of the exam. You are tested on virtually every possible component of the protocol.

Objectives for Installation and Configuration

- Given a scenario, select the appropriate services to install when using Microsoft TCP/IP on a Microsoft Windows NT Server computer.
- On a Windows NT Server computer, configure Microsoft TCP/IP to support multiple network adapters.
- Configure scopes by using DHCP Manager.
- Install and configure a WINS server.
- Import LMHOSTS files to WINS.
- Run WINS on a multihomed computer.
- Configure WINS replication.
- Configure static mappings in the WINS database.
- Configure subnet masks.
- Configure a Windows NT Server computer to function as an IP router.
- Install and configure the DHCP Relay Agent.
- Install and configure the Microsoft DNS Server service on a Windows NT Server computer.
- Integrate DNS with other name servers.
- Connect a DNS server to a DNS root server.

- Configure DNS server roles.

- Configure HOSTS and LMHOSTS files.

- Configure a Windows NT Server computer to support TCP/IP printing.

- Configure SNMP.

Connectivity

The Connectivity component of the *Internetworking with Microsoft TCP/IP on Microsoft Windows NT 4.0* certification exam concentrates on how to use the various interconnecting components of TCP/IP.

Objectives for Connectivity

- Given a scenario, identify which utility to use to connect to a TCP/IP-based UNIX host.

- Configure a RAS server and Dial-Up Networking for use on a TCP/IP network.

- Configure and support browsing in a multiple-domain routed network.

Monitoring and Optimization

The Monitoring and Optimization component of the *Internetworking with Microsoft TCP/IP on Microsoft Windows NT 4.0* certification exam has only one objective.

Objective for Monitoring and Optimization

- Given a scenario, identify which tool to use to monitor TCP/IP traffic.

Troubleshooting

The Troubleshooting component of the *Internetworking with Microsoft TCP/IP on Microsoft Windows NT 4.0* certification exam has four components, running the entire gamut of troubleshooting.

Objectives for Troubleshooting

- Diagnose and resolve IP addressing problems.

- Use Microsoft TCP/IP utilities to diagnose configuration problems.

- Identify which Microsoft TCP/IP utility to use to diagnose IP configuration problems.

- Diagnose and resolve name resolution problems.

Hardware and Software Recommended for Preparation

The *MCSE TestPrep: TCP/IP* is meant to help you review concepts with which you already have training and hands-on experience. To make the most of the review, you need as much background and experience as possible. The best way to do this is to combine studying with working on real networks using the products on which you will be tested. This section gives you a description of the minimum computer requirements you will need to build a solid practice environment.

Computers

The minimum computer requirements to ensure that you can study everything on which you'll be tested are one or more workstations running Windows 95 or NT Workstation and two or more servers running Windows NT Server, all connected by a network.

Workstations: Windows 95 and Windows NT

- Computer on the Microsoft Hardware Compatibility list
- 486DX 33MHz
- 16MB of RAM
- 200MB hard disk
- 3.5-inch 1.44MB floppy drive
- VGA video adapter
- VGA monitor
- Mouse or equivalent pointing device
- Two-speed CD-ROM drive
- Network Interface Card (NIC)
- Presence on an existing network, or use of a hub to create a test network
- Microsoft Windows 95 or NT Workstation 4.0

Servers: Windows NT Server

- Two computers on the Microsoft Hardware Compatibility list
- 486DX2 66MHz
- 32MB of RAM
- 340MB hard disk
- 3.5-inch 1.44MB floppy drive
- VGA video adapter
- VGA monitor
- Mouse or equivalent pointing device
- Two-speed CD-ROM drive
- Network Interface Card (NIC)
- Presence on an existing network, or use of a hub to create a test network
- Microsoft Windows NT Server 4.0

## CHAPTER 1

Planning

This chapter helps you prepare for the exam by covering the following objective:

- Given a scenario, identify valid network configurations

1.1   Introduction

Operating systems, networks, and protocols are designed with a particular framework, or architecture, in mind. Although they may vary from vendor to vendor, this fundamental architecture defines how all the components of a machine, operating system, and protocol fit together.

All computers in a network environment rely on network protocols to enable them to communicate with one another. Network protocols are designed and written to fit into the overall computing framework, or architecture, of the operating system running on a machine. Defining how these protocols are developed has always been important, and after operating systems such as Microsoft Windows NT began to support multiple protocols running on a machine at the same time, having a clear idea of how various protocols function in relation to the operating system, and with each other, became even more critical.

Without an understanding of networks in general, an appreciation of how TCP/IP works is much more difficult to reach.

1.2   Introductory Concepts—Network Basics

The subjects covered in this section represent the basic knowledge required to understand the architecture of TCP/IP. This section on network basics reviews basic network concepts and provides the larger picture within which the TCP/IP architecture comes together.

1.2.1   The Components of a Network

Put simply, a network is a collection of machines that have been linked together both physically and through software components to facilitate communication and sharing of information among them.

Unless you plan to run a wireless network, the first requirement for a network is a physical connection between machines for transferring data back and forth. A number of communication methods can be used to establish a physical connection: 10BASE-T Ethernet, 10BASE2 Ethernet, token ring, FDDI, and others. Each connection type has pros and cons in terms of ease of installation, maintenance, and expense. Table 1.1 summarizes the features of each type of media as a means to connect computers.

Table 1.2.1   Network Connection Types

Connection Type	Installation	Maintenance	Expense	Notes
10BASE2 coaxial cable	Easy	Easy	Cheap	Traffic seen by all machines on a coax segment
10BASE-T unshielded twisted pair	Moderately easy	Easy	Moderately inexpensive	Traffic can be easily isolated
Token ring	Moderately difficult	Difficult	Expensive	Traffic isolated, large data throughput
FDDI (Fiber)	Difficult	Difficult	Very expensive	Immune to electrical disturbances, very large data throughput

The second requirement for a network is appropriate hardware, such as a network card in the machine that acts as the machine's interface to the network. The hardware provides the connection the machine needs to communicate with other machines across the wire. Physical networks can have different connection methods, depending on what has been installed. For example, if the physical network consists of coaxial cable, a BNC connector attaches the machines to the network; on the other hand, if the physical network uses unshielded twisted-pair cabling, RJ-45 connectors connect the machines to the network. Connecting an unshielded twisted-pair network card to a network that uses coaxial cable, and vice versa, is very difficult. Although you can purchase conversion devices and intermediary pieces to handle this kind of mixing, you're generally better off buying a network card that supports your physical media inherently. This approach prevents an additional source of error when troubleshooting network connection problems.

Some network cards support multiple connection types for easy implementation. Naturally, a network card in the machine requires machine resources, including interrupts and memory addresses. These features need to be available for the network card to function.

Your third requirement in setting up a network is to install a network protocol. A network protocol is software installed on a machine that determines the agreed-upon set of rules for two or more machines to communicate with each other. One way to describe different protocols is to compare them to human languages.

Think of a group of people in the same room who know nothing about each other. In order for them to communicate, this group has to determine which language to speak, how to handle identifying each other, whether to make general announcements or to have private conversations, and so on. A situation in which machines are using different protocols is equivalent to a conversation in which one person is speaking French and another person is speaking Spanish. Machines that have different protocols installed are not able to communicate with each other. Common protocols in the Microsoft family include NetBEUI (NetBIOS frame), NWLink (the NDIS-compliant version of Novell's IPX/SPX), Data Link Control (DLC), AppleTalk File Protocol (AFP), and Transmission Control Protocol/Internet Protocol (TCP/IP).

The fourth and final key to the networking equation is an operating system that is network aware. Examples of operating systems that are network aware include Windows NT, Windows 95, Windows for Workgroups, DOS (with additional drivers loaded), UNIX, and Novell. Most operating systems are network aware, but until now almost all applications were written to ask for local resources (hard drives) on the machine. Applications have only recently become fully network aware and still generally use local drives to access resources.

Because applications still use local drives, the operating system must be able to redirect (thus the name of *redirector*) local resource requests to other machines on the network.

1.2.2 The Physical Address

As long as the four criteria discussed in the preceding section are met, creating a network is relatively simple. All you need now is some way to distinguish machine A from machine B in a way the network cards can understand. This job falls to the *physical address,* the unique identifier assigned to a network card. This unique identifier is often referred to as the MAC address, the hardware address, or the Ethernet address, but all these terms represent the same thing. For simplicity, this chapter refers to this unique identifier as the physical address.

A physical address is a 48-bit address represented by six sections of two hexadecimal values, for example 00-C0-DF-48-6F-13. It is assigned by the manufacturer of the network card before it is shipped from the factory. This unique identifier is often used to help identify a single machine on a network. At this level of the networking model, the physical layer, data being passed over the network appears to be nothing more than the transmission and error checking of voltage (ones and zeroes) on the wire. These ones and zeroes are transmitted in groups of a certain sequence based on the type of network in use. This sequence is referred to as a *frame*. Within the frame, various pieces of information can be deciphered. The first active component to receive and process the voltage being transmitted onto the network is the network card.

The network card is responsible for determining whether the voltage is intended for it or some other machine. Each network card has a set of rules that it must obey. First, it listens to the preamble to synchronize itself so it can determine where the data within the frame begins. After it determines where the data begins, it discards both the preamble and the frame check sequence before continuing to the next process. In the second process, the network card deciphers the data to determine the physical address of the frame's destination. If the destination address matches the physical address of the network card, it continues to process the information and pass the remaining data on for further action. If the destination address specifies some other machine's physical address, the network card silently discards the data within the frame and starts listening for other messages.

Determining the physical address of a machine running Windows NT 4.0 is relatively easy. Complete the following steps:

1.   From the Start menu, select Programs | Command Prompt.

2.   After the command prompt window appears, type IPCONFIG /all.

3.   Read the information provided by the IPCONFIG utility until you see a section called "Ethernet Address." The value represented is the physical address of the machine.

If a network card discards the preamble and determines that the destination physical address is a broadcast, the message is intended for all machines connected on that network segment. Whenever a network card receives a broadcast, it assumes that the data is relevant and passes the data to the rest of the system for further processing. Network protocols such as NetBEUI use broadcasts to begin communication with a single machine on the network, requiring all machines on the network segment to listen, process the frame, and allow higher layers in the networking model to discard the information. Network protocols such as TCP/IP, although capable of broadcasting, typically determine the specific physical address of the destination machine, eliminating a great deal of broadcast traffic.

Saying that TCP/IP does not use any broadcasts to communicate would be unfair, but in general, machines on a network using NetBEUI spend more time deciphering broadcast traffic than do machines on a TCP/IP network. This situation occurs primarily because NetBEUI is optimized for use on a local area network (LAN) where bandwidth (or the amount of sustainable data transfer rate) and resources are plentiful. NetBEUI is also extremely easy to install and configure and requires almost no ongoing intervention on behalf of the user. Its only significant weakness is that it is not a routable protocol, meaning that it has no addressing characteristics that allow packets to be moved from one logical network to another.

TCP/IP, on the other hand, is designed for wide area network (WAN) environments where routers are the common connection method between two locations. Because of its routability and almost surgical (precise and efficient) use of bandwidth resources, TCP/IP is clearly the favorite for this type of environment. However, TCP/IP does require significant expertise and experience on the users' part to install and configure it correctly, which is probably why Microsoft deems it necessary to test users' and administrators' knowledge of this protocol (that is, Microsoft doesn't have a test dedicated to NetBEUI or NWLink).

1.2.3   Network Topologies

In the seemingly never-ending competition to maximize the amount of data that can be pushed through a piece of wire, numerous network topologies have been tried and tested. Initially, companies offered wholesale solutions for customers wanting to use various software packages. The problem was that these solutions typically required certain network protocols and certain hardware to be in place before anything would work. This approach was often referred to as "monolithic" networking because these solutions were rarely interoperable with other applications or hardware.

After a company committed to a particular type of network, it was stuck with that network; and if a really useful application was released for a different network architecture, that company was out of luck. Accommodating a brand new application or suite of applications sometimes required removing the old network and installing another one. Administrators therefore wanted to make sure that they were planning for the longest term possible. In an effort to sell administrators on the benefits of a particular networking package, companies developed network configurations for maximizing network performance. Performance was typically rated by how well a network architecture maximized available bandwidth. The strategies and implementation details for achieving these goals could be broken down into three general configurations, which evolved into the bus, ring, and star configurations.

The Bus Configuration

The bus configuration has its roots with coaxial cable in simple networks in which desktop machines are connected so that they can share information. *Traffic,* here defined as voltage applied to the wire by any machine that needs to communicate, is applied to the bus, or the wire connecting the machines.

Any time a machine needs to access information from another machine, it simply sends out a sequenced variation of voltage in a frame that the destination machine can understand, process, and respond to.

One problem with this type of network architecture occurs when two machines try to communicate and send their frames on the wire at the same time. This event is the electrical equivalent of a train wreck for ones and zeroes, or what is commonly referred to as a "collision" on the network. Any machine listening on the network for frames has no idea what to make of the chaotic confusion that results from a collision. Imagine trying to listen to 15 or 20 people trying to talk at the same time to different people, possibly even in different languages.

Thankfully, network cards are designed with algorithms to alleviate some of the chaos surrounding collisions and with ground rules for avoiding collisions in the future. One common design called carrier sense multiple access with collision detection (CSMA/CD) implements a standard set of rules for the transmission of frames on a network.

CSMA/CD defines the relative politeness of machines on the network. When a network card wants to use the wire to transmit data, it listens first to determine whether another machine is already in the process of transmitting. If the network is idle (silent), the machine may transmit its own frames. If, in the course of transmitting, another network card also begins to transmit, a collision occurs. Each network card is instructed to stop transmitting, wait a random amount of time, and then listen again before trying to retransmit the data.

At the blazing speeds at which data is transferred, collisions might not seem to be a problem, and on small networks they aren't; however, as networks grow in size and as the data being transferred between machines increases, the number of collisions also increases. It is possible to put so many machines on a network segment that the capability of machines to communicate is slowed down, if not stopped altogether. If too many machines try to communicate at the same time, it is nearly impossible for network cards to transmit data without collisions. This scenario is often referred to as *saturating your bandwidth* and should be avoided if at all possible.

As an example, imagine how the traffic on any rural road increases as the surrounding area becomes more developed. More and more people move into the area and use the road until it becomes congested. A trip to the store that once took five minutes now takes 15 minutes, despite the fact that the distance hasn't changed. Further development and growth of the area into, say, a metropolitan city, leads to more people and more traffic until the same trip eventually takes two hours because of the constant traffic jams. The usual effect is frustration and a commitment not to go to the store during rush hours.

This scenario can happen with computer networks as well. The inability to access resources in a timely manner because of saturated bandwidth can lead to productivity losses and frustrated users. One way to reduce collisions is to specify a smaller frame size for sending data. This approach forces network cards to stop more often to give other network cards the opportunity to transmit. Consequently, computers can send only a small amount of data at any one time.

The Ring Configuration

The ring configuration provides an alternative method for the transmission of data from one computer to another over a network segment. This configuration relies on a token-passing method. In this type of network, one machine is designated to be the creator of a token. The *token* is the vehicle that carries all network communication, and it is sent from one machine to another in a circular loop until it travels all the way around.

A token has two basic states: In Use and Free. If a network card receives the token and the token is Free, the card has permission to place data in the token, address the token for a destination address, and flag the token as In Use. This token is passed from network card to network card, each silently ignoring it, until it reaches its destination. The destination address receives the frame, formulates a reply, readdresses the token, and returns it to the originator of the message. Again, the token is passed from one network card to another until the token reaches its origin. Assuming that communication between the two machines is completed, the originator of the communication releases the token by setting its flag to Free and passes the token on to the next network card.

To conceptualize this method, think of a classroom of five students. At any one time, a shoe box (the token) is in the hands of one of the students. It starts off empty (no lid, no tag) and is passed around from student to student. After a student decides to send a message, he or she assembles the message, places it inside the shoe box, and puts a lid on the shoe box with a tag indicating who is to receive the message.

Each time a student receives the shoe box, he or she checks to see whether the box has a lid and a tag. If it does have a lid, the student looks at the tag to determine for whom the message is intended. If the lid is on, but the tag isn't addressed to her, the student simply passes it to the next student. A student can put a message into the shoe box only when he receives the shoe box and it is empty.

The only student who can remove the lid permanently is the original sender. After the communication is complete, the sender removes the lid and passes the empty shoe box to the next student. Notice the absence of any type of collision detection. In a ring-based network, the only communication occurring on the network is by the machine that currently has control of the token. The

1

risk of collisions has been completely eliminated. In addition, the absence of collisions means that network cards don't have to be quite so polite and can send much larger frames. Larger frame sizes equates to much larger amounts of data being transmitted at any one time.

So where is the drawback? Look at the example again. Student 4 passes the shoe box with a message to student 5. The shoe box is sitting on student 5's desk, but student 5 actually skipped school that day. The ring has essentially been broken (machine crash), and the communications network is down. Without the capability to pass the token to student 1, the other students are out of luck. Also, imagine that the students are wearing blindfolds and can only identify the students to their immediate left and their immediate right through touch. Therefore, if a student (or machine) on a ring-based network is moved, the student has to learn who its neighbors are before communications can be reestablished.

As with bus-based networks, software and hardware implementations have been developed to eliminate some of these problems. However, compared to those networks, ring networks are typically more expensive and more difficult to maintain and service. The main selling point behind this type of configuration is the amount of data that can be transferred at one time through the significantly larger frame sizes.

The Star Configuration

The star configuration is designed primarily to reduce the traffic with which any one machine has to compete to communicate on the network. It operates in almost the same way as the bus configuration, with one exceptional difference. Through the implementation of smart hardware, such as a fast switch, machines never have to worry about collisions with each other. The switch isolates the network segments so that collisions do not occur between network cards. All data is designed to flow through the switch. A virtual circuit is created between two machines to allow them to communicate with each other, and this virtual circuit lasts only as long as is necessary to transfer data. After the machines finish communicating, the virtual circuit is destroyed and the segments are isolated from each other again.

To visualize this type of network, you might think of the switch in the middle acting as telephone operators did back in the days when connections were made between a caller and receiver by plugging the cables into their respective sockets. Switches are performing essentially the same task but at a significantly quicker pace than a person can do it. Again, the connection lasts only as long as the two machines are communicating.

When the machines stop, the connection is broken and the path between the two machines no longer exists. In a very small environment, each machine is assigned a port on the switch; in most situations, however, this method is not terribly practical. Switches of this kind are typically very expensive and would not be used for a small number of machines. Most switches are used in hybrid configurations where additional hubs can provide more available bandwidth to hundreds of machines.

The key characteristic of this type of configuration is that each machine with its own port receives the maximum sustainable bandwidth that the medium can carry because each machine only sees the traffic for the connections it has established. This solution is one of the more expensive ways to minimize bandwidth bottlenecks, but it works very well when implemented.

Hybrid Configurations

These three basic network configurations have been modified and hybridized in recent years so that each has several variations. But in the past, businesses had to choose which configuration they were going to use based not only on the merits of each implementation but also on which software they intended to use. This situation didn't make too many people in the industry happy. A company producing network interface cards had to know exactly what kinds of programs its customers would run so that it could support those applications. Similarly, a programmer or software company couldn't complete work on its software before knowing what kind of physical network the software would be running on.

Hardware companies were unhappy; software companies were unhappy; and businesses faced with millions of dollars of upgrade investment every time there was a software or operating system conversion were decidedly unhappy.

This universal unhappiness forced the industry to create several models for developing networks. These models typically include agreed-upon layers that distribute tasks among various manufacturers and programmers in the industry. Consequently, software companies can spend their time worrying about improving their software, not about network card standards. And network card manufacturers can spend their time learning to get more throughput from their cards, rather than worrying about whether a card can support the most popular application of the day. One of the most well-known network development model is the Open Systems Interconnect (OSI) model.

1.2.4   The OSI Model

The OSI model divides networking tasks into seven fundamentally different layers to make it easier for the industry to move forward and evolve. With the tasks segregated into functional units, a person writing the code for a network card doesn't have to worry about what applications are going to be run over it; conversely, a programmer writing an application doesn't have to worry about who manufactured the network card. However, to make this system work, everything must be written to comply with the boundary specifications between each of the seven layers of the model. Although the TCP/IP protocol suite only maps to a four-layer model, these four layers provide the same functionality as the seven layers of the OSI model.

The Physical Layer

The first layer is the physical layer. This layer is the only one truly connected to the network in the sense that it is the only layer concerned with how to interpret the voltage on the wire—the ones and zeroes. This layer is responsible for understanding the electrical rules associated with devices and for determining what kind of medium is actually being used (cables, connectors, and other mechanical distinctions). TCP/IP does not function at the physical level, leaving these tasks instead for the network cards to handle.

The Data Link Layer

The second layer is the data link layer. This layer is responsible for the creation and interpretation of different frame types based on the actual physical network being used. For instance, Ethernet and token-ring networks support different and numerous frame types, and the data link layer must understand the difference between them.

This layer is also responsible for interpreting what it receives from the physical layer, using low-level error detection and correction algorithms to determine when information needs to be resent. Network protocols, including the TCP/IP protocol suite, do not define physical standards at the physical or data link layer, but instead are written to make use of any standards that may currently be in use.

The boundary between the data link layer and network layer defines a group of agreed-upon standards for how protocols communicate and gain access to these lower layers. As long as a network protocol is appropriately written to this boundary layer, the protocols should be able to access the network regardless of what media type is being used.

The Network Layer

The third layer of the OSI model is the network layer. This layer is mostly associated with the movement of data by means of addressing and routing. It directs the flow of data from a source to a destination, despite the fact that the machines may not be connected to the same physical wire or segment, by finding a path or route from one machine to another.

If necessary, this layer can break data into smaller chunks for transmission. This step is sometimes necessary when transferring data from one type of physical network to another, for instance, token ring (which supports larger frame sizes) to Ethernet (which supports smaller frame sizes). Of course, it is also responsible for reassembling those smaller chunks into the original data after the data has reached its destination. A number of protocols from the TCP/IP protocol suite exist in this layer, but the network protocol that is responsible for routing and delivery of packets is the IP protocol.

The Transport Layer

The fourth layer is the transport layer. This layer is primarily responsible for guaranteeing delivery of packets transmitted by the network layer, although it does not always have to do so. Depending on the protocol being used, delivery of packets may or may not be guaranteed. When it is responsible for guaranteeing the delivery of packets, it does so through various means of error control, including verification of sequence numbers for packets and other protocol-dependent mechanisms. TCP/IP has two protocols at this layer of the model, Transmission Control Protocol (TCP) and User Datagram Protocol (UDP). UDP may be used for non-guaranteed delivery of packets, and TCP may be used to guarantee the delivery of packets.

The Session Layer

The fifth layer is the session layer. This layer is responsible for managing connections between two machines during the course of communication between them. The session layer determines whether it has received all pertinent information for the session and whether it can stop receiving or transmitting data. This layer also has built-in error correction and recovery methods. TCP/IP uses two Application Programming Interfaces (APIs)—Windows Sockets and NetBIOS—to determine whether all information has been sent and received between two connected machines.

The Presentation Layer

The sixth layer is the presentation layer. This layer is primarily concerned with the conversion of data formats from one machine to another. One common example is the sending of data from a machine that uses the ASCII format for characters to a machine that uses the EBCDIC format for characters, typically IBM mainframes. (EBCDIC and ASCII are standards for translating characters to hexadecimal code.) Letters, numbers, and symbols in one format must be translated when communicating with machines using a different format. The presentation layer is responsible for picking up differences such as these and translating them to compatible formats.

The Application Layer

The seventh layer is the application layer. This is the last layer of the model, and it acts as the arbiter or translator between users' applications and the network. Applications that want to use the network to transfer data must be written to conform to networking APIs supported by the machine's networking components, such as Windows Sockets and NetBIOS. After the application makes an API call, the application layer determines with which machine it wants to communicate, whether a session should be set up between the communicating machines, and whether the delivery of packets needs to be guaranteed.

The Layer Relationship

Between each layer is a common boundary layer. For instance, between the network layer and the transport layer is a boundary that both layers must be able to support. These boundary layers enable one layer of the networking model to communicate and share valuable and necessary information with the layer above or below it. In fact, each time a layer passes data to the layer below, the sending layer adds information to it; similarly, each time a layer receives data, it strips off its own information and passes the rest up the protocol stack.

One of the most common and useful ways to describe the networking model is to imagine the process a letter goes through to get to its destination.

Messages from one layer are packaged and placed into the next layer. Each step of the process has little to do with the preceding or following step. The kind of envelope has nothing to do with either the language in which the message is written or its content. In the same way, the actual address on the envelope—be it California, Florida, or Hawaii—has absolutely nothing to do with the color of the envelope. The only common link between the address and the message is the envelope itself. Finally, the method of delivery—whether the postal service uses a boat, plane, or train—doesn't matter, as long as the envelope gets to its destination address. Each layer depends on the other layers, but is only mildly related to the functionality of the others.

This introduction to networks and networking should help you understand and appreciate the architecture of TCP/IP.

1.3   Introduction to TCP/IP

TCP/IP is an industry-standard suite of protocols designed to be routable, robust, and functionally efficient. TCP/IP was originally designed as a set of WAN protocols for the express purpose of maintaining communication links and data transfer between sites in the event of a atomic/ nuclear war. Since those early days, development of the protocols has passed from the hands of the government to the Internet community.

1

The evolution of these protocols from a small four-site project into the foundation of the world-wide Internet has been extraordinary. But despite more than 25 years of work and numerous modifications to the protocol suite, the inherent spirit of the original specifications is still intact.

Installing Microsoft's TCP/IP as a protocol on your machine or network provides the following advantages:

- An industry-standard protocol. Because TCP/IP is not maintained or written by one company, it is not proprietary or subject to as many compatibility issues as other protocols. The Internet community as a whole decides whether a particular change or implementation is worthwhile. Naturally, this process slows down the implementation of new features and characteristics compared to how quickly a particular company might make changes, but it does guarantee that changes are well thought out and provide functionality with most, if not all, other implementations of TCP/IP and that a set of publicly available specifications can be referenced at any time over the Internet, detailing how the protocol suite should be used and implemented.

- A set of utilities for connecting dissimilar operating systems. Many connectivity utilities have been written for the TCP/IP suite, including the File Transfer Protocol (FTP) and Terminal Emulation Protocol (Telnet). Because these utilities use the Windows Sockets API, connectivity from one machine to another does not depend on the network operating system used on either machine. For example, a Microsoft FTP client could access a UNIX FTP server to transfer files without either party having to worry about compatibility issues. This functionality also enables a Windows NT machine running a Telnet client to access and run commands on an IBM mainframe running a Telnet server, for example.

- A scalable, cross-platform client/server architecture. Consider what happened during the initial development of applications for the TCP/IP protocol suite. Vendors wanted to be able to write their own client/server applications, for instance, SQL server and Simple Network Management Protocol (SNMP). The specification for how to write applications was also up for public perusal. Which operating systems would be included?

   Users everywhere wanted to be able to take advantage of the connectivity options promised through the use of TCP/IP regardless of the operating system they were currently running. Therefore, the Windows Sockets API was established so that applications using the TCP/IP protocol could write to a standard, agreed-upon interface. Because the contributors included everyone, and therefore every kind of operating system, the specifications for Windows Sockets on TCP/IP were written to make the operating system transparent to the application. Microsoft TCP/IP includes support for Windows Sockets and for connectivity to other Windows Sockets–compliant TCP/IP stacks.

- Access to the Internet. TCP/IP is the de facto protocol of the Internet and allows access to a wealth of information that can be found at thousands of locations around the world. To connect to the Internet, though, a valid IP address is required. Because IP addresses have become more and more scarce, and as security issues surrounding access to the Internet have been raised, many creative alternatives have been established to allow connections to the Internet. However, all these implementations use gateways or firewalls that act on behalf of the requesting machines.

Now that you understand the benefits of installing TCP/IP, you are ready to learn about how the TCP/IP protocol suite maps to a four-layer model.

1.3.1   The Four Layers of TCP/IP

TCP/IP maps to a four-layer architectural model. This model is called the Internet protocol suite and is broken into the network interface, Internet, transport, and application layers. Each layer corresponds to one or more layers of the OSI model. The network interface layer of TCP/IP corresponds to the physical and data link layers of OSI. The Internet layer corresponds to the network layer. The transport layer corresponds to the transport layer, and the application layer corresponds to the session, presentation, and application layers of the OSI model.

Each of the four layers of the TCP/IP model is responsible for all the activities of the layers to which it maps.

The network interface layer is responsible for communicating directly with the network. It must understand the network architecture being used, such as token ring or Ethernet, and provide an interface allowing the Internet layer to communicate with it. The Internet layer is responsible for communicating directly with the network interface layer.

The Internet layer is primarily concerned with the routing and delivery of packets through the Internet Protocol (IP). All the protocols in the transport layer must use IP to send data. The Internet Protocol includes rules for how to address and direct packets, fragment and reassemble packets, provide security information, and identify the type of service being used. However, because IP is not a connection-based protocol, it does not guarantee that packets transmitted onto the wire will not be lost, damaged, duplicated, or out of order. This task is the responsibility of higher layers of the networking model, such as the transport layer or the application layer. Other protocols that exist in the Internet layer are the Internet Control Messaging Protocol (ICMP), Internet Group Management Protocol (IGMP), and the Address Resolution Protocol (ARP).

The transport layer maps to the transport layer of the OSI model and is responsible for providing communication between machines for applications. This communication can be connection based or nonconnection based. The primary difference between these two types of connections is whether a mechanism exists for tracking data and guaranteeing the delivery of the data to its destination. TCP is the protocol used for connection-based communication between two machines providing reliable data transfer. UDP is used for nonconnection-based communication with no guarantee of delivery.

The application layer of the Internet protocol suite is responsible for all the activities that occur in the session, presentation, and application layers of the OSI model. Numerous protocols have been written for use in this layer, including SNMP, FTP, Simple Mail Transfer Protocol (SMTP), as well as many others.

The interface between each of these layers is written to have the capability to pass information from one layer to the other.

The interface between the network interface layer and the Internet layer does not pass a great deal of information, although it must follow certain rules. Namely, it must listen to all broadcasts and send the rest of the data in the frame up to the Internet layer for processing, and if it receives any frames that do not have an IP frame type, they must be silently discarded.

The interface between the Internet layer and the transport layer must be able to provide each layer full access to such information as the source and destination addresses, whether TCP or UDP should be utilized in the transport of data, and all other available mechanisms for IP. Rules and specifications for the transport layer include giving the transport layer the capability to change these parameters or to pass parameters it receives from the application layer down to the Internet layer. The most important thing to remember about all of these boundary layers is that they must use the agreed upon rules for passing information from one layer to the other.

The interface between the transport layer and the application layer is written to provide an interface to applications, whether they are using the TCP or UDP protocol for transferring data. The interface uses the Windows Sockets and NetBIOS APIs to transfer parameters and data between the two layers. The application layer must have full access to the transport layer to change and alter parameters as necessary.

The layers provide guidelines only; the real work is done by the protocols that are contained within the layers. This section describes the TCP/IP protocol as being a suite of protocols, not just two (TCP and IP). In fact, six primary protocols are associated with TCP/IP:

- Transmission Control Protocol (TCP)
- User Datagram Protocol (UDP)
- Internet Protocol (IP)
- Internet Control Message Protocol (ICMP)
- Address Resolution Protocol (ARP)
- Internet Group Management Protocol (IGMP)

Transmission Control Protocol

The first protocol that lives in the transport layer is the TCP. This protocol is a connection-based protocol and requires the establishment of a session before data is transmitted between two machines. TCP packets are delivered to sockets or ports. Because TCP sets up a connection between two machines, it is designed to verify that all packets sent by a machine are received on the other end. If, for some reason, packets are lost, the sending machine resends the data. Because a session is established and delivery of packets is guaranteed, using TCP to transmit packets involves additional overhead.

To understand TCP further, you must understand ports and sockets, connection-oriented communications, sliding windows, and acknowledgments. The following sections cover these areas.

Ports and Sockets

The communication process between the transport layer and the application layer involves identifying the application that has requested either a reliable or unreliable transport mechanism. Port assignments are the means used to identify application processes to the transport layer. Ports identify to which process on the machine data should be sent for further processing. Specific port numbers have been assigned, specifically those from 1 to 1,023, by the Internet Assigned Numbers Authority (IANA). These port assignments are called the *well-known ports* and represent the ports to which standard applications listen.

Defining these standard port numbers helps eliminate guessing to which port an application is listening so that applications can direct their queries or messages directly. Port numbers above the well-known port range are available for running applications, and work in exactly the same way. In this case, however, the client or user must be able to identify to which port the application is connecting. Ports can be used by both TCP and UDP for delivering data between two machines. Ports themselves do not care whether the data they receive is in order or not, but the applications running on those ports might.

To identify both the location and application to which a stream of data needs to be sent, the IP address (location) and the port number (application) are often combined into one functional address called a socket.

Connection-Orientation Communication

The TCP is a connection-based protocol that establishes a connection, or session, between two machines before any data is transferred. TCP exists within the transport layer, between the application layer and the IP layer, providing a reliable and guaranteed delivery mechanism to a destination machine. Connection-based protocols guarantee the delivery of packets by tracking the transmission and receipt of individual packets during communication. A session is able to track the progress of individual packets by monitoring when a packet is sent, in what order it was sent, and by notifying the sender when the packet is received so the sender can send more.

The first step in the communication process is to send a message indicating a desire to synchro-nize the systems. This step is equivalent to dialing a phone number and waiting for someone to answer. The second step is for the machine to send an acknowledgment that it is listening and willing to accept data. This step is equivalent to a person answering the phone and then waiting for the caller to say something. The third step is for the calling machine to send a message indicating that it understands the receiving machine's willingness to listen and that data transmis-sion will now begin.

After the TCP session has been created, the machines begin to communicate just as people do during a phone call. In the example of the telephone, if the caller uses a cellular phone and some of the transmission is lost, the user indicates she did not receive the message by saying, "What did you say? I didn't hear that." This messages tells the sender to resend the data.

Included in the header are sections defining the sequence numbers and acknowledgment num-bers that help verify the delivery of a datagram. A datagram or packet is simply the data that is being transferred to the destination machine. This data often has to be broken up into smaller pieces (datagrams) because the underlying network can transmit only a limited amount of data at one time.

Other parameters include the SYN and FIN options for starting and ending communication sessions between two machines, the size of the window to be used in transferring data, a checksum for verifying the header information, and other options that can be specific implemen-tations of TCP/IP.

The last part of the frame is the actual data being transmitted. A full discussion of these param-eters is beyond the scope of this book or the TCP/IP test. More academic texts and Requests for Comment (RFCs) on the Internet describe in fuller detail the specifications for each parameter.

During the initialization of a TCP session, often called the "three-way handshake," both machines agree on the best method to track how much data is to be sent at any one time, acknowledgment numbers to be sent upon receipt of data, and when the connection is no longer necessary because all data has been transmitted and received. It is only after this session is created that data transmission begins. To provide reliable delivery, TCP places packets in sequenced order and requires acknowledgments that these packets reached their destination before it sends new data. TCP is typically used for transferring large amounts of data or when the application requires acknowledgment that data has been received. Given all the additional overhead information that TCP needs to keep track of, the format of a TCP packet can be somewhat complex.

Sliding Windows

TCP uses the concept of sliding windows for transferring data between machines. In the UNIX environment, sliding windows are often referred to as *streams*. Each machine has both a send window and a receive window that it uses to buffer data and to make the communication process more efficient. A window represents the subset of data that is currently being sent to a destination machine and is also the amount of data that is being received by the destination machine. At first this method seems redundant, but it really isn't. Not all data that is sent is guaranteed to be received, so both machines must keep track of the data. A sliding window allows a sending machine to send the window data in a stream without having to wait for an acknowledgment for every single packet.

A receiving window allows a machine to receive packets out of order and reorganize them while it waits for more packets. Reorganization may be necessary because TCP uses IP to transmit data, and IP does not guarantee the orderly delivery of packets. By default, window sizes in Windows NT are a little more than 8KB, representing eight standard Ethernet frames. Standard Ethernet frames are a little more than 1KB apiece.

Packets do not always make it to their destination, though. TCP has been designed to recover in the event that packets are lost along the way, perhaps by busy routers. TCP keeps track of the data that has been sent out, and if it doesn't receive an acknowledgment for that data from the destination machine in a certain amount of time, the data is re-sent. In fact, until acknowledgment for a packet of data is received, further data transmission is halted completely.

Acknowledgments

Acknowledgments ensure the reliable delivery of packets. As the receiving window receives packets, it sends acknowledgments to tell the sending window that the packets arrived intact. When the sending window receives acknowledgments for data it has sent, it slides the window to the right so that it can send any additional data stored in memory. But it can only slide over by the number of acknowledgments it has received. By default, a receive window sends an acknowledgment for every two sequenced packets it receives.

As long as the acknowledgments begin flowing back regularly from the receiving machine, data flows smoothly and efficiently. However, on busy networks, packets can get lost and acknowledgments may be delayed. Because TCP guarantees delivery and reliability of traffic flow, the window cannot slide past any data that has not been acknowledged. If the window cannot slide beyond a packet of data, no more data beyond the window is transmitted, TCP eventually has to shut down the session, and the communication fails.

Each machine is therefore instructed to wait a certain amount of time before either retransmitting data or sending acknowledgments for packets that arrive out of sequence. Each window is given a timer: the send window has the retransmit timer and the receive window has the delayed acknowledgment timer. These timers help define what to do when communication isn't flowing very smoothly.

In the sending window, a retransmit timer is set for each packet, specifying how long to wait for an acknowledgment before assuming that the packet did not get to its destination. After this timer has expired, the send window is instructed to resend the packet and wait twice as long as the time set on the preceding timer. The default starting point for this timer is approximately three seconds but is usually reduced to less than a second almost immediately.

Each time an acknowledgment is not received, the retransmit timer doubles. For instance, if the retransmit timer started at approximately one second, the second retransmit timer is set for two seconds, the third for four seconds, and the fourth for eight seconds, up to a fifth attempt that waits 16 seconds. The number of attempts can be altered in the Registry, but if after these attempts an acknowledgment still cannot be received, the TCP session is closed and errors are reported to the application.

In the receiving window, a delayed acknowledgment timer is set for those packets that arrive out of order. Remember, by default an acknowledgment is sent for every two sequenced packets, starting from the left side of the window. If packets arrive out of order (if, for instance, packet 1 and 3 arrive but packet 2 is missing), an acknowledgment for two sequenced packets is not possible. When packets arrive out of order, a delayed acknowledgment timer is set on the first packet in the pair.

In the preceding example, a timer is set on packet 1. The delayed acknowledgment timer is hard-coded for 200 milliseconds, or one-fifth the retransmit timer. If packet 2 does not show up before the delayed acknowledgment timer expires, an acknowledgment for packet 1, and only packet 1, is sent. No other acknowledgments are sent, including those for packets 3 through 8 that might have appeared. Until packet 2 arrives, the other packets are considered interesting but useless. As data is acknowledged and passed to the application layer, the receive window slides to the right, enabling more data to be received. Again though, if a packet doesn't show up, the window is not enabled to slide past it.

User Datagram Protocol

The second protocol that lives in the transport layer is the UDP. This protocol is a nonconnection-based protocol and does not require a session to be established between two machines before data is transmitted. UDP packets are still delivered to sockets or ports, just as they are in TCP. But because UDP does not create a session between machines, it cannot guarantee that packets are delivered or that they are delivered in order or retransmitted if the packets are lost. Given the apparent unreliability of this protocol, you may wonder why UDP was developed.

One of the main reasons for its development is that sending a UDP datagram involves very little overhead. A UDP datagram has no synchronization parameters or priority options. It doesn't have to keep track of sequence numbers, retransmit timers, delayed acknowledgment timers, and retransmission of packets. All that exists is the source port, destination port, the length of the data, a checksum for verifying the header, and then the data. UDP is quick and extremely streamlined functionally; it's just not guaranteed. Therefore, UDP is perfect for communications that involve broadcasts, general announcements to the network, or real-time data.

Another really good use for UDP is in streaming video and streaming audio. Not only does the nonguaranteed delivery of packets enable more data to be transmitted (because a broadcast has little to no overhead) but also the retransmission of a packet is pointless. In a streaming broadcast, users are more concerned with what's coming next than with trying to recover a packet or two that may not have made it. Compare the situation to listening to a music CD and a piece of dust gets stuck in one of the little grooves. The small omission is usually imperceptible; your ear barely notices, and your brain probably filled in the gap for you. Imagine instead that your CD player decides to guarantee the delivery of that one piece of data that it can't quite get and ends up skipping and skipping indefinitely. This technique can definitely ruin your day; in fact, dealing with an occasional packet dropping out provides a much more fulfilling listening experience. Thankfully, UDP was developed for applications to use in this fashion.

Internet Protocol

A number of protocols are found in the Internet layer, including the most important protocol in the entire suite, the Internet Protocol, or IP. The reason that the IP is probably the most important protocol is that the transport layer cannot communicate at all without communicating through IP in the Internet layer.

Addressing

The most fundamental element of the IP is the address space that IP uses. Each machine on a network is given a unique 32-bit address called an Internet address or IP address. Addresses are divided into five categories, called classes, currently known as classes A, B, C, D, and E. The unique address given to a machine is derived from the class A, B, or C address. Class D addresses are used for combining machines into one functional group; class E addresses are considered experimental and are not currently available. For now, the most important concept to understand is that each machine requires a unique address and IP is responsible for maintaining, utilizing, and manipulating it to provide communication between two machines. The whole concept behind uniquely identifying machines is to be able to send data to one machine and one machine only, even if the IP stack has to broadcast at the physical layer.

If IP receives data from the network interface layer that is addressed to another machine or is not a broadcast, IP's directions are to silently discard the packet and not continue processing it.

IP receives information in the form of packets from the transport layer, from either TCP or UDP, and sends out data in what are commonly referred to as datagrams. The size of a datagram depends on the type of network that is being used, such as token ring or Ethernet. If a packet has too much data to be transmitted in one datagram, it is broken into pieces and transmitted through several datagrams. Each of these datagrams has to then be reassembled by TCP or UDP.

Broadcasts

Despite the fact that IP was designed to be able to send packets directly to a particular machine, at times it is preferable to send a message to all machines connected to a physical segment. IP supports broadcasts at the Internet layer; if IP receives a broadcast datagram from the network interface layer, IP must process the packet as if the packet had been addressed to IP itself.

Fragmentation and Reassembly

Fragmentation and reassembly occur when data is too large to be transmitted on the underlying network. Combining a token-ring and Ethernet network is the most common example. Token-ring networks support much larger frame sizes and therefore support larger datagram sizes. Alternatively, the transport layer may send the Internet layer more data than one datagram can handle. In either of these cases, IP must break down the data into manageable chunks through a process called fragmentation.

After data is fragmented, each datagram gets a fragment ID, identifying it in the sequence so that each fragment can be reassembled at the destination machine. This whole process is transparent to the user.

After the fragments have been received and reassembled at the destination machine, the data can be sent up to the higher layers for processing.

Routability

IP is responsible for routing IP datagrams from one network to another. Machines on a network can be configured to support routing. With routing, when a machine receives a datagram that is neither addressed to it nor is a broadcast, the machine has to try to find where the datagram should be sent so that it can reach its destination. Not all machines on a TCP/IP network are routers. But all routers can forward datagrams from one network to another. Connections to the Internet are often through some form of router.

Time to Live

The Time to Live (TTL) specification is set in Windows NT to a default of 128. This setting represents 128 hops, 128 seconds, or a combination of the two. Each time a router handles a datagram, it decrements the TTL by a minimum of one. If a datagram is held up at a router for longer than one second before it is transmitted, the router can decrement the TTL by more than one.

One way to visualize how the TTL works is to think of a deadly poison. Each time a datagram is sent out on to the network, it is injected with this deadly poison. The datagram has only the length of time specified in the TTL to get to its destination and receive the antidote for the poison. If the datagram gets routed through congested routers, traffic jams, narrow bandwidth communication avenues, and so on, it might not make it. If the TTL expires before the datagram reaches its destination, it is discarded from the network.

Although this concept may seem strange at first, in reality it prevents datagrams from running around a network indefinitely wreaking havoc with bandwidth and the synchronization of data. Imagine a scenario in which 100 datagrams are sent to a machine. Twenty-five of them have to be re-sent because the retransmit timer on the sending machine expired. After the communication is complete and the session broken down, suddenly 25 packets appear out of nowhere hitting the destination machine. These 25 packets may have been rerouted through some extremely slow network path and were never discarded. At least in this case, the destination machine can just ignore the datagrams. However, in routed environments it would be pretty easy to set up infinite loops where packets would bounce between two routers indefinitely.

TCP, UDP, and IP work together to provide both connection-oriented and nonconnection-oriented communication. These three protocols work together to provide communication between two machines.

Internet Control Message Protocol

ICMP is part of the Internet layer and is responsible for reporting errors and messages regarding the delivery of IP datagrams. It can also send "source quench" and other self-tuning signals during the transfer of data between two machines without the intervention of the user. These signals are designed to fine-tune and optimize the transfer of data automatically. ICMP is the protocol that warns you when a destination host is unreachable or informs you how long it took to get to a destination host.

ICMP messages can be broken down into two basic categories: error messages and general queries. Error messages include the following:

- Destination unreachable—ICMP generates the destination unreachable error message when an IP datagram is sent out and the destination machine either cannot be located or does not support the designated protocol. For instance, a sending machine may receive a destination host unreachable message when trying to communicate through a router that does not know to which network to send a datagram.

- Redirect—The first important thing to realize about redirect messages is that these are only sent by routers in a TCP/IP environment, not individual machines. A machine may have more than one default gateway defined for redundancy. If a router detects a better route to a particular destination, it forwards the first packet it receives but sends a redirect message to the machine to update its route tables. In this way, the machine can use the better route to reach the remote network.

- Source quench—Sometimes a machine has to drop incoming datagrams because it has received so many it can't process them all. In this case, a machine can send a source quench message to the source, telling the source to slow down transmission. The source quench message can also be sent by a router between the source and destination machines that is having trouble routing all the packets in time. Upon receiving a source quench message, the source machine immediately reduces its transmissions. However, it continues to try to increase the amount of data to the original quantity.

- Time exceeded—The time exceeded error message is sent by a router whenever it drops a packet because the TTL expired. This error message is sent to the source address to notify the machine of a possible infinite routing loop or that the TTL is set too low to get to the destination.

ICMP also includes general message queries. The two most commonly used are the following:

- Echo request
- Echo reply

The most familiar tool for verifying that an IP address on a network actually exists is the Packet Internet Groper (PING) utility. This utility uses the ICMP echo request and reply mechanisms. The echo request is a simple directed datagram that asks for acknowledgment that a particular IP address exists on the network. If a machine with this IP address exists and receives the request, it is designed to send an ICMP echo reply. This reply is sent back to the destination address to notify the source machine of its existence. The PING utility reports the existence of the IP address and how long it took to get there.

Internet Group Management Protocol

IGMP is a protocol and set of specifications that enable machines to be added and removed from IP address groups, utilizing the class D range of addresses mentioned earlier. IP allows the assignment of class D addresses to groups of machines so that they may receive broadcast data as one functional unit. Machines can be added and removed from these units or groups, or be members of multiple groups.

Most implementations of the TCP/IP protocol stack support IGMP on the local machine; however, routers designed to broadcast IGMP messages from one network to another are still in the experimental stage. Routers are designed to initiate queries for multicast groups on local network segments to determine whether they should be broadcasting on that segment. If at least one member of an IGMP group exists or responds with an IGMP response, the router processes IGMP datagrams and broadcasts them on the segment.

Address Resolution Protocol

Unless IP is planning to initiate a full broadcast on the network, it has to have the physical address of the machine to which it is going to send datagrams. For this information, it relies on ARP. ARP is responsible for mapping IP addresses on the network to physical addresses in memory. This way, whenever IP needs a physical address for a particular IP address, ARP can deliver. But ARP's memory does not last indefinitely, and occasionally IP will ask for an IP address that is not in ARP's memory. When this happens, ARP has to find one.

ARP is responsible for finding a map to a local physical address for any local IP address that IP may request. If ARP does not have a map in memory, it has to find one on the network. ARP uses local broadcasts to find physical addresses of machines and maintains a cache in memory of recently mapped IP addresses to physical addresses. Although this cache does not last indefinitely, it enables ARP to not have to broadcast every time IP needs a physical address.

As long as the destination IP address is local, all ARP does is a local broadcast for that machine and returns the physical address to IP. IP, realizing that the destination IP address is local, simply formulates the datagram with the IP address above the physical address of the destination machine.

But IP does not always need to send datagrams to local IP addresses. In fact, often the destination address is on a remote network where the path may include several routers along the way. The hardest thing to realize conceptually is that ARP operates so close to the network interface layer that it is really only good for finding local physical addresses—even in environments where routers exist. ARP never reports a physical address that exists on a remote network to IP.

To get the packet to the other network, the router is supposed to listen to the packet and forward it. The only way to get the router to listen to the packet, though, is to either do a broadcast or send the packet to the router's physical address. IP is smart enough to realize that the destination IP address is on a remote network and that the datagram must be sent to the router. However, it has no idea what the physical address of the router is and thus relies on ARP for that information.

To route a packet, IP asks ARP whether it has the physical address of the router, not of the destination machine. This technique is one of the more subtle and elegant features of the TCP/IP suite in that it cleverly redirects packets based on the layer that is being communicated with. After IP receives the physical address of the router from ARP, IP formulates the datagram, placing the destination IP address directly above the router's physical address.

The Network APIs, Windows Sockets, and NetBIOS

The application layer provides the interface between applications and the transport protocols. Microsoft supports two APIs for applications to use: Windows Sockets and NetBIOS. This functionality is included because Microsoft networks still use NetBIOS for much of the internal networking within the Windows NT operating system. It is also used because it provides a standard interface to a number of other protocols. TCP/IP, NetBEUI, and NWLink all have a NetBIOS interface to which applications can be written to use networking protocols. Strict UNIX flavors of TCP/IP may not support the NetBIOS interface and may only support Windows Sockets as their API; Microsoft's implementation of TCP/IP therefore includes support for both.

The Windows Sockets interface defines an industry-standard specification for how Windows applications communicate with the TCP/IP protocol. This specification contains definitions for how to use the transport protocols and how to transfer data between two machines, including the establishment of connection-oriented sessions (TCP three-way handshake) and nonconnection-oriented datagrams (broadcasts). The Windows Sockets API also defines how to uniquely address packets destined for a particular application on another machine.

The concept of a socket (the combination of the TCP/IP address and the port number) is a common example of the relative ease of uniquely identifying a communications path. Because of the ease and standardization of the Windows Sockets specifications, this API is enjoying a tremendous amount of exposure and success, particularly in Internet applications.

Windows Sockets uniquely identifies machines through their IP address, so machine names in the TCP/IP environment are entirely optional. Given that it is tremendously more difficult for users to remember a hundred IP addresses than to remember some form of an alias for these machines, a name space was created to help identify machines on a TCP/IP network. A *name space* is a hierarchical naming scheme that uniquely identifies machine aliases to IP addresses.

This scheme allows two machines to have the same alias as long as the machines are in different domains. This approach is very useful for people; however, it is entirely unnecessary for applications because they can use the IP address. However, this naming scheme enables you to use any alias you wish to establish a connection to a particular machine. As long as the name resolution method (DNS, hosts file) returns a valid IP address, a communication path can be created. The IP address is what's most important.

With the NetBIOS API, the IP address is only part of the information necessary to establish communication between two machines, and the name of the machine is required.

The NetBIOS API was developed on local area networks and has evolved into a standard interface for applications to use to access networking protocols in the Transport Layer for both connection-oriented and nonconnection-oriented communications. NetBIOS interfaces have been written for the NetBEUI, NWLink, TCP/IP, and other protocols so that applications need not worry about which protocol is providing the transport services. (Any protocol that NT uses will have a Transport Driver Interface to translate between the NetBIOS world of NT and the native capabilities of the protocol.) Because each of these protocols supports the NetBIOS API, all the functionality for establishing sessions and initiating broadcasts is provided. Unlike Windows Sockets, NetBIOS requires not only an IP address to uniquely identify a machine but a NetBIOS name as well.

Every machine on a network must be uniquely identified with a NetBIOS name. This name is required for establishing a NetBIOS session or sending out a broadcast. When using names through a NetBIOS session, the sending machine must be able to resolve the NetBIOS name to an IP address. Because both an IP address and name are needed, all name resolution methods have to supply the correct IP address before successful communication can occur.

The Microsoft TCP/IP stack supports connection-oriented and nonconnection-oriented communications established through either of these popular APIs. Microsoft includes NetBT (NetBIOS over TCP/IP) for applications that want to use the NetBIOS API over a TCP/IP network. This small, seemingly insignificant piece of software prevents your machine from having to run two protocols, one for Windows Sockets and one for NetBIOS. By providing NetBT with Microsoft's TCP/IP protocol stack, all NetBIOS calls an application may initiate are supported.

1.4   Exercises

1.4.1   Exercise 1: Using NETSTAT to Generate Statistics (TCP)

1.   From the Start menu, choose Programs | Command Prompt.

2.   At the command prompt, type > `netstat -s -p tcp`.

The result is a statistics report for the TCP protocol as well as for displaying any TCP sessions that are currently in use.

1.4.2   Exercise 2: Using NETSTAT to Generate Statistics (UDP)

1.   From the Start menu, choose Programs | Command Prompt.

2.   At the command prompt, type > `netstat -s -p udp`.

The result is a statistics report for the UDP protocol.

1.4.3   Exercise 3: Using NETSTAT to Generate Statistics (IP)

1. From the Start menu, choose Programs | Command Prompt.

2. At the command prompt, type > `netstat -s -p ip`.

The result is a statistics report for the IP protocol.

1.4.4   Exercise 4: Using NETSTAT to Generate Statistics (ICMP)

1. From the Start menu, choose Programs | Command Prompt.

2. At the command prompt, type > `netstat -s -p icmp`.

The result is a statistics report for the ICMP protocol.

1.4.5   Practice Problems

1. You're talking with a few of the programmers in your department about an application they are working on. They tell you it is designed to use a connection-oriented protocol to communicate over the network. Which protocol in the TCP/IP protocol suite provides connection-oriented communications?

    A. Transmission Control Protocol

    B. User Datagram Protocol

    C. Internet Control Message Protocol

    D. Address Resolution Protocol

2. Several machines on the network use DHCP and WINS to get their IP address information and to resolve NetBIOS names to IP addresses. What protocol allows these machines to resolve an IP address to a hardware address?

    A. Internet Control Protocol

    B. DHCP address resolution manager

    C. WINS address resolution manager

    D. Address Resolution Protocol

3. An NT server in your environment must communicate with other machines on the Internet using a DNS server to resolve names to IP addresses. Which command-line utility tells you whether a machine has been configured with the IP address of a DNS server?

    A. NETSTAT –N

    B. NBTSTAT –N

    C. IPCONFIG

    D. PING

4. Several programmers are discussing the design of a new application to be written for your company and a heated debate ensues over whether the application should use Windows Sockets or NetBIOS. Half the programmers think TCP/IP supports Windows Sockets only, and half think TCP/IP supports both Windows Sockets and NetBIOS. Who is correct in this argument?

    A. Programmers who say Windows Sockets only

    B. Programmers who say NetBIOS only

    C. Programmers who say neither

    D. Programmers who say both

5. One of your users cannot connect to the network. The user can't log on to the NT domain and can't use Network Neighborhood. As part of your troubleshooting routine, you find out that the user can ping every IP address on the network successfully. In addition, the user seems to be able to FTP, HTTP, and Telnet without a problem. Which of the following do you think might be the source of the error?

    A. NetBIOS API isn't functioning properly.

    B. DNS isn't configured.

C.   Telnet is an unpredictable program.

D.   Windows sockets isn't functioning properly.

6.   Kristin in the advertising department is writing a very important document in Word. She must transfer it immediately to the remote office. Which of the following protocols is the best protocol for this type of transfer?

A.   User Datagram Importance Protocol

B.   Internet Control Messaging Protocol

C.   Transmission Control Protocol

D.   Important Packet Protocol

7.   Paul is having trouble connecting to another network segment on the other side of a router. Despite repeated attempts to route packets to the other side, Paul is unsuccessful. In an attempt to help Paul, you will need to determine which layer is responsible for the routing of IP packets. Which layer would that be?

A.   Network layer

B.   Transport layer

C.   Internet layer

D.   Application layer

8.   During the troubleshooting of a problem, you take a *trace* (capture the network traffic) to discover what is going on. As you are analyzing the packets, you discover a "redirect" packet that appears to have come from a router. Which protocol can generate such a packet?

A.   Transmission Control Protocol

B.   User Datagram Protocol

C.   Internet Group Management Protocol

D.   Internet Control Message Protocol

1.4.6   Practice Problems: Answers and Explanations

1.   **A**   The Transmission Control Protocol (TCP) is connection oriented.

2.   **D**   The Address Resolution Protocol (ARP) resolves IP addresses to hardware addresses.

3.   **C**   IPCONFIG is used to display machine configuration.

4.   **D**   Both Windows Sockets and NetBIOS are supported.

5.   **A**   The most likely cause is that NetBIOS isn't functioning properly.

6.   **C**   The Transmission Control Protocol would be best for this type of transfer.

7.   **C**   The Internet layer is the layer to select.

8.   **D**   The Internet Control Message Protocol can generate the packet described.

## CHAPTER 2

Installation and Configuration

This chapter helps you prepare for the exam by covering the following objectives:

- Given a scenario, select the appropriate services to install when using Microsoft TCP/IP on a Microsoft Windows NT Server computer

- On a Windows NT Server computer, configure Microsoft TCP/IP to support multiple network adapters

- Configure scopes by using DHCP Manager

- Install and configure a WINS server

- Import LMHOSTS files to WINS

- Run WINS on a multihomed computer

- Configure WINS replication

- Configure static mappings in the WINS database

- Configure subnet masks

- Configure a Windows NT Server computer to function as an IP router

- Install and configure the DHCP relay agent

- Install and configure the Microsoft DNS server service on a Windows NT Server computer

- Integrate DNS server with other name servers

- Connect a DNS server to a DNS root server

- Configure DNS server roles

- Configure HOSTS and LMHOSTS files

- Configure a Windows NT Server computer to support TCP/IP printing

- Configure SNMP

2.1   Installing Services When Using Microsoft TCP/IP on Windows NT

When installing the TCP/IP protocol, you have the choice of installing and using several different services that work with it. The following list describes the services that you may want or need to install:

- Internet Information Server (IIS)—Enables you to share information with types of computers that can use the TCP/IP protocol. IIS includes FTP, Gopher, and WWW servers.

- Line Printer server daemon—Enables you to share your printers with many different types of hosts including mainframes and UNIX-based hosts.

- Dynamic Host Configuration Protocol (DHCP)—Provides automatic configuration of remote hosts, making management of a TCP/IP environment easy.

- DHCP relay agent—Extends the capabilities of the DHCP service by allowing it to work across various subnets.

- Windows Internet Name Service (WINS)—If you couldn't find another computer on the network, you would never be able to communicate. The WINS server provides a centralized method of name management that is both flexible and dynamic.

- Simple Network Management Protocol (SNMP) agent—In areas where you will use SNMP managers, or even if you want to track the performance of your TCP/IP protocols, you will want to install the SNMP agent.

- Domain Name Server (DNS)—Whereas the WINS server enables you to find NetBIOS names, the DNS server works with host names, which means that you can integrate your systems into the Internet or resolve hosts on the Internet.

IIS is covered in great detail in its own certification exam; the Line Printer daemon is covered in detail in section 2.17, and SNMP is covered in 2.18. The next few sections examine DHCP, WINS, and DNS.

2.1.1   Understanding DHCP

The configuration of Microsoft TCP/IP involves your knowing the correct values for several fields for each TCP/IP host and entering them manually. At the minimum, the host IP address and subnet mask need to be configured. In most cases, other parameters, such as WINS and DNS server addresses, also need to be configured on each host. DHCP relieves the need for manual configuration and provides a method of configuring and reconfiguring all the TCP/IP-related parameters.

The correct TCP/IP address must be configured on each host; otherwise, hosts on the internetwork might

- Fail to communicate

- Fail to initialize

- Cause other hosts on the internetwork to hang

DHCP is an open industry standard that enables the automatic TCP/IP configuration of DHCP client computers. The use of Microsoft's DHCP server greatly reduces the administrative overhead of managing TCP/IP client computers by eliminating the need to manually configure clients. The DHCP server also allows greater flexibility and mobility of clients on a TCP/IP network without administrator intervention. If used correctly, DHCP can eliminate nearly all the problems associated with TCP/IP. The administrator enters the valid IP addresses or ranges of IP addresses (called a *scope*) in the DHCP server database, which then assigns (or leases) the IP addresses to the DHCP client hosts.

Storing all the TCP/IP configuration parameters on the DHCP server provides the following benefits:

- The administrator can quickly verify the IP address and other configuration parameters without having to go to each host. Also, reconfiguration of the DHCP database is accomplished at one central location, thereby eliminating the need to manually reconfigure each host.

- DHCP does not lease the same IP address from a scope to two hosts at the same time; if used properly, this feature can prevent duplicate IP addresses.

> **DHCP cannot detect which IP addresses are already being used by non-DHCP clients. If a host has a manually configured IP address and a DHCP scope is configured with that same address, the DHCP server may lease the address to a DHCP client, creating a duplicate IP address on the network. To prevent this situation, you must exclude all manually configured IP addresses from any scopes configured on the DHCP server.**

- The DHCP administrator controls which hosts use which IP addresses. DHCP uses local network broadcasts to lease IP addresses to client hosts. If a second DHCP server resides on the same local network segment, the DHCP client can communicate with either server and may receive an IP address lease from the unintended DHCP server.

- The chance of clerical and typing errors is reduced because all TCP/IP configuration parameters are entered in the DHCP server database.

- Several options can be set for each DHCP scope (or globally for all scopes) that is configured on the client along with the IP address, for example, default gateway, and WINS server addresses.

- An IP address may be leased for a limited time. Therefore, the DHCP client must periodically renew its lease before the lease expires. If the host is no longer using the IP address (is no longer running TCP/IP or is powered off), the lease expires and can then be assigned to another TCP/IP host. This feature is useful if the number of hosts requesting IP addresses is larger than the number of available valid IP addresses (such as when the network is part of the Internet). This practice is not recommended, however, and you should always have more IP addresses than you have clients.

- If a host is physically moved to another subnet, the DHCP server on that subnet automatically reconfigures the host with the proper TCP/IP configuration information for that subnet.

What DHCP Servers Can Do

To enable automatic TCP/IP configuration by using DHCP, the DHCP administrator first enters the valid IP addresses as a scope in the DHCP server database and then activates the scope.

The DHCP administrator now enters other TCP/IP configuration information that will be given to the clients. The administrator or user then selects the Enable Automatic DHCP Configuration option on the client (found in their network configuration).

When a DHCP client host starts, TCP/IP initializes and the client requests an IP address from a DHCP server by issuing a DHCPDISCOVER packet. The DHCPDISCOVER packet represents the client's IP lease request.

After a DHCP server receives the DHCPDISCOVER packet, the DHCP server offers (DHCPOFFER) one of the unassigned IP addresses from the scope of addresses that are valid for that host. This procedure ensures that no two DHCP clients on that subnet have the same IP address. This DHCPOFFER information is sent back to the host. If your network contains more than one DHCP server, the host may receive several DHCPOFFERs. In most cases, the host or client computer accepts the first DHCPOFFER that it receives. The client then sends a DHCPREQUEST packet containing the IP address offered by the DHCP server.

The DHCP server now sends the client an acknowledgment (DHCPACK) that contains the IP address originally sent and a lease for that address. The DHCP server leases the IP address to the DHCP client host for the specified period. The DHCP client must renew its lease before the lease expires. During the life of the lease, the client attempts to renew the lease.

The renewal request is sent automatically if the host still has TCP/IP initialized, can communicate with the DHCP server, and is still on the same subnet or network. After 50% of the lease time expires, the client attempts to renew its lease with the DHCP server that assigned its TCP/IP configuration. At 87.5% of the active lease period, the client, if unable to contact and renew the lease with the original DHCP server, attempts to communicate with any DHCP server to renew its configuration information. If the client cannot make contact with a DHCP server and consequently fails to maintain its lease, the client must discontinue use of the IP address and begin the entire process again by issuing a DHCPDISCOVER packet.

Limitations of DHCP

Although DHCP can substantially reduce the headaches and time required to administer IP addresses, you should note a few limiting characteristics of DHCP:

- DHCP does not detect IP addresses already in use on a network by non-DHCP clients. These addresses should be excluded from any scopes configured on the DHCP server.

- A DHCP server does not communicate with other DHCP servers and cannot detect IP addresses leased by other DHCP servers. Therefore, two DHCP servers should not use the same IP addresses in their respective scopes.

- DHCP servers cannot communicate with clients across routers unless BOOTP forwarding is enabled on the router or the DHCP relay agent is enabled on the subnet.

- As with manually configured TCP/IP, incorrect values configured for a DHCP scope can cause unexpected and potentially disastrous results on the internetwork.

Other than the IP address and subnet mask, any values configured manually through the Network Control Panel applet or Registry Editor of a DHCP client override the DHCP server scope settings. If you intend to use the server-configured values, be sure to clear the values from the host TCP/IP configuration dialog boxes. Enabling DHCP on the client host does not automatically clear any preexisting values with the exception of the IP address and subnet mask.

Planning a DHCP Implementation

As with all network services that you will use, you should plan the implementation of DHCP. The next two sections cover the network and client requirements.

Network Requirements

Your network must meet the following requirements to implement Microsoft TCP/IP using DHCP:

- The DHCP server service must be running on a Windows NT Server.

- The DHCP server must have a manually configured IP address.

- A DHCP server must be located on the same subnet as the DHCP clients, the clients subnet must have a DHCP relay agent running, or the routers connecting the two subnets involved must be able to forward DHCP (BOOTP) datagrams.

- Pools of IP addresses (that is, scopes) must be configured on the DHCP server.

The easiest way to implement DHCP is with only one DHCP server on a subnet (local network segment). If more than one DHCP server is configured to provide addresses for a subnet, then either could provide the address—there is no way to specify which server to use (as you can in WINS). Because DHCP servers do not communicate with each other, a DHCP server has no way of knowing whether an IP address is leased to a client from another DHCP server.

To prevent two DHCP servers from assigning the same IP address to two clients, you must ensure that each IP address is made available in a scope on only one DHCP server on the internetwork. In other words, the IP address scopes cannot overlap or contain the same IP addresses.

If no DHCP server is available to lease an IP address to a DHCP client—because of hardware problems, for example—the client cannot initialize. For this reason, you may want to have a second DHCP server, with unique IP address scopes, on the network. This scenario works best when the second DHCP server is on a different subnet connected by a router that forwards DHCP datagrams.

A DHCP client accepts the first IP address offer it receives from a DHCP server. This address would normally be from the DHCP server on the local network because the IP address request broadcast would reach the local DHCP server first. However, if the local DHCP server is not responding and if the DHCP broadcasts were forwarded by the router, the DHCP client could accept a lease offer from a DHCP server on a remote network.

Finally, the DHCP server must have one or more scopes created by using the DHCP Server Manager application (Start | Programs | Administrative Tools | DHCP Manager). A *scope* is a range of IP addresses available for lease by DHCP clients; for example, 200.20.5.1 through 200.20.5.20 may be a scope for a given subnet, and 200.20.6.1 through 200.20.6.50 may be a scope for another subnet.

Client Requirements

A Microsoft TCP/IP DHCP client can be any of the following Microsoft TCP/IP clients:

- Windows NT Server 3.5 or later that is not a DHCP server

- Windows NT Workstation 3.5 or later

- Windows 95

- Windows for Workgroups 3.11 running the Microsoft TCP/IP-32 software from the Windows NT Server CD-ROM

- Microsoft Network Client for MS-DOS 3.0 from the Windows NT Server CD-ROM

- LAN Manager server for MS-DOS 2.2c from the Windows NT Server CD-ROM

If some clients on the network do not use DHCP for IP address configuration—because they do not support DHCP or otherwise need to have TCP/IP manually configured—the IP addresses of these non-DHCP clients must not be made available for lease to the DHCP clients. Non-DHCP clients can include clients that do not support Microsoft DHCP (see the preceding list), and clients that must always use the same IP address, such as Windows Internet Name Service (WINS) servers, Domain Name System (DNS) servers, and other DHCP servers.

Using Multiple DHCP Servers

Having more than one DHCP server on a subnet is not recommended, because you cannot control which DHCP server gives a client an IP address lease. Any DHCP server that receives a client's DHCP request broadcast can send a DHCP offer to that client. The client accepts the first lease offer it receives from a DHCP server.

If more than one subnet exists on a network, the general recommendation is to have a DHCP server on each subnet. However, if the DHCP relay agent or routers that support the forwarding of BOOTP broadcasts are used, then a single DHCP server can handle the requests for DHCP addresses.

A DHCP server has an IP address scope configured for each subnet to which it sends DHCP offers. If the DHCP server receives a relayed DHCP request from a remote subnet, it offers an IP address lease from the scope for that subnet. To ensure that a DHCP client can receive an IP address lease even if a DHCP server is not functioning, you should configure an IP address scope for a given subnet on more than one DHCP server. Thus if a DHCP client cannot obtain a lease from the local DHCP server, the DHCP relay agent or router passes the request to a DHCP server on a remote network that can offer a DHCP lease to the client.

For example, consider a network with two subnets, each with a DHCP server, joined by an RFC 1542-compliant router. For this scenario, Microsoft recommends that each DHCP server contain approximately 75% of the available IP addresses for the subnet the DHCP server is on and 25% of the available IP addresses for the remote subnet. Most of the IP addresses available for a subnet can be obtained from the local DHCP server. If the local DHCP server is unavailable, the remote DHCP server can offer a lease from the smaller range of IP addresses available from the scope on the remote DHCP server.

If the range of IP addresses available is 120.50.7.10 through 120.50.7.110 for subnet A and 120.50.8.10 through 120.50.8.110 for subnet B, you could configure the scopes on each DHCP server as follows:

Subnet	DHCP Server A	DHCP Server B
A	120.50.7.10—120.50.7.84	120.50.7.85—120.50.7.110
B	120.50.8.10—120.50.8.34	120.50.8.35—120.50.8.110

2

> You must ensure that no IP address is duplicated on another DHCP server. If two DHCP servers contain the same IP address, that IP address could potentially be leased to two DHCP clients at the same time. Therefore, IP address ranges must be split between multiple DHCP servers, as shown in the preceding example.

How DHCP Works

DHCP client configuration is a four-part process:

1. When the DHCP client initializes, it broadcasts a request for an IP lease from a DHCP server called a DHCPDISCOVER.

2. All DHCP servers that receive the IP lease request respond to the DHCP client with an IP lease offer known as a DHCPOFFER. This includes DHCP servers on the local network and on remote networks when the relay agent is used on a router that passes BOOTP requests.

3. The DHCP client selects the first offer it receives and broadcasts an IP lease selection message specifying the IP address it has selected. This message is known as a DHCPREQUEST.

4. The DHCP server that offered the selected lease responds with a DHCP lease acknowledgment message known as a DHCPACK. The DHCP server then updates its DHCP database to show that the lease can no longer be offered to other DHCP clients. The DHCP servers offering leases that were not selected can offer those IP addresses in future lease offers.

DHCPACK Phase

After the server that offered the lease receives the DHCPREQUEST message, it checks its DHCP database to ensure that the IP address is still available. If the requested lease remains available, the DHCP server marks that IP address as being leased in its DHCP database and broadcasts a DHCPACK to acknowledge that the IP address has been leased to the DHCP client. The DHCPACK contains the same information as the DHCPOFFER sent plus any optional DHCP information that has been configured for that scope as a scope option.

If the requested lease is no longer available, the DHCP server broadcasts a DHCP negative acknowledgment (DHCPNACK) containing the DHCP client's hardware address. When the DHCP client receives a DHCPNACK, it must start the lease request process over with a DHCPDISCOVER message. After receiving a DHCPACK, the DHCP client can continue to initialize TCP/IP, and it updates its Registry with the IP addressing information included with the lease. The client continues to use the leased IP address information until the lease expires, the command `ipconfig/release` is typed from a command prompt, or it receives a DHCPNACK from the DHCP server after unsuccessfully renewing its lease.

DHCP Lease Renewal

The DHCP client attempts to renew its IP address lease after 50% of its lease time has expired (or when manually requested to renew the lease by the `ipconfig/renew` command from a command prompt).

To renew the lease, a DHCP client sends a DHCPREQUEST directly to the DHCP server that gave it the original lease. Again, the DHCPREQUEST contains the hardware address of the client and the requested IP address, but this time uses the DHCP server IP address for the destination and the DHCP client IP address for the source IP address in the datagram. If the DHCP server is available and the requested IP address is still available (has not been removed from the scope), the DHCP server responds by sending a DHCPACK directly to the DHCP client. If the server is available but the requested IP address is no longer in the configured scopes, a DHCPNACK is sent to the DHCP client, which then must start the lease process again with a DHCPDISCOVER. A DHCPNACK can be sent for the following reasons:

- The IP address requested is no longer available because the lease was manually expired on the server and given to another client.

- The IP address requested has been removed from the available scopes on the DHCP server.

- The DHCP client has been physically moved to another subnet that will use a different scope on the DHCP server for that subnet. Hence, the IP address changes to a valid IP address for the new subnet. If the server does not respond to the DHCPREQUEST sent after the lease is 50% expired, the DHCP client continues to use the original lease until it is seven-eighths expired (87.5% of the lease time has expired). Because this DHCPREQUEST is broadcast rather than directed to a particular DHCP server, any DHCP server can respond with a DHCPACK or DHCPNACK to renew or deny the lease. Only the server holding that address in its scope, however, can ultimately renew it.

Installing the DHCP Server Service

The DHCP server service can be installed on a computer running Microsoft TCP/IP and Windows NT Server version 3.5 or later.

1. Open the Control Panel and double-click the Network icon.

2. From the Network settings dialog box, choose the Services tab and then click Add.

3. Choose Microsoft DHCP Service from the list that appears and click OK. When prompted, enter the directory for the NT source files.

4. Click Close on the Network Settings dialog box and, when prompted, restart your computer.

The DHCP server must have a manually configured IP address, subnet mask, and default gateway. It cannot be assigned an address from another DHCP server even if an address is reserved for the DHCP server.

> Here is something important to remember for the exam: a DHCP server cannot be a DHCP client.

Configuring the DHCP Server

After a DHCP server has been installed on an internetwork, you need to configure the following items:

- One or more IP address scopes (ranges of IP addresses to be leased) must be defined on the DHCP server.

- Non-DHCP client IP addresses must be excluded from the defined scopes.

- The options for the scope must be configured—for example, the default gateway for a subnet.

- IP address reservations for DHCP clients requiring a specific IP address to be assigned must be created.

- The DHCP clients must have Automatic DHCP Configuration enabled and should have Unwanted Manually Configured TCP/IP Parameters deleted.

2.1.2   Understanding WINS

WINS is used to dynamically map NetBIOS (computer) names to IP addresses. In the absence of a WINS server, the same function can be performed with LMHOSTS files (discussed in section 2.16), but the files are static and do not incorporate changes. The only time a WINS server automatically collects entries is when a WINS client is configured with that WINS server's address. When the client starts up, it sends a registration request to the WINS server.

After a client registers its NetBIOS name with a WINS server, the client is responsible for renewing that registration. The WINS server does not initiate any registration renewals with clients. The registration is released if not renewed by the time the TTL expires. However, the entry is not scavenged until the Extinction Interval and the Extinction Timeout have expired.

WINS writes its error messages to the Windows NT Event Log. However, because WINS uses a Joint Engine Technology (JET) database to store its entries, messages are written in the Application Log instead of the System Log.

You can also enable non-WINS clients to use a WINS server to resolve NetBIOS names by installing a *WINS proxy agent*. By definition, a non-WINS client cannot directly communicate with a WINS server to resolve a name. The non-WINS client resolves names by resorting to a b-node broadcast. If you install a WINS proxy agent, it forwards any broadcasts for name resolution to the WINS server. The proxy agent must be located on the same subnet as non-WINS clients so the proxy agent receives the broadcast for name resolution.

When a non-WINS client broadcasts a name resolution request, a proxy agent that hears the broadcast checks its own NetBIOS name cache to see whether an entry exists for the requested name. If the entry doesn't exist, the proxy agent adds to the cache an entry for that name with the status of pending. The proxy agent then sends a name resolution request for the same name to the WINS server. After the WINS server responds with the name resolution, the proxy agent adds the entry to its cache and then removes the pending status from the entry. The proxy agent does not forward the response to the non-WINS client making the request. When the non-WINS client broadcasts another request for the name resolution, the proxy agent now finds an entry for the name in its cache and can respond to the non-WINS client with a successful name resolution response.

The WINS proxy agent also forwards registration requests to the WINS server. However, registration requests for non-WINS clients are not added to the WINS server's database. The WINS server uses these forwarded registration requests to check for any potential conflicts in its database with the requested name registration. You must still add static entries to the WINS database so names of non-WINS clients can be resolved.

You must place a WINS proxy agent on each subnet where non-WINS clients are located so those clients have access to the WINS server. Because those clients resolve names only by using broadcasts, which are not typically routed, those broadcasts never go beyond the subnet. With a proxy agent on each subnet, broadcasts on each subnet can then be forwarded to the WINS server. You can have two proxy agents on a subnet, but you shouldn't exceed this limit. Even having more than one proxy agent on a subnet can generate excessive work for the WINS server because each proxy agent forwards name resolution and name registration requests to the WINS server. The WINS server has to respond to duplicate messages from proxy agents if more than one proxy agent is on a subnet.

Any Windows-based WINS client can be a WINS proxy agent. To configure a Windows NT Server or Workstation to be a proxy agent, you must turn on a parameter in the Registry. This proxy agent cannot be a WINS server. Windows 95 and Windows for Workgroups computers are more easily configured by turning on a switch in the TCP/IP configuration.

After you configure a WINS client to be a proxy agent, you must reboot the machine for this change to take effect. No other configuration is needed for this proxy agent. This WINS client remains a proxy agent until you turn off the proxy agent parameter and reboot the computer.

Configuring a Client for WINS

To manually configure a WINS client, you specify the WINS server address as part of the TCP/IP configuration. Open the TCP/IP properties in the Protocol tab of the Network Properties dialog box (opened via Control Panel | Network). Select the WINS tab in the TCP/IP Properties dialog box and simply specify the address of a primary WINS server. If you are using a secondary WINS server (recommended for every 10,000 clients), you should also type in the IP address of the secondary WINS server.

To configure a DHCP client to be a WINS client, you must add two properties to the DHCP scope created on the DHCP server. Under the DHCP scope options, add the following parameters:

- 044 WINS/NBNS Servers—Configure this parameter with the address of the primary WINS server and a secondary WINS server if desired.

- **046 WINS/NBT Node**—By default, this parameter is set to 1, a b-node broadcast. WINS clients use h-node broadcasts, so you must change the value of this parameter to 8.

Files Used for WINS

The WINS database is stored in the path \WINNT\SYSTEM32\WINS, and several files make up the WINS database:

- **WINS.MDB**—The WINS database.

- **WINSTMP.MDB**—A temporary working file used by WINS. This file is deleted when the WINS server is shut down normally, but a copy could remain in the directory after a crash.

- **J50.LOG**—The transaction log of the WINS database.

- **J50.CHK**—A checkpoint file used by the WINS database. This file is equivalent to a cache for a disk drive.

Backing Up the WINS Database

The database can be backed up automatically when WINS shuts down. You also can schedule backups or manually start a backup. All these backups are copied to the backup directory specified in the Advanced Configuration options. You can manually start a WINS backup from the Mappings menu in the WINS Manager. To automatically schedule backups, configure the path for a backup directory. After you set this path, the WINS server automatically backs itself up every 24 hours.

You should also back up the WINS subkey in the Registry. This subkey has the configuration settings for WINS, but does not contain any entries from the WINS database. The regular backup for WINS makes a copy of the database.

Restoring the WINS Database

You can restore the WINS database from the backup files. To restore the database, from the Mappings menu in WINS Manager, choose Restore database.

WINS also can automatically restore the database. If the WINS service detects a corrupted database on startup, WINS automatically restores a backup from the specified backup directory. If you suspect the database is corrupt, you can stop and start the WINS service via Control Panel | Services to force this automatic restoration.

Compacting the WINS Database

You can compact the WINS database to reduce its size. However, WINS under Windows NT 4.0 is designed to automatically compact the database, so you shouldn't have to compact it. To force a manual compaction of the database, use the JETPACK utility in the \WINNT\SYSTEM32\WINS directory. (The WINS database is a JET database, so this utility packs that database.) To pack the database, you must first stop the WINS service. You cannot pack an open database. Then type the following command:

```
jetpack WINS.mdb temp.mdb
```

This command compacts the database into the file `temp.mdb`, copies the compacted database to `WINS.mdb`, and deletes the temporary file. After the database is compacted, you can restart the WINS service via Control Panel | Services.

2.1.3 Understanding DNS

DNS (which stands for Domain Name System) is one way to resolve host names in a TCP/IP environment. In non-Microsoft environments, host names are typically resolved through host files or DNS. In a Microsoft environment, WINS and broadcasts are also used. DNS is the primary system used to resolve host names on the Internet.

DNS began when the Internet was still a small network established by the Department of Defense for research. This network linked computers at several government agencies with a few universities. The host names of the computers in this network were registered in a single HOSTS file located on a centrally administered server. Each site that needed to resolve host names downloaded this file. Few computers were being added to this network, so the HOSTS file wasn't updated too often and the different sites only had to download this file periodically to update their own copies. As the number of hosts on the Internet grew, managing all the names through a central HOSTS file became more and more difficult. The number of entries was increasing rapidly, changes were being made frequently, and the server with the central HOSTS file was being accessed more and more often by Internet sites trying to download a new copy.

DNS was introduced in 1984 as a way to resolve host names without relying on one central HOSTS file. With DNS, the host names reside in a database that can be distributed among multiple servers, decreasing the load on any one server and also allowing more than one point of administration for this naming system. The name system is based on hierarchical names in a tree-type directory structure. DNS allows more types of registration than the simple host-name-to-TCP/IP-address mapping used in HOSTS files and allows room for future defined types. Because the database is distributed, it can support a much larger database than can be stored in a single HOSTS file. In fact, the database size is virtually unlimited because more servers can be added to handle additional parts of the database.

History of Microsoft DNS

DNS was first introduced in the Microsoft environment as part of the Resource Kit for Windows NT Server 3.51. It was not integrated with the Windows NT source files until version 4.0. Although DNS is not installed by default as part of a Windows NT 4.0 Server installation, you can specify that DNS be included as part of a Windows NT installation or you can add DNS later just as you would any other networking service that is part of Windows NT.

Microsoft DNS is based on Request for Comments (RFCs) 974, 1034, and 1035. A popular implementation of DNS is the Berkeley Internet Name Domain (BIND), developed at UC Berkeley for its version of UNIX. However, BIND is not totally compliant with the DNS RFCs. Microsoft's DNS does support some features of BIND, but Microsoft DNS is based on the RFCs, not on BIND.

> You can read these RFCs, or any other RFC, by going to the Internet Network Information Center (InterNIC) Web site at `http://ds.internic.net/ds/rfc-index.html`.

The Structure of DNS

Some host-name systems, like NetBIOS names, use a flat database. With a flat database, all names exist at the same level, so there can't be any duplicate names. These names are like Social Security numbers—every participant in the Social Security program must have a unique number. Because Social Security encompasses all workers in the United States, it must use an identification system that uniquely identifies each individual in the United States.

DNS names are located in hierarchical paths, like a directory structure. You can have a file called `TEST.TXT` in `C:\` and another file called `TEST.TXT` in `C:\ASCII`. In a network using DNS, you can have more than one server with the same name, as long as each is located in a different path.

DNS Domains

The InterNIC controls the top-level domains. These have names like `com` (for businesses), `edu` (for educational institutions such as universities), `gov` (for government organizations), and `org` (for nonprofit organizations). There are also domains for countries. You can visit the InterNIC Web site at `http://www.internic.com/`. Table 2.1.2 summarizes common Internet domains.

Table 2.1.1   Common Internet Domains

Name	Type of Organization
com	Commercial organizations
edu	Educational institutions
org	Nonprofit organizations
net	Networks (the backbone of the Internet)
gov	Nonmilitary government organizations
mil	Military government organizations
num	Phone numbers
arpa	Reverse DNS
xx	Two-letter country code

DNS Host Names

To refer to a host in a domain, use a fully qualified domain name (FQDN), which completely specifies the location of the host. An FQDN specifies the host name, the domain or subdomain the host belongs to, and any domains above that in the hierarchy until the root domain in the organization is specified. On the Internet, the root domain in the path is something like `com`, but on a private network the top-level domains may be named according to some internal naming convention. The FQDN is read from left to right, with each host name or domain name specified by a period. The syntax of an FQDN follows:

```
host name.subdomain. … .domain
```

An example of an FQDN is www.microsoft.com, which refers to a server called www located in the subdomain called microsoft in the domain called com. Referring to a host by its FQDN is similar to referring to a file by its complete directory path. However, a complete filename goes from general to specific, with the filename at the right-most part of the path. An FQDN goes from specific to general, with the host name at the left-most part of the name. Fully qualified domain names are more like addresses. An address starts with the most specific information: who is to receive the letter. Then the address specifies the house number in which the recipient lives, the street on which the house is located, the city where the street is located, and finally the most general location, the state in which that city is located.

Zone Files

The DNS database is stored in files called *zones*. It's possible, even desirable, to break the DNS database into a number of zones. Breaking the DNS database into zones was part of the original design goals of DNS. With multiple zones, the load of providing access to the database is spread among a number of servers. Also, the administrative burden of managing the database is spread out because different administrators manage only the parts of the DNS database stored in their own zones. A zone can be any portion of the domain name space; it doesn't have to contain all the subdomains for that part of the DNS tree. Zones can be copied to other name servers through replication. With multiple zones, smaller amounts of information are copied when zone files are replicated than would be the case if one zone file held the entire domain.

Reverse Lookup

Looking up an IP address to find the host name is exactly the same as looking up an FQDN using a DNS server (only backwards). An FQDN starts with the specific host and then the domain; an IP address starts with the network ID and then the host ID. Because you want to use DNS to handle the mapping, both must go the same way, so the octets of the IP address are reversed. That is, 148.53.66.7 in the inverse address resolution is 7.66.53.148.

Now that the IP address is reversed, it is going the same way as an FQDN. Now you can resolve the address using DNS. You need to create a zone with a particular name. To find the name, take the assigned portion of the address—for example, in 148.53.66.7 the portion that was assigned is 148.53, and for 204.12.25.3 it is 204.12.25. Now, create a zone in which these numbers are reversed and to which you add in-addr.arpa—that is, 53.148.in-addr.arpa or 25.12.204.in-addr.arpa, respectively.

2.1.4   Exercises

Excercise 1: Backing Up the WINS Server

Prerequisites: You have installed WINS on a Windows NT 4.0 Server.

Purpose: To configure the WINS server for automatic backup and to manually back up the WINS server.

1.   Choose Start | Programs | Administrative Tools.

2.   From the Administrative Tools menu, choose WINS Manager.

3.   From the Server menu in the WINS Manager window, choose Configuration.

4. Choose Advanced.

5. In the Database Backup Path box, browse to find the System32\WINS subdirectory under the root of the Windows NT installation.

6. Choose OK. A path similar to C:\WINNT\SYSTEM32\WINS should appear in the Database Backup Path box.

7. Note the Backup on Termination option in the Advanced WINS Server Configuration box. When this option is checked, WINS automatically backs up the WINS database when the WINS service is stopped. However, the WINS server does not back up the database when the Windows NT Server is shut down.

8. Choose OK to close the WINS Server Configuration dialog.

9. From the Mappings menu of the WINS Manager window, choose Backup Database.

10. Choose OK to back up the database to the path entered in the Advanced Configuration settings. You can also choose to save the backup in a different directory.

11. A message appears indicating the backup is successful.

Exercise 2: Restoring the WINS Database Backup

Prerequisites: You have installed WINS on a Windows NT 4.0 Server. You have completed Exercise 1—Backing Up the WINS Server.

Purpose: To manually restore a WINS database backup.

1. Choose Start | Settings | Control Panel.

2. From the Control Panel window, choose Services.

3. From the Services windows, select Windows Internet Name Service.

4. Choose Stop.

5. Choose Start | Programs | Administrative Tools.

6. From the Administrative Tools menu, choose WINS Manager.

7. From the Mappings menu in the WINS Manager windows, choose Restore Local Database.

> **This option is grayed out if the WINS service is started. The WINS service must be stopped to restore the WINS database.**

8. Choose OK to restore a backup from the path specified in the Advanced Configuration settings. You can also choose to restore a backup from a different directory.

9. A message indicating a successful restoration should appear.

10. Choose Start | Settings | Control Panel.

11. From the Control Panel window, choose Services.

12. From the Services dialog, choose Windows Internet Name Service.

13. Choose Start.

14. A message indicating that WINS started successfully should appear.

2.1.5 Practice Problems

1. IIS enables you to share information to any type of computer that can use the TCP/IP protocol. IIS includes which three servers?

    A. FTP

    B. Gopher

    C. SMTP

    D. WWW

2. Which server enables you to share your printers with UNIX-based hosts?

    A. Dynamic Host Configuration Protocol

    B. Line Printer daemon

    C. DHCP relay agent

    D. WINS

    E. SNMP

3. Which server provides automatic configuration of remote hosts?

    A. Dynamic Host Configuration Protocol

    B. Line Printer daemon

    C. DHCP relay agent

    D. WINS

    E. SNMP

4. Which server provides a centralized method of name management?

    A. Dynamic Host Configuration Protocol

    B. Line Printer daemon

    C. DHCP relay agent

    D. WINS

    E. SNMP

5. Which service should you use to track the performance of your TCP/IP protocols?

    A. Dynamic Host Configuration Protocol

    B. Line Printer daemon

    C. DHCP relay agent

    D. WINS

    E. SNMP

6. The primary purpose of DHCP relay agent is

    A. To provide name resolution

    B. To track TCP/IP performance

    C. To extend the DHCP service across subnets

    D. To allow UNIX-based hosts to print on Windows NT printers

7. What does the SNMP acronym stand for?

    A. System Network Monitoring Protocol

    B. Simple Network Monitoring Protocol

    C. System Network Management Protocol

    D. Simple Network Management Protocol

8. Which service resolves host names to IP addresses?

    A. DNS

    B. DHCP

    C. WINS

    D. BDC

9. Which service resolves NetBIOS names to IP addresses?

    A. DNS

    B. DHCP

    C. WINS

    D. BDC

10. How does a WINS server gather entries to add to its database?

    A. It examines each packet sent on the network.

    B. It receives a copy of the browse list from the Master Browser on each network segment.

    C. WINS clients send a name registration to the WINS server.

    D. It retrieves a copy of the computer accounts in each domain.

11. Where does a client first look to resolve a NetBIOS name?

    A. In the NetBIOS cache on the WINS server

    B. In the NetBIOS cache on the WINS proxy agent

    C. In the NetBIOS cache on the Primary Domain Controller

    D. In the NetBIOS cache on the client

12. What type of names are registered by WINS clients? (Select all that apply.)

    A. The computer name

    B. The domain name of a domain controller

    C. Share names created on that computer

    D. The names of network services

13. How do you configure automatic backup of the WINS database?

    A. Use the AT command to schedule the backup

    B. Specify the name of the backup directory in WINS Manager

    C. Specify the backup interval in WINS Manager

    D. Install a tape device through Control Panel | SCSI Adapters

14. When does a WINS client try to renew its registration?

    A. After three days

    B. One day before the registration expires

    C. Every 24 hours

    D. When half of the registration life has expired

15. By default, where does the WINS server first write changes to the database?

    A. To the log file

    B. To the database

    C. To the Registry

    D. To the temporary database

16. Where can you see a record of WINS server error messages?

    A. In the Windows NT System Event Log

    B. In the ERROR.LOG file in the WINS directory

    C. In the Windows NT Application Event Log

    D. In the Error Log in WINS Manager

17. What does a WINS server do if it receives a name registration request for a host name already in its database?

    A. It replaces the old entry with the newer one.

    B. It queries the host of the existing registration to see whether the registration is still valid.

    C. It denies the registration request.

    D. It adds the registration as an alternative address for the existing name.

18. How do you install a WINS proxy agent?

    A. From Control Panel | Network. Then choose Services.

B. From Control Panel | Add Programs.

C. By changing a Registry entry.

D. By running the Network Client Administration tool from the WINS program group.

19. How does a client decide which WINS server to use?

A. The first WINS server that responds to a broadcast

B. The WINS server that wins an election

C. The initial WINS server configured in TCP/IP

D. The primary WINS server specified in the DHCP scope options

20. What happens to a name registration when the host crashes?

A. The WINS server marks the record as released after it queries the client at half of TTL.

B. The name is marked as released after three renewal periods are missed.

C. The name is scavenged after the registration expires.

D. The name is released after the TTL is over.

21. On which platform can you install a WINS server? (Select all that apply.)

A. On a Windows NT 3.51 member server

B. On a Windows NT 4.0 Workstation running the WINS proxy agent

C. On a Windows NT 4.0 Backup Domain Controller

D. On a Windows NT 4.0 Primary Domain Controller

22. How many WINS servers should be installed?

A. One primary for each subnet and one secondary for every two subnets

B. One primary for every 2,000 clients and one secondary for each additional 2,000 clients

C. One primary and one secondary for every 10,000 clients

D. One primary and one secondary for each domain

23. Where should a WINS proxy agent be located?

A. On the same subnet as non-WINS clients

B. On the same subnet as the DHCP server

C. On the same subnet as the DNS server

D. On the same subnet as the DHCP relay agent

24. How can the WINS clients of one WINS server resolve the addresses of clients registered with another WINS server?

A. The WINS server can be configured for recursive lookup to the other WINS server.

B. The WINS server can be a replication partner of the other server.

C. The client can be configured with the address of the other WINS server as its secondary WINS server.

D. The WINS servers automatically synchronize their databases.

25. Where is WINS configuration information stored?

A. In the \WINNT\SYSTEM32\WINS directory

B. In the Registry

C. In the WINS.CFG file in the WINNT directory

D. In the J50.CHK file in the WINS directory

26. Your organization uses primarily Microsoft operating systems and you want to provide reverse DNS lookup for the hosts in your organization for servers on the Internet. Your organization uses DHCP to assign IP addresses. How can you provide reverse-lookup capabilities?

A. Reserve a DHCP address for each client and enter this information into the DNS server.

B. Set up the clients to use DNS for WINS resolution.

C. Add an @ IN WINS record in the DNS database.

D. This is not possible.

27. Your organization currently uses a UNIX server for DNS. The server is fully configured using BIND files. In which two ways can you configure your Microsoft DNS server so you will not need to reenter any information?

A. Set up Microsoft DNS as the primary and transfer the zone to the UNIX system

B. Set up Microsoft DNS as the secondary and transfer the zone from the UNIX system

C. Configure the Microsoft DNS server as an IP forwarder

D. Configure the Microsoft DNS server as a caching only server

28. Which of the following is *not* part of a Fully Qualified Domain Name? (Choose all that apply.)

A. Type of organization

B. Host name

C. Company name

D. CPU type

29. What are the benefits of DNS? (Select all that apply.)

A. It allows a distributed database that can be administered by a number of administrators.

B. It allows host names that specify where a host is located.

C. It allows WINS clients to register with the WINS server.

D. It allows queries to other servers to resolve host names.

30. With what non-Microsoft DNS platforms is Microsoft DNS compatible?

A. Only UNIX DNS servers that are based on BIND

B. Only UNIX DNS servers that are based on the DNS RFCs

C. UNIX DNS servers that are either BIND based or RFC based

D. Only other Microsoft DNS servers

31. In the DNS name www.microsoft.com, what does microsoft represent?

A. The last name of the host

B. The domain in which the host is located

C. The IP address of the building in which the host is located

D. The directory in which the host name file is located

2.1.6   Practice Problems: Answers and Explanations

1. **A, B, D**   IIS includes FTP, Gopher, and WWW servers.

2. **B**   The Line Printer daemon enables you to share your printers with UNIX-based hosts.

3. **A**   DHCP provides automatic configuration of remote hosts.

4. **D** WINS server provides a centralized method of name management that is both flexible and dynamic.

5. **E** SNMP is used to track the performance of your TCP/IP protocols.

6. **C** The DHCP relay agent extends the capabilities of the DHCP service by allowing it to work across various different subnets.

7. **D** Simple Network Management Protocol.

8. **A** The DNS server resolves host names to IP addresses.

9. **C** The WINS server resolves NetBIOS names to IP addresses.

10. **C** The only time a WINS server automatically collects entries is when a WINS client is configured with that WINS server's address. When the client starts up, it sends a registration request to the WINS server

11. **D** A client always tries to resolve a NetBIOS name through its own name cache. If the entry is not found, then the client sends a name resolution request to the WINS server. The WINS server looks in the WINS database for the resolution at that point.

12. **A, B, D** All networking services register with WINS. A domain controller must also register its domain name with WINS, along with its computer name, so clients of that domain can log on.

13. **B** You can back up the WINS database only through the WINS Manager. Once you specify the path of the backup directory, backups automatically take place every 24 hours. The only backup interval you can specify is 24 hours. However, you can do a manual backup through WINS Manager.

14. **D** A client first tries to renew its registration when half of the Time to Live has expired. Although the default Time to Live

is six days, the more correct answer is half of the TTL because the default TTL could have been changed.

15. **A** The WINS database is a transactional database in which changes are first written to a log file and then to the database. This technique gives the database a backup source for all its changes.

16. **C** WINS writes its error messages to the Windows NT Event Log. However, because WINS uses a JET database to store its entries, messages are written in the Application Log instead of the System Log.

17. **B** When a WINS server receives a registration request that conflicts with an existing entry, the server tries to resolve the conflict by querying the owner of the original registration. If the owner responds, the WINS server denies the new registration request. If the owner doesn't respond, the WINS server successfully registers the client and replaces the old entry with the new one.

18. **C** You must change a Registry entry to turn on the WINS proxy agent for an existing WINS client. When that client reboots, it notes the new Registry setting and makes that client into a WINS proxy agent.

19. **D** A WINS client communicates only with WINS servers for which the client is configured. You can configure these WINS servers in one of two ways. You can manually specify a WINS server with the primary WINS server address in TCP/IP, or you can specify the primary WINS server address through the scope options of DHCP for clients that receive their TCP/IP addresses from DHCP.

20. **D** After a client registers its NetBIOS name with a WINS server, it is the client's responsibility to renew that registration. The WINS server does not initiate any registration renewals with clients. The registration is released if not renewed by the time the TTL expires. However, the

entry is not scavenged until the Extinction Interval and the Extinction Timeout have expired.

21. **A, C, D**   You can install a WINS server on any Windows NT Server platform.

22. **C**   You should have one primary and one secondary WINS server for every 10,000 WINS clients. Although the secondary server is not required, it can serve as a backup if the primary WINS servers goes down.

23. **A**   You should locate a WINS proxy agent on each subnet that has non-WINS clients. Non-WINS clients resort to b-node broadcasts to resolve NetBIOS names, yet these broadcasts are typically forwarded by routers. The only way to have the request forwarded to a WINS server is to have a WINS proxy agent on the subnet so it can hear the broadcast.

24. **B**   WINS clients register their addresses only with the primary WINS server. If the registration succeeds, the clients won't attempt to contact the secondary WINS server. WINS servers copy entries to their replication partners, but it doesn't happen automatically; the copying process must be configured.

25. **B**   The WINS database, with its associated files, is stored in the \WINNT\ SYSTEM32\WINS directory. However, the WINS configuration information is stored in the Registry.

26. **C**   Adding an @ IN WINS record in the DNS database will provide reverse lookup capability.

27. **B, C**   Set up DNS as the secondary and transfer the zone from the UNIX system or you can configure the DNS server as a caching only server.

28. **D**   CPU type is not a component of a FQDN.

29. **A, B, D**   Although DNS on a Windows NT Server can be configured to query the WINS server for a name resolution, WINS clients do not register themselves directly with the DNS server.

30. **C**   NT DNS is based on the RFCs for DNS but is designed to be compatible with DNS servers based on BIND as well.

31. **B**   The path specifies a host named www in a domain microsoft. The domain microsoft is located in the top-level domain com.

2.1.7   Keywords

DHCP   Dynamic Host Configuration Protocol

DNS   Domain Name Server

IIS   Internet Information Server

SNMP   Simple Network Management Protocol

WINS   Windows Internet Name Service

2.2   Installing TCP/IP

Installation of the TCP/IP protocol and support on a Windows NT Server computer is a very straightforward operation. Follow these steps:

1. Open the Network Settings dialog box (double-click the Network icon in the Control Panel).

2. Click Add in the Protocols tab to open the Select Network Protocol dialog box.

3. Select TCP/IP Protocol in the Network Protocol list and choose OK.

4. The next prompt asks whether you wish to use DHCP. If this computer will obtain its IP address from DHCP, choose Yes. If this computer will be configured with a static IP address, choose No.

5. When prompted, supply the path where Setup can locate the driver files.

6. Choose Close to exit the Network settings dialog box. After it recalculates the bindings, Setup shows you a blank Microsoft TCP/IP Properties dialog box.

7. If more than one adapter has been installed, select the adapter to be configured in the Adapter list. (Note: You should configure each adapter with a valid IP address for the subnet it is on.)

8. If this computer will obtain its address configuration from DHCP for the network adapters, click the Obtain an IP address from a DHCP Server radio button.

9. If this computer will be configured with static addresses, click the Specify an IP Address radio button and complete the following fields:

   IP Address (Required)

   Subnet Mask (Required. Setup will suggest the default subnet mask appropriate for the IP address you enter.)

   Default Gateway

10. Choose OK and restart the computer to activate the settings.

2.2.1   Practice Problems

1. To install TCP/IP support on Windows NT Server 4.0, which utility in the Control Panel must you select?

   A. Services

   B. System

   C. Network

   D. Hardware

2. After having chosen the utility in question 1, which tab must you select?

   A. Protocols

   B. Adapter

   C. Bindings

   D. Information

3. Selecting which service prevents you from needing to supply TCP/IP configuration information?

   A. WINS

   B. DNS

   C. DHCP

   D. PDC

4. When manually configuring TCP/IP, which of the following fields are required entries? (Select two.)

   A. IP Address

   B. TCP Address

   C. Subnet Mask

   D. Default Gateway

2.2.2   Practice Problems: Answers and Explanations

1. **C**   Begin installation from the Network icon in the Control Panel.

2. **A**   Click Add in the Protocols tab to open the Select Network Protocol dialog box.

3. **C**   The DHCP service prevents you from needing to manually enter TCP/IP configuration information.

4. **A, C**   If a computer will be configured with static addresses, you must specify the IP Address and Subnet Mask fields.

2.3   Configuring Scopes

For a DHCP server to lease IP addresses to the DHCP clients, a range of valid IP addresses for those clients must be configured on the DHCP server. Each range of IP addresses is called a scope. One scope must be configured on the server for each subnet to which the DHCP server provides IP address leases. The DHCP server is normally configured with a scope for the local subnet (the subnet the DHCP server is on) and, optionally, with a scope for each remote subnet for which it will provide addresses. Configuring scopes for remote subnets on a DHCP server has two benefits:

- The DHCP server can provide IP address leases to clients on remote subnets. This feature is especially useful as a backup in case another DHCP server is not available. If no DHCP server is available with an IP address lease for a DHCP client, the client cannot initialize TCP/IP. To prevent the inability to lease to a client when a server is down, you may want to have more than one DHCP server that can provide a DHCP client with a lease. You must ensure, however, that the scopes on each DHCP server have unique IP address ranges so that no duplicate IP addresses are on the internetwork.

- You can create separate scope options for each subnet. For example, each subnet could have a default gateway that can be configured individually for each scope. After installing the DHCP server and restarting the computer, you must create an IP address scope.

To create a scope on a DHCP server, you must have the DHCP server service installed and running. You also should know a range of IP addresses that you can use to create a DHCP scope, as well as the IP addresses that should be excluded from that range.

Follow these steps to configure a scope on the DHCP server:

1. Start DHCP Manager (Start | Programs | Administrative Tools | DHCP Manager).

2. Select the local DHCP server Local Machine by clicking the entry and choosing Create from the Scope menu. The Create Scope dialog box is displayed. (This dialog box will be displayed automatically the first time you run the DHCP Manager.)

3. Type the starting and ending IP addresses for the first subnet in the Start Address and the End Address fields of the IP address pool.

4. Type the subnet mask for this scope in the Subnet Mask field.

5. If required, type a single IP address or a range of IP addresses to be excluded from the IP. The IP address that is not used in the address pool in the Exclusion Range Start Address scope is added to the Excluded Addresses list. Choose Add. Repeat if required.

> **If any hosts are not using DHCP but have an IP address that falls within the IP address pool, the IP addresses of these hosts must be excluded from the scope. If the IP address is not excluded, DHCP does not know that the IP address is already in use and might assign the IP address to a DHCP client, causing a duplicate IP address on the network. If you want certain DHCP clients to use a specific IP address out of the scope, you can assign this address from the Add Reservations dialog box as described later in this section.**

6. If you do not want the IP address leases to expire, select the Unlimited option under Lease Duration. (If you choose this option, then the configuration of the client will never be updated.) If you want to force the DHCP clients to renew their leases periodically (to ensure that the client is still using the IP address), choose the Limited To: option and type the lease duration in days, hours, and minutes. By default, the lease duration is three days. If you have a large ratio of available IP addresses to hosts on the network, you may want to use a longer lease duration to reduce broadcast traffic. If hosts are regularly coming and going and changing subnets on the network, such as with laptops and docking stations, you want a relatively short lease duration so the DHCP server can recover previously used IP addresses fairly quickly.

7. In the Name field, type the name to be used for referring to the scope in the DHCP Manager, for example, `subnet 200.20.1.0`.

8. In the Comment field, type an optional descriptive comment for the scope, for example, `Third floor - west side`.

2.3.1 Scope Options

Each DHCP scope can have several options that are configured on the client along with the IP address, such as default gateway and WINS server addresses. DHCP Manager includes many scope options that can be configured and sent to the DHCP clients; however, if TCP/IP configuration has been manually entered, then the client will ignore everything except the IP address and subnet mask.

Two types of DHCP scope options are available:

- Global options, which are set for all scopes in DHCP Manager
- Scope options, which are set for a selected scope in DHCP Manager

The value set in a scope option overrides a value set for the same DHCP option in a global option. Any values manually configured on the DHCP client—through the Network Control Panel applet Microsoft TCP/IP Configuration dialog box, for example—override any DHCP configured options.

To view and define options for a DHCP server, follow these steps:

1. Start the DHCP Manager tool.

2. Choose either Scope or Global from the DHCP Options menu.

3. Configure the desired DHCP options:

    1. From the unused Options list, select an option and click Add. The option is added to the Active Options list.

    2. Choose Value to display the value for the option.

    3. You can now edit the value. Three types of values can be edited: strings (such as domain name), which you can simply enter; hexadecimal values (such as NetBIOS node type), which you can enter; and IP address ranges. For these, click Edit Array and another dialog box appears in which you can enter one or more IP addresses.

4. When all the required options are entered, click OK and exit DHCP Manager.

2.3.2   Address Reservations

If a DHCP client requires a specific IP address to be assigned to it each time it renews its IP address lease, that IP address can be reserved for the DHCP client through the DHCP Manager tool. Following are the most common examples of clients that should have an IP address reservation:

- Servers on a network with non-WINS–enabled clients. If a server on such a network does not always lease the same IP address, the non-WINS clients might not be able to connect to the servers using NetBIOS over TCP/IP (NetBT).

- Any other host that is expected to have a specific IP address to which hosts connect.

To reserve an IP address from a scope for a specific DHCP client, follow these steps:

1. Determine the hardware address for the DHCP client with the IP address to be reserved from the scope. You can do so by typing **ipconfig/all** at a client's command prompt. A sample ipconfig/all output is shown here:

   ```
   Ethernet adapter NDISLoop1:
           Description . . . . . . . . : MS LoopBack Driver
           Physical Address. . . . . . : 20-4C-4F-4F-50-20
           DHCP Enabled. . . . . . . . : No
           IP Address. . . . . . . . . : 200.20.1.30
           Subnet Mask . . . . . . . . : 255.255.255.0
           Default Gateway . . . . . . : 200.20.1.1
   ```

2. Start DHCP Manager and select the DHCP server to be configured.

3. Select the scope containing the IP address to be reserved.

4. Choose Add Reservations from the Scope menu. The Add Reserved Clients dialog box is displayed.

5. In the IP Address field, type the IP address to be reserved for the DHCP client.

6. In the Unique Identifier field, type the hardware address of the network card for the IP address used. The hardware address should be typed without hyphens (-).

7. In the Client Name field, type a name for the client to be used only in DHCP Manager. This value is purely descriptive and does not affect the client in any way.

8. In the Client Comments field, type any comments for the client reservation. (This step is optional.)

9. Choose Add. The reservation is enabled.

10. Choose Active Leases from the Scope menu of DHCP Manager. The Active Leases dialog box is displayed and the reservations are shown.

2.3.3   DHCP Clients

For a client to use DHCP to obtain IP address information, automatic DHCP configuration must be enabled at the client. The procedure is slightly different for Windows NT and Windows for Workgroups clients.

Windows NT and Windows 95 as DHCP Clients

You can enable Automatic DHCP configuration either before or after Microsoft TCP/IP is installed. To ensure that the DHCP TCP/IP parameters are used instead of any configured manually on the host, you should preferably enable automatic DHCP configuration before Microsoft TCP/IP is installed. To enable automatic DHCP configuration after TCP/IP is installed, follow these steps:

1. Double-click the Network icon in Control Panel. The Network settings dialog box will be displayed.

2. Select the Protocols tab. From the list of installed protocols, select TCP/IP and choose the Properties button. The TCP/IP configuration dialog box appears.

3. Select the Enable Automatic DHCP Configuration check box. The previous IP address and subnet mask values disappear. Ensure that all other configuration parameters you want DHCP to supply are cleared.

4. Close the TCP/IP configuration dialog box and the Network Setting dialog box. Restart the system when prompted.

Windows for Workgroups as a DHCP Client

Configuring Windows for Workgroups as a DHCP client is simple:

1. Double-click the Network Setup icon in the Network program group of the Windows for Workgroups client.

2. Choose the Drivers button, select Microsoft TCP/IP, and choose the Setup button. The TCP/IP Configuration dialog box is displayed.

3. Select the Enable Automatic DHCP Configuration check box and choose Continue. The dialog box closes, and you are prompted to restart the computer.

4. Do not configure any other parameters, unless you want to override the options set in the DHCP scope—which is not recommended.

2.3.4   Using Scope Options

Each time a DHCP client initializes, it requests an IP address and subnet mask from the DHCP server. The server is configured with one or more scopes, each containing a range of valid IP addresses, the subnet mask for the internetwork, and additional optional DHCP client configuration information, known as scope options. For example, the default gateway for a subnet is often configured as a scope option for a given subnet. If any scope options are configured on the DHCP server, these are given to the DHCP client along with the IP address and subnet mask to be used by the client. The common scope options supported by Microsoft DHCP clients are shown in Table 2.3.1.

Table 2.3.1   Scope Options Supported by Microsoft DHCP Clients

Scope Option	Option Number
Router	3
DNS server	6

Scope Option	Option Number
DNS domain name	15
NetBIOS name server (WINS)	44
NetBIOS node type	46
NetBIOS scope ID	47

The Scope Options Configuration dialog box in the DHCP Manager application contains many other scope options (such as Time Server) that can be sent to the clients along with the other TCP/IP configuration information. The Microsoft DHCP clients, however, ignore and discard all the scope option information except for the options listed in Table 2.3.1.

2.3.5   Compacting the DHCP Database

Entries in the DHCP database are continually being added, modified, and deleted throughout the IP address leasing process. When entries are deleted, the space is not always completely filled with a new entry, due to the different sizes of each entry. After some time, the database contains unused space that can be recovered by compacting the database. This process is analogous to defragmenting a disk drive.

Microsoft recommends compacting the DHCP database from once every month to once every week, depending on the size of the internetwork. This compaction increases transaction speed and reduces the disk space used by the database.

The JETPACK utility compacts the DHCP database (DHCP.mdb) into a temporary database, which is then automatically copied to DHCP.mdb and deleted. The command used is jetpack DHCP.mdb temp_name.mdb, where temp_name.mdb is any filename specified by the user, with extension .mdb.

Here's how to compact the DHCP database:

1. Stop the DHCP server service by using either the Control Panel, Server Manager, or a command prompt.

2. To stop the service from a command prompt, type **net stop dhcpserver service**. This command stops the DHCP server.

3. Type **cd \systemroot\system32\dhcp**, where **systemroot** is WINNT. This changes to the DHCP directory.

4. Type **jetpack dhcp.mdb temp.mdb**. This command compacts DHCP.mdb into temp.mdb, copies it back to DHCP.mdb, and automatically deletes temp.mdb.

5. Type **net start dhcpserver**. This command restarts the DHCP server service.

2.3.6   Backing Up the DHCP Database

By default, the DHCP database is automatically backed up at a specific interval. You can change the default interval by editing the DHCP server BackupInterval parameter value contained in the Registry:

```
SYSTEM\current\currentcontrolset\services\DHCPServer\Parameters
```

Backing up the DHCP database enables recovery from a system crash or DHCP database corruption. You can change the default backup interval of 60 minutes by following these steps:

1. Stop the DHCP server service from a command prompt by typing **net stop dhcpserver**.

2. Start the Registry Editor (REGEDT32.EXE).

3. Open the HKEY_LOCAL_MACHINE\SYSTEM\CurrentControlSet\Services\DHCPserver\Parameters key and double-click to select BackupInterval.

4. In the Radix, make a selection, and configure the entry to the desired value. Close the Registry Editor.

5. Restart the DHCP server service from a command prompt by typing **net start dhcpserver**.

2.3.7   Restoring a Corrupt DHCP Database

If the DHCP database becomes corrupt, it can be restored from a backup in one of the following ways:

- It can be restored automatically.

- You can use the RestoreFlag key in the Registry.

- You can manually replace the corrupt database file.

Automatic Restoration

The DHCP server service automatically restores the backup copy of the database if it detects a corrupt database. If the database has become corrupt, stop and restart the DHCP server service. You can do so by typing **net stop dhcpserver** and then **net start dhcpserver** at a command prompt.

Registry RestoreFlag

If a corrupt DHCP database is not automatically restored from a backup when the DHCP server service is started, you can force the database to be restored by setting the RestoreFlag key in the Registry. Follow these steps:

1. Stop the DHCP server service from a command prompt by typing **net stop dhcpserver**.

2. Start the Registry editor (REGEDT32.EXE).

3. Open the HKEY_LOCAL_MACHINE\SYSTEM\CurrentControlSet\Services\DHCPserver\Parameters key and select RestoreFlag.

4. Change the value to 1 in the data field and click OK. Close the Registry editor.

5. Restart the DHCP server service from a command prompt by typing **net start dhcpserver**. The database is restored from the backup, and the RestoreFlag entry in the Registry automatically resets to 0.

Copying from the Backup Directory

You can manually replace the corrupt database file with a backed-up version by following these steps:

1. Stop the DHCP server service from a command by typing **net stop dhcpserver**.

2. Change to the DHCP directory by typing **cd \systemroot\system32\dhcp\backup\jet**, where **systemroot** is WINNT, for example.

3. Copy the contents of the directory to the \systemroot\system32\DHCP directory.

4. Type **net start dhcpserver** from a command prompt to restart the DHCP server service.

2.3.8   Exercises

Exercise 1: Installing the DHCP Server

In this exercise, you install the DHCP service. If the DHCP service is already installed, move to the next exercise.

1. Open the Networking Setting dialog box and, from the Services tab, choose Add.

2. Select Microsoft DHCP server and click OK.

3. Enter the path for your Windows NT source files. Close the Network Setting dialog box and restart your computer.

4. From the Start menu, choose Programs | Administrative Tools. Verify that DHCP Manager is installed.

Exercise 2: Configuring a DHCP Scope

In this exercise, you configure a scope on the DHCP server.

1. Start the DHCP Manager. Double-click the Local Machine to ensure you're connected to it.

2. Choose Scope | Create from the menu. You should see the Create Scope dialog box.

3. Enter the following information for the IP Address Pool:

Start Address	**148.53.66.1**
End Address	**148.53.127.254**
Subnet Mask	**255.255.192.0**

4. To add an exclusion, enter **148.53.90.0** into the Start Address and **148.53.90.255** into the End Address. Click the Add button.

5. Leave the duration at default and enter **Test Subnet 1** as the name. Click OK.

6. Choose Yes when prompted to activate the scope.

Exercise 3: Adding Scope and Global Options in the DHCP Server

Now you add options to the scope you configured.

1. Click the scope that was created in the previous exercise.

> If you get an error, click OK to continue—this event is an undocumented feature (a.k.a. a bug). Close the DHCP Manager and reopen it to stop this.

2. From the menu, choose DHCP Options | Scope.

3. From the list of unused options, choose 003 Router and click Add.

4. Click the Values button to see the rest of the dialog box. Currently, no router is listed.

5. Choose Edit Array. In the dialog box that appears, enter **148.53.64.1** in the IP Address field. Click Add to add the address to the list.

6. Click OK to close the IP Address Array Editor and then click OK to close the DHCP Options: Scope dialog box.

   The router option should appear in the Options Configuration panel.

7. Choose DHCP Options | Global from the menu and add the following options:

   006 DNS servers

   015 Domain name

   044 WINS/NBNS servers (you will get a message when you add this one)

   046 WINS/NBT node type

8. When the options are in, add the following configuration information:

DNS server	**148.53.64.8**
Domain name	**scrimtech.com**
WINS/NBNS servers	**198.53.64.8**
WINS/NBT node type	**0x8**

9. Click OK.

Exercise 4: Configuring a Second DHCP Scope

In this exercise, you configure a second scope of addresses.

1. Add the following information to the second DHCP scope:

   IP Address Pool

Start Address	**148.53.140.0**
End Address	**148.53.191.255**
Subnet Mask	**255.255.192.0**

2. Set the lease duration for 14 days and name the scope **Test Subnet 2**.

   A number should be listed for each scope in DHCP Manager. That number is the subnet ID for the scope. This scenario used a class B address, which is split into two subnets: **148.53.64.0** and **148.53.128.0**.

3. Set the default gateway for this scope to **148.53.128.1**.

4. This scope will not be used immediately; therefore, you want to deactivate it. Choose Scope | Deactivate.

Exercise 5: Adding Client Reservations

Finally, you add a client reservation:

1. Highlight the first subnet (**148.53.64.0**).

2. Choose Scope | Add Reservations from the menu.

3. In the Add Reserved Clients dialog box, change the IP address to **148.53.66.7**.

4. Enter the unique identifier, **0000DE7342FA**, and enter the client name as **Rob**.

5. Click Add.

6. Enter the IP address **148.53.66.9** with the unique identifier **00D4C9C57D34**. The client name is **Judy**. Click add.

7. Choose Done.

2.3.9   Practice Problems

1. Before a client can receive a DHCP address, what must be configured on the DHCP server?

    A. The DHCP relay agent

    B. A scope for the client's subnet

    C. A scope for the server's subnet

    D. A host name

2. What is the recommended method of providing backup to the DHCP server?

    A. Configure two DHCP servers with the same scope.

    B. Configure a BOOTP server.

    C. Replicate the database using directory replication.

    D. Configure two DHCP servers with different sections of the scope.

3. What is the effect of a lease duration of Unlimited?

    A. DHCP configuration options will never be updated.

    B. There is no effect.

    C. Network traffic will increase.

    D. Addresses cannot be shared dynamically.

4. In what environment is it advisable to have a short lease duration?

    A. In static environments where addresses don't change often

    B. When you have fewer hosts than IP addresses

    C. In environments where you have hosts moving and many changes to IP addresses

    D. When you have more hosts than IP addresses

5. What portions of the DHCP process are initiated by the server?

    A. Lease acquisition

    B. Lease renewal

    C. Lease release

    D. None

6. How must an NT Server be configured before you install a DHCP server?

  A. The WINS server must be installed.

  B. The server requires a static IP configuration.

  C. TCP/IP must not be installed.

  D. The server must be a Backup Domain Controller.

7. What information is required to define a scope?

  A. Starting and ending address and the subnet mask

  B. Subnet ID and the number of addresses to lease

  C. Number of hosts to be leased

  D. The name of the scope

8. Which clients cannot use a DHCP server?

  A. MS LAN Manager for DOS 2.2c

  B. Windows NT Workstation

  C. MS LAN Manager for OS/2 2.2c

  D. Windows 95

9. How do you configure a client to use DHCP?

  A. Install the DHCP client service.

  B. Select the Automatic Configuration icon from the Control Panel.

  C. DHCP automatically configures all clients.

  D. Select Obtain IP address automatically in the TCP/IP configuration.

10. What is the difference between a Global option and a Scope option?

  A. Global options affect all systems on the network whether DHCP clients or not.

  B. Scope options are set in the DHCP Manager for individual scopes.

  C. Global options affect the clients on scopes where no scope options are configured.

  D. There is no difference in the options, just in how they are entered.

11. Why would you use a client reservation?

  A. To provide dynamic configuration of TCP/IP options with a static IP address.

  B. To be able to control all the IP addresses.

  C. It is required for any host that cannot be a DHCP client but that uses an address in the scopes range.

  D. You cannot reserve addresses.

12. What is required for a client reservation?

  A. The NetBIOS name of the client

  B. The HOST name of the client

  C. The MAC address of the client

  D. The WINS address of the client

13. What happens to the client if you delete its lease?

  A. It immediately stops using the address.

  B. It will not be able to initialize at next startup.

  C. Nothing until it attempts to renew the address.

  D. The host stops working.

2.3.10 Practice Problems: Answers and Explanations

1. **B** A scope for the client's subnet must be configured on the DHCP server.

2. **D** Configuring two DHCP servers with different sections of the scope is the recommended method of providing backup to a DHCP server.

3. **A** DHCP configuration options will never be updated if the lease is set to Unlimited.

4. **C** Short lease durations are ideal for environments where you are moving hosts often.

5. **D** All processes are initiated by the client and not the server.

6. **B** A DHCP server cannot be a DHCP client and must have a static address.

7. **A, D** Starting and ending addresses and the subnet mask and the name of the scope are required to define a scope.

8. **C** MS LAN Manager for OS/2 2.2c clients cannot use DHCP.

9. **D** Select Obtain IP Address Automatically in the TCP/IP configuration to configure a client to use DHCP.

10. **B** Scope options are set in DHCP Manager for individual scopes.

11. **A** A client reservation provides a static IP address.

12. **C** The MAC address of a client must be given to configure a client reservation.

13. **C** If you delete a client's lease, nothing will happen until it attempts to renew the address.

2.3.11 Keywords

DHCP Manager Utility for administering scopes

Reservation Reserved IP address excluded from the scope

Scope A range of addresses issued by DHCP

2.4 Installing and Configuring a WINS Server

WINS must be installed on a Windows NT Server version 3.5x or 4.0. WINS servers on any version are compatible with the others; that is, you can mix a Windows NT 3.51 WINS server with a Windows NT 4.0 WINS server, including using them as replication partners. You can install WINS on any configuration of Windows NT Server—a member server, a Backup Domain Controller, or a Primary Domain Controller. The WINS server should have a static TCP/IP address with a subnet mask and default gateway along with any other TCP/IP parameters required for your network (such as a DNS server address). You can assign a DHCP address to the WINS server (the address should be reserved so the WINS server always receives the same address), but using a static address is the recommended option. Also, you should specify a WINS server address; in this case, the address is the same machine.

The WINS service is installed as a network service. After it is installed, it is immediately available for use. However, until WINS clients are configured with the TCP/IP address of the WINS server, they cannot register their names or use the WINS server for name resolution. In fact, if no clients are configured with this WINS server's address, the WINS database remains empty unless you add static entries or set up replication with another WINS server.

2.4.1 WINS Clients

Almost any Microsoft client capable of networking can be a WINS client:

- Windows NT Server 3.5x, 4.0
- Windows NT Workstation 3.5x, 4.0

- Windows 95
- Windows for Workgroups with TCP/IP-32
- Microsoft Network Client 3.0 for MS-DOS
- LAN Manager 2.2c for MS-DOS

However, only the Windows-based clients can register their names with the WINS server. The DOS-based clients can use the WINS server for name resolution, but you must add static entries for DOS clients to the WINS server so their names can be resolved.

To enable these clients for WINS, the address of the primary WINS server must be specified on the client. The client can also have the address of a secondary WINS server configured. The client can have this configuration information manually entered at the client or it can receive the configuration information with its TCP/IP address from a DHCP server.

2.4.2   Configuring WINS to Be Used by Non-WINS Clients

A WINS server interacts in two ways with WINS clients. First, it registers the names of those clients. Second, it answers requests for name resolutions (name queries). You can enable both functions for non-WINS clients through additional configuration.

2.4.3   Exercises

Exercise 1: Installing a WINS Server

Prerequisites: You have installed Windows NT 4.0 Server with the TCP/IP protocol. The Windows NT Server can be a member server, a Backup Domain Controller, or a Primary Domain Controller.

Purpose: Install the WINS service and configure your WINS server to function as the primary WINS server.

1. Right-click Network Neighborhood and choose Properties from the menu. (Network properties can also be accessed from the Network icon in Control Panel.)

2. Select the Services tab; then choose Add. From the Network Service box, select Windows Internet Name Service and then choose OK.

3. Select the Protocols tab, select TCP/IP Protocol, and then choose properties.

4. Select the WINS Address tab. Type the TCP/IP address of your Windows NT Server as the primary WINS server.

5. Choose OK; then choose Close to close the Network Properties dialog box.

6. Choose Yes when prompted to reboot your server.

Exercise 2: Manually Configuring a WINS Client

Prerequisites: You have installed WINS on a Windows NT 4.0 Server.

Purpose: To manually configure a TCP/IP client to be a WINS client. You configure the WINS server to be a WINS client, but the same process is used to configure other WINS clients—that is, you specify the address of the primary WINS server in the specified box and, if desired, the address of a secondary WINS server in the specified box.

1. Right-click Network Neighborhood. From the menu, choose Properties. (You also can access the Network Properties dialog box via Control Panel | Network.)

2. Select the Protocols tab.

3. Select TCP/IP Protocol; then choose Properties.

4. Select the WINS Address tab.

5. Type the address of your WINS server in the primary WINS server box.

6. Choose OK; then choose Close.

7. Reboot your computer when prompted. You have now configured your computer manually to be a WINS client.

Exercise 3: Configuring a DHCP Client to Be a WINS Client

Prerequisites: You have installed WINS on a Windows NT 4.0 Server. You have installed a DHCP server with a scope.

Purpose: To configure DHCP clients to receive WINS client configuration automatically through the DHCP scope

1. Choose Start | Programs | Administrative Tools.

2. From the Administrative Tools menu, choose DHCP Manager.

3. In the DHCP Manager window, choose the local machine.

4. Select the scope created under the local machine.

5. From the DHCP Options menu, select Scope.

This option is grayed out unless you have selected the scope.

---

6. In the Unused Options box, select 044 WINS/NBNS servers; choose Add.

7. In the Unused Options box, select 046 WINS/NBNS Node Type; choose Add.

8. From the Active Options box, select 044 WINS/NBNS servers; choose Value.

9. Choose Edit Array, type the address of your WINS server, and then choose Add.

10. Click OK to close the IP Address Array Editor.

11. From the Active Options box, select 046 WINS/NBNS Node Type.

12. In the Byte box, change the value 0x1 (b-node broadcast) to 0x8 (h-node broadcast).

13. Click OK. The scope options are now set for DHCP clients from this scope to automatically become clients of your WINS server.

2.4.4 Practice Problems

1. WINS must be installed on a Windows NT Server version:

   A. 3.1 or greater

   B. 3.5 or greater

   C. 3.51 or greater

   D. 4.0 or greater

2. WINS can be installed on which of the following? (Select all correct choices.)

   A. Windows NT Workstation

   B. Member server

   C. Backup Domain Controller

   D. Primary Domain Controller

3. To use WINS, clients need to know the _____ of the WINS server:

   A. Host name

   B. Subnet mask

   C. Default gateway

   D. IP address

4. Which of the following can be WINS clients? (Select all correct answers.)

   A. Windows NT Server 3.5

   B. Windows NT Workstation 3.5

   C. Windows 95

   D. Microsoft Network Client 2.0 for MS-DOS

   E. LAN Manager 2.2c for MS-DOS

2.4.5 Practice Problems: Answers and Explanations

1. **B** WINS must be installed on a Windows NT Server version 3.5*x* or 4.0.

2. **B, C, D** You can install WINS on any configuration of Windows NT Server—a member server, a Backup Domain Controller, or a Primary Domain Controller.

3. **D** Until WINS clients are configured with the IP address of the WINS server, they can neither register their names nor use the WINS server for name resolution.

4. **A, B, C, E** Any Microsoft client capable of networking can be a WINS client:

   • Windows NT Server 3.5*x*, 4.0

   • Windows NT Workstation 3.5*x*, 4.0

   • Windows 95

   • Windows for Workgroups with TCP/IP-32

   • Microsoft Network Client 3.0 for MS-DOS

   • LAN Manager 2.2c for MS-DOS

2.5 Importing LMHOSTS Files to WINS

The LMHOSTS file is a static file that can be used in place of WINS for NetBIOS name resolution. It is discussed in greater detail in section 2.16. If you have been using LMHOSTS files and decide to implement WINS, you can copy entries from an LMHOSTS file to a WINS server. Any entries copied this way are considered static entries. To copy the entries, follow these steps:

1. Choose Start | Programs | Administrative Tools.

2. From the Administrative Tools menu, choose WINS Manager.

3. From the Mappings menu in WINS Manager, choose Static Mappings.

4. Choose the Import Mappings button.

5. Browse to find the LMHOSTS file you modified and then choose that file.

6. Choose Open.

7. Note the names from the LMHOSTS file that have been added to the static mappings.

8. Close the Static Mappings dialog box.

9. From the Mappings menu, choose Show Database.

10. Note that the mappings you added from the LMHOSTS file are now in the WINS database.

2.5.1 Practice Problem

1. How can you add entries for non-WINS clients to a WINS server's database? (Select all that apply.)

   A. Configure the WINS server to be a pull partner for a DNS server.

   B. Import an LMHOSTS file.

   C. Install the WINS proxy agent on the segment with non-WINS clients.

   D. Add the entries with WINS Manager.

2.5.2 Practice Problem: Answer and Explanation

1. **B, D** An LMHOSTS file can be imported to a WINS server, which adds all the entries in the LMHOSTS file as static entries in the WINS database. You can also add static entries through WINS Manager. A WINS server can be a replication partner only with another WINS server, not a DNS server. A WINS proxy agent can help non-WINS clients resolve NetBIOS names, but non-WINS clients cannot automatically register their names with a WINS server even if a WINS proxy agent is installed.

2.5.3 Keywords

LMHOSTS Static file used for NetBIOS name resolution

NetBIOS Microsoft computer name convention

static entries Not dynamic

2.6 Running WINS on a Multihomed Computer

A *multihomed computer* contains more than one network interface card (NIC) that participates on more than one network. For example, a Windows NT Server can have two NIC cards. One NIC card can have the address 192.2.2.1 and communicate with the network of hosts from 192.2.2.2 to 192.2.2.200. The other NIC card can have the address 160.2.2.1 and communicate with the network of hosts from 160.2.2.2 to 160.2.2.200.

The common object between these two networks is the multihomed host, and as such, it can act as a router between the two networks. This method is most useful when you have two different physical types of networks—such as Ethernet and token ring.

Normally, the WINS service should not be run on a multihomed computer because the WINS server always registers its names in the local database. Therefore, you will have a problem if you run DOS clients, as they always try the first address that they receive from the WINS server. Because the WINS server registers its cards in order, the DOS client might not be able to reach resources on the WINS server from a network other than the one on which the first card is located.

2.6.1 Practice Problems

1. A multihomed host must have two:

    A. Protocols

    B. Topologies

    C. Network cards

    D. Operating systems

2. A good use for a multihomed host is to connect networks with dissimilar:

    A. Physical topologies

    B. Network cards

    C. Operating systems

    D. Protocols

3. Running WINS on a multihomed host is

    A. Encouraged

    B. Possible, but discouraged

    C. Necessary

    D. The only way WINS can run

2.6.2 Practice Problems: Answers and Explanations

1. **C** A multihomed host must have two network cards.

2. **A** A good use for a multihomed host is to connect networks with dissimilar physical topologies.

3. **B** Running WINS on a multihomed host is possible, but discouraged.

2.7 Configuring WINS Replication

Because WINS clients are configured to communicate only with specified WINS servers, the database on each WINS server may not have entries for all the WINS clients in the network. In fact, many TCP/IP implementations divide WINS clients among different WINS servers to balance the load. Unfortunately, WINS clients cannot resolve addresses registered with another WINS server unless the registrations from that server are somehow copied to the client's WINS server. *WINS replication* is the process used to copy one WINS server's database to another WINS server.

You can configure a WINS server so that it replicates its database with another WINS server. In this way, clients registered with one WINS server can be added to the database of another server. Static mappings entered on one server are also replicated to replication partners. In fact, you can enter static entrieson only one WINS server and yet these entries can be propagated to any number of WINS servers through replication.

After you enable replication, clients seeking name resolution can see not only entries from their server but also entries of the replication partners. Remember that clients register their names with the WINS server for which the clients are configured. WINS registrations are not done through broadcasts (in fact, one of the main benefits of WINS is the reduction of broadcast traffic). Because one WINS server is collecting registrations just for its clients, the only way for its clients to resolve names registered with another WINS server is for replication to be configured between the servers.

To set up replication, you must configure aWINS server as either a push partner or a pull partner. A *push partner* sends its entries to another server; for example, you can send a copy of the database from this WINS server to the other WINS server. A *pull partner* retrieves entries from another server; for example, one server can receive a copy of the database from another WINS server. You must always configure WINS servers in pairs; otherwise, replication won't work.

At the very least, one WINS server must be a push partner to send its entries, whereas the other WINS server must be a pull partner to receive the entries. Replication does not occur unless both WINS servers are properly configured. If both WINS servers are configured as push and pull partners, then each server ends up with entries from the other server. In theory, the combined database on each WINS server should be the same. However, because of the lag time in replication, this condition doesn't always happen.

Deciding which WINS server will be a push partner and which will be a pull partner is often determined by performance considerations. You often use a pull partner across slow wide area network (WAN) links because you can configure a pull partner to replicate only at certain times, such as at night when the WAN link is not in heavy use. In this case, you could make the WINS server on each side of the WAN link a pull partner with the other WINS server. This setup is known as *pull-pull replication*.

On faster links, you can use push partners. Push partners replicate when a specified number of changes, or updates, are made to the database. These updates can happen fairly frequently, but are not too large because you are not waiting to replicate a whole day's worth of changes. If you want two WINS servers to have identical databases, you must configure each WINS server to be a push and a pull partner for the other server.

You can configure a replication partner to start replication in several ways:

- When the WINS server starts, you can configure it as either a push or a pull partner.

- At a specified interval, such as every 24 hours. This option applies to pull replication.

- When a push partner reaches a specified number of changes to the database. These changes include name registrations and name releases. When this threshold is reached, the push partner notifies all its pull partners that it has changes for replications.

- Manually. You can force replication from the WINS Manager.

WINS can automatically replicate with other WINS servers if your network supports multi-casting. By default, every 40 minutes each WINS server sends a multicast to the address 224.0.1.24. Any servers found through this multicast are automatically configured as push and pull partners with replication set to occur every two hours. If the routers on your network do not support multicasting, the WINS servers see only other servers on the same subnet.

You can turn off this multicasting feature by editing the Registry in the following location:

```
HKEY_LOCAL_MACHINE\System\CurrentControlSet\Services\NetBT\Parameters
```

Change the value of UseSelfFndPnrs to 0.

Change the value of McastIntvl to a large number.

2.7.1   The Replication Process

A WINS server replicates only its active and extinct entries; released entries are not replicated. A replication partner can have entries that are marked active even though they have been released by its partner. To reduce the traffic from computers booting and shutting down each day, released entries are not replicated. However, if a registration changes, it is considered a new entry and it is replicated. The following example shows how records are replicated between replication partners.

2.7.2   Using the WINS Manager

As you install WINS, a WINS Manager tool is added to the Administrative Tools group. You can use this tool to manage the local WINS server and remote WINS servers as well. You can use WINS Manager to view the WINS database, add static entries to the database, configure push and pull partners for replication, and back up and restore the WINS database.

WINS Manager Configuration Dialog

You can use the WINS Manager Configuration dialog to configure how long entries stay in the WINS database. The following four parameters control the life of entries:

- Renewal Interval—The interval given to a WINS client after it successfully registers its name. The client begins renewing the name registration when half this time has expired. The default is six days.

- Extinction Interval—The amount of time that must pass before the WINS server marks a released entry as extinct. An extinct entry is not immediately deleted. The default is six days. The time until removal is controlled by the following parameter.

- Extinction Timeout— The amount of time WINS waits before removing (scavenging) entries that have been marked extinct. The default is six days.

- Verify Interval—The interval at which the WINS server verifies that names in its database that came from other servers are still valid. The default is 24 days and cannot be set below this value. This parameter applies if WINS servers are set up for replication.

Initial Replication Configuration

You can configure whether the WINS server replicates with its replication partners when it starts. Check the Initial Replication option under Pull Parameters on the WINS Server Configuration dialog box to have a pull replication partner replicate on startup. You can also specify the number of times the pull partner tries to contact the other WINS server as the pull partner does the startup replication.

For a push partner, you can also configure it to replicate upon startup by checking the Initial Replication option under Push Parameters. You can also specify that the push partner replicate when it has an address change.

Advanced Configuration Options

You can turn on or turn off the logging of entries to the WINS database. This log file records changes that are made to the WINS database before they are made. By default, logging is on, which gives the WINS server a backup via the log file. If you turn off the logging, the WINS server registers names more quickly, but you lose the backup support of the log file. These settings are configured through the WINS Advanced Configuration dialog.

The following are the advanced settings you can configure:

- Log Detailed Events—This option makes the logging of WINS events in Event Viewer more verbose. That is, you get more useful troubleshooting information from the log file. However, some performance degradation occurs when verbose logging is turned on.

- Replicate Only with Partners—By default, WINS replicates only with other WINS servers that are specifically configured as push or pull partners. If you want the WINS server to replicate automatically, you must turn off this setting.

- Backup on Termination—If you set this option, the WINS database is automatically backed up when the WINS service is stopped. However, the database is not backed up when the Windows NT Server is shut down.

- Migrate On/Off—If this switch is on, static entries that have the same address as a WINS client requesting registration are overwritten. This option is helpful if you are converting a computer from a non–Windows NT machine to a Windows NT machine with the same TCP/IP address. To have addresses resolved for this non–Windows NT machine in the past, you may have added a static entry to the WINS database. With the option on, the new dynamic entry can overwrite the old static entry. It is usually best to turn off this switch after you have migrated (upgraded) the new Windows NT machine. This switch is off by default so static entries are not overwritten.

- Starting Version Count—This option specifies the largest version ID number for the database. Each entry in the database is assigned a version ID. Replication is based on the version ID. A replication partner checks its last replicated entries against the version IDs of the records in the WINS database. The replication partner replicates only records with a later version ID than the last records it replicated from this partner. Usually, you don't need to change this parameter. However, if the database becomes corrupted, you may need to adjust this number so a replication partner replicates the proper entries.

- Database Backup Path—When the WINS database is backed up, it is copied to a local hard drive. This entry specifies the path to a directory on a local drive where the WINS backups are stored. This directory can also be used to automatically restore the WINS database. You must specify a local drive path.

2.7.3 Exercises

Exercise 1: Configuring Replication Partners

Prerequisites: You have installed WINS on a Windows NT 4.0 Server. The best way to do this exercise is to have another WINS server, but you can go through the steps of setting up replication without one. However, you will not be able to see the results of replication.

Purpose: To set up replication with another WINS server

1. Choose Start | Programs | Administrative Tools.

2. From the Administrative Tools menu, choose WINS Manager.

3. If you don't have another WINS server, skip to step 5. If you have another WINS server, do step 4.

4. From the Server menu, choose Add Server. Type the TCP/IP address of the other WINS server and then choose OK.

5. Select your WINS server in the WINS Manager window.

6. From the Server menu, choose Replication Partners.

7. From the Replication Partners box, select the other WINS server.

8. In the Replication Options box, select the other WINS server to be both a push and a pull partner.

9. Choose Configuration for a Push Partner. Note that push replication is triggered when an update count is reached.

10. Choose Configuration for a Pull Partner. Note that pull replication is started at a specific time and then from an offset time after the initial replication time.

11. Note that in this dialog box you can also manually trigger replication by choosing the Push or the Pull button in the Send Replication Trigger Now box.

Exercise 2: Viewing the WINS Database Mappings

Prerequisites: You have installed WINS.

Purpose: To see the database mappings collected by the WINS server

1. Choose Start | Programs | Administrative Tools.

2. From the Administrative Tools menu, choose WINS Manager.

3. In the WINS Manager window, note the statistics for your WINS server. The items listed are the latest starting time of the WINS service (typically the last boot); the last registration time; and the total queries, releases, and registrations.

4. From the Server menu, choose Detailed Information.

5. Note that you can see some total statistics about the WINS database from the Detailed Information window.

6. Choose Close.

7. From the Mappings menu in WINS Manager, choose Show Database. Note: If the menu is gray, select your WINS server in the WINS Manager window before choosing Show Database.

8. Note the different numbers registered for each machine name. See whether you can find the registration for your computer's name, your computer's server service, your computer's workstation service, and your user name.

9. Try the different sort order options to see how they affect the display.

10. Note the time stamp for each entry as well as the version ID. The time stamp specifies when the current status of the entry expires. The version ID is used to determine whether the record is replicated.

11. Close the Show Database window.

Exercise 3: Configuring the WINS Server

Prerequisites: You have installed WINS on a Windows NT 4.0 Server.

Purpose: To see the different configuration options in WINS Manager

1. Choose Start | Programs | Administrative Tools.

2. From the Administrative Tools menu, choose WINS Manager.

3. From the Server menu, choose Configuration.

4. Note the default times for the renewal interval, the extinction interval, and the extinction timeout. Each of these values is six days (144 hours). These times dictate how quickly a WINS database entry moves from active to released (renewal interval), from released to extinct (extinction interval), and from extinct to being removed from the database (extinction timeout). Microsoft recommends that you do not modify these values.

5. Note: The default time for the verify interval is 24 days (576 hours). This item specifies when a WINS server verifies that entries that it does not own (entries added to the database due to replication) are still active. The minimum value you can set for this parameter is 24 days.

6. Note the check box to do push or pull replication when the WINS server initializes.

7. Choose the Advanced button.

8. Note two of the settings here that can affect WINS performance—Logging Enabled and Log Detailed Events. With Logging Enabled, WINS must first write any changes to the WINS database to the JET.LOG file. Then the changes are made to the database. This log file serves as an ongoing backup to the database should it crash during the write process. However, if a number of changes are being made to the database simultaneously, logging can slow WINS performance—for example, when many people power up their computers in the morning and the clients try to register at the same time. With Log Detailed Events turned on, more detailed messages are written to the Event Log. Note that both settings are turned on by default.

9. Note the default setting for Replicate Only with Partners. WINS replicates only with specified partners unless you turn off this setting. When turned off, WINS tries to replicate with all the WINS servers it can locate through broadcasts.

10. Choose OK to close the Configuration dialog.

2.7.4 Practice Problems

1. How do you configure replication to occur at specified intervals?

    A. Configure a WINS server to be a pull partner.

    B. Use the AT command to schedule replication.

    C. Configure a WINS server to be a push partner.

    D. Edit the ReplIntrvl parameter in the Registry.

2. How can you configure a WINS server to automatically replicate its database with any other WINS servers?

    A. Specify All servers as push partners for replication.

    B. Turn on the Migrate On/Off switch in WINS Manager.

    C. Change the UseSelfFndPnrs parameter in the Registry to 0.

    D. Turn off the Replicate Only with Partners switch in WINS Manager.

3. Which replication option is best for WINS servers separated by a slow WAN link?

    A. Pull replication configured to replicate after 100 changes

    B. Push replication configured to replicate after 100 changes

    C. Pull replication configured to replicate at 6 a.m. and 6 p.m.

    D. Push replication configured to replicate at 6 a.m. and 6 p.m.

2.7.5   Practice Problems: Answers and Explanations

1. **A**   Only pull partners can have replication occur at specified times. Push replication occurs after a specified number of changes have been made to the WINS database. The `ReplIntrvl` parameter in the Registry doesn't exist.

2. **D**   A WINS server can automatically replicate with any other WINS server. However, WINS is configured by default to replicate only with specified partners. You must turn off this parameter to enable the automatic replication.

3. **C**   The best way to manage traffic on a slow WAN link is to schedule replication during slow traffic times. The only type of replication that supports scheduling is pull replication.

2.7.6   Keywords

extinction interval   The amount of time that must pass before the WINS server marks a released entry as extinct

extinction timeout   The amount of time WINS waits before removing (scavenging) entries that have been marked extinct

pull partner   Receives entries from another server

push partner   Sends its entries to another server

renewal interval   Interval given to a WINS client after it successfully registers its name

verify interval   Interval at which the WINS server verifies that names in its database that came from other servers are still valid

WINS Manager   Tool used to manage the local WINS server and remote WINS servers

WINS replication   The process used to copy one WINS server's database to another WINS server

2.8   Configuring Static Mappings in the WINS Database

You can register a non-WINS client with a WINS server by adding a static entry to the WINS database. With entries added for non-WINS clients, a WINS client can resolve more names without having to look up the entries in an LMHOSTS file. In fact, by adding entries for all non-WINS clients, you can eliminate the need for an LMHOSTS file. Static entries are added through the WINS Manager.

There are several types of static mappings. The following table summarizes the types that you can add.

Table 2.8.1   Types of Static Mappings

Type of Mapping	Explanation
Normal group	Group names don't have an address; rather, the WINS server returns 255.255.255.255 (the broadcast address). This type of mapping forces the client to broadcast on the local subnet to resolve the name.
Multihomed	A multihomed name is used to register a computer with more than one network card. It can contain up to 25 addresses.

Type of Mapping	Explanation
Domain name	In Windows NT 3.51, the domain name mapping was known as an Internet group. This entry contains a maximum of 25 IP addresses for the Primary or Backup Domain Controllers in a domain. This type of mapping enables client computers and servers to locate a domain controller for logon validation and pass through authentication.
Internet group	An Internet group mapping name is a user-defined mapping used to store addresses for members of a group other than a domain (such as a workgroup).

2.8.1 Exercise

Exercise: Adding Static Entries to a WINS Database

Prerequisites: You have installed WINS on a Windows NT 4.0 Server.

Purpose: To add static entries manually to the WINS database through WINS Manager

1. Choose Start | Programs | Administrative Tools.

2. From the Administrative Tools menu, choose WINS Manager.

3. From the Mappings menu in WINS Manager, choose Static Mappings.

4. Choose Add Mappings.

5. In the computer box, type **ABDCE**.

6. In the IP Address box, type **131.107.2.25**.

7. In the Type box, select Unique.

8. Choose Add to save the entry.

9. Add an entry for a computer named **FGHIJ** with an IP address of **133.107.4.53** and Type: Group.

10. Add an entry for a computer named **KLMNO** with an IP address of **136.107.3.34** and Type: Domain Name. Note that with the domain name mappings you must also move the IP address down with the arrow before you can save it because you can have multiple addresses (for multiple domain controllers) associated with a domain name.

11. Close the Add Static Mappings dialog. Note the mappings you have added in the Static Mappings dialog.

12. Try editing each of the entries. Note that the type of each entry differs. Note also that the Edit Static Mapping dialog for the domain mapping differs from the dialogs for the unique and group types.

13. Close the Static Mappings dialog after exploring the Edit Static Mapping dialogs.

14. In the WINS Manager window, choose Show Database from the Mappings menu.

15. Scroll down the mappings database and note the static entries you added. The static mappings are marked with a check in the S column.

16. Sort the database by expiration date. Scroll to the bottom of the database and note that the static mappings are there with a time stamp that won't let these entries expire.

17. Close the Show Database window.

2.8.2 Practice Problems

1. You can register a non-WINS client with a WINS server by

   A. Adding a static entry to the WINS database

   B. Creating a reservation for the entry

   C. Modifying the scope to exclude the address

   D. Manually editing the cache

2. With entries added for non-WINS clients, a WINS client can resolve more names without having to look up the entries in a(n) _____ file.

   A. HOSTS

   B. SERVICES

   C. LMHOSTS

   D. NETWORKS

3. Static entries are added through the

   A. Entry Manager

   B. ARP cache

   C. HOSTS file

   D. WINS Manager

2.8.3 Practice Problems: Answers and Explanations

1. **A** You can register a non-WINS client with a WINS server by adding a static entry to the WINS database.

2. **C** With entries added for non-WINS clients, a WINS client can resolve more names without having to look up the entries in an LMHOSTS file.

3. **D** Static entries are added through the WINS Manager.

2.9 Configuring Subnet Masks

Communication in a TCP/IP network is based on sending messages back and forth between computers and network devices. The messages contain a sender and a recipient address, known as IP addresses. The IP addresses are in an octet-based form such as 100.34.192.212. The first octet dictates the "class" of network that is being referred to, and as such, administrators can use three classes:

- 01–126   class A
- 128–191   class B
- 192–223   class C

Thus, the address 100.34.192.212 is clearly a class A address, whereas 220.34.192.212 is a class C address. The class is important because it indicates the maximum number of hosts that a network can have according to the following rules:

- Class A   16,777,214
- Class B   65,534
- Class C   254

Although the existing shortage of addresses has made it impossible to obtain a class A address for some time, imagine the difficulties inherent in trying to network 16 million hosts on a single segment; it is virtually impossible. At the same time, networking 254 hosts, although not impossible, is rarely done on a single segment. Typically, hosts are spread out across several physical locations often within the same building, campus, or other geographical area.

For that reason, and to make routing practical and possible, subnets are used to divide the network (and network numbers) into smaller portions. This discussion assumes that you have some familiarity with the basics of TCP/IP and addressing and concentrates on looking at subnetting—one of the most misunderstood components of addressing.

Simply put, *subnetting* is a mechanism for using some bits in the host ID octets as a subnetID. Without subnetting, an IP address is interpreted as two fields:

    netid + hostid

With subnetting, an IP address is interpreted as three fields:

    netid + subnetid + hostid

2.9.1   Subnet Masks, Host IDs, and Network IDs

Subnets are created in a TCP/IP internetwork by choosing the IP addresses and subnet masks used—a process known as subnet addressing or subnetting. The term *network* is used when it is not necessary to distinguish between individual subnets and internetworks. A *subnet* is simply a subdivision of a network. The term *subnetworking* or *subnetting* is used when a single network ID is subdivided into multiple network IDs by applying a custom subnet mask.

The subnet mask, like the IP address, is a 32-bit number often shown in dotted decimal notation. When shown in binary notation, the subnet mask has a 1-bit for each bit corresponding to the position of the network ID in the IP address, and a 0-bit for each bit corresponding to the position of the host ID in the IP Address (in binary notation). An example of a subnet mask is `11111111111111110000000000000000`, or `255.255.0.0` in dotted decimal notation.

A binary number is made up of bits. A bit can be either a `1` or a `0`, where `1` represents TRUE and `0` represents FALSE. All computer operations are performed using binary numbers because the bits are easily represented by electrical charges. Huge binary numbers are usually fairly meaningless to the average person, so the computer converts them to more human-friendly states such as decimal numbers and characters.

Any decimal number is represented in binary notation, using ones and zeroes. Each bit with a one represents 2 raised to the power of n-1 $[2^{(n-1)}]$, where n is the position of the bit from the right. Each bit with a `0` represents a 0 in decimal notation as well. The decimal number results from adding together all the 1 bits after converting each to $2^{(n-1)}$.

For example, the binary number `100` is 2^2, which means the decimal equivalent is 4.

The binary number `101` would be 2^2+0+2^0, or 5 in decimal notation.

With TCP/IP, use 8-bit binary numbers are often used in IP addresses, also called octets or bytes.

An example is

```
11111111
```

Each bit in position *n* from the right gives a value of $2^{(n-1)}$. Therefore the first bit represents a 1, the second bit a 2, the third a 4, the fourth an 8, and so on , so that you have

```
11111111          (binary)

128+64+32+16+8+4+2+1 = 255     (decimal)
```

Keep in mind that any 0 bits do not add to the total, so the following representations are equal:

```
11001001          (binary)

128+64+0 +0 +8+0+0+1 = 201     (decimal)
```

Memorizing the decimal equivalent number of each character in the 8-bit number is much simpler. Remembering the value 201 is easier than remembering 11001001.

Decimal to Binary

1	1	1	1	1	1	1	1
128	64	32	16	8	4	2	1

The preceding table makes it extremely easy to convert between binary and decimal quickly. For example, the number

```
01111111
```

should be easily recognized as 127, by taking the maximum value (255) and subtracting the missing digit (128). Likewise,

```
11011111
```

is quickly converted to 223 by subtracting the value of the missing digit (32) from the maximum value (255).

The 0 bits of the subnet mask essentially mask out, or cover up, the host ID portion of an IP address. Thus, the subnet mask is used to determine on which network or subnet the address being referred to is found. When one host sends a message to another host, the TCP/IP protocol must determine whether the hosts are on the same subnet and can communicate by broadcasts or whether they are on different subnets and the message should be sent via a router to the other subnet. You cannot determine whether two IP addresses are on the same subnet just by looking at the IP addresses without the subnet mask. For example, if the host at `192.20.1.5` sends a message to the host at `192.20.6.8`, should it be sent by broadcast or to a router connecting to another subnet?

The answer depends on the subnet mask being used on the network. If the subnet mask is 255.255.255.0, then the network ID of the first host would be 192.20.1 and the network ID of the second host would be 192.20.6, which are on different subnets; therefore, they must communicate via a router. On the other hand, if the subnet mask is 255.255.0.0, then both hosts would be on subnet 192.20 and could communicate by using local broadcasts and local address resolution.

When the subnet mask is one of 255.0.0.0, 255.255.0.0, or 255.255.255.0, it is fairly obvious which part of the IP address is the network ID. (These subnet masks are the defaults for class A, B, and C networks, respectively). However, which part of the IP address is the network becomes less apparent when other subnet masks are used (such as 255.255.248.0). In this case, if both the IP address and subnet mask are converted to binary, then the answer becomes more apparent. (The 1 bits of the subnet mask correspond to the network ID in the IP address.)

By figuring out what subnet a host is on from the IP address and subnet mask, routing a packet to the proper destination becomes easier. Fortunately, all you have to do is supply the proper IP addresses with one subnet mask for the entire internetwork, and the software determines which subnet the destination is on. If the destination address is on a different subnet than the sender, then it is on a remote network and the packet is routed appropriately, usually by being sent to the default gateway.

If a network has a small number of hosts and they are all on the same segment without any routers, they are likely given the same network ID (the network portion of an IP address). If the network is larger, however, with remote segments connected by routers (an internetwork), then each individual subnet needs a different network ID. Therefore, when assigning IP addresses and subnet masks, the network administrator must know how many subnets are required and the maximum number of hosts that are on each subnet.

Depending on the subnet mask, the internetwork can have either many different network IDs with a smaller number of hosts on each subnet or a smaller number of network IDs with a larger number of hosts on each subnet. The reasons for these results will become clearer as you read further. The following table shows the maximum number of hosts and subnets available per the number of bits used.

Additional Bits Required	Number of Possible Subnets	Maximum C Hosts	Maximum B Hosts	Maximum A Hosts	Subnet Mask
0	0	254	65,534	16,777,214	0
1	invalid	invalid	invalid	invalid	invalid
2	2	62	16,382	4,194,302	192
3	6	30	8,190	2,097,150	224
4	14	14	4,094	1,048,574	240
5	30	6	2,044	524,286	248
6	62	2	1,022	262,142	252
7	126	invalid	510	131,070	254
8	254	invalid	254	65,534	255

2.9.2   Purpose of Subnet Masks

By specifying the correct subnet mask for addresses, you are telling the TCP/IP software which part of the address refers to the host and which part refers to the specific subnet on which the host is located. As mentioned previously, the IP address and subnet mask are made up of four 8-bit octets that are most often shown in decimal, rather than binary, format for ease of reading. Here's an example of an IP address and subnet mask in binary format::

IP address	`11001000 00010100 00010000 00000101`
Subnet mask	`11111111 11111111 11111111 00000000`
Network ID	`11001000 00010100 00010000 00000000`
Host ID	`00000000 00000000 00000000 00000101`

Notice that the network ID is the portion of the IP address corresponding to a bit value of 1 in the subnet mask.

In the preceding example, you could have a maximum of 254 different hosts on the network `192.20.16` (`192.20.16.1` through `192.20.16.254`). If you wanted to have more hosts on one network, then you have to use a different addressing scheme. For example, using a subnet mask of `255.255.0.0` gives the following results:

IP address	`192.20.16.5`
Subnet mask	`255.255.0.0`
Network ID	`192.20`
Host ID	`16.5`

A common convention in TCP/IP is to omit the trailing zero octets in a network ID and the leading zero octets in a host ID. Therefore, the network ID `192.20` really represents `192.20.0.0`, and the host ID `16.5` really represents `0.0.16.5`.

Because the host ID in this example is a 16-bit value, you can have (256×256)-2 hosts on the network `192.20`. The two addresses that must be subtracted from the possibilities are `0` (consisting of all zeroes) and `255` (consisting of all ones)—both reserved addresses. The `0` is used to define the network, whereas `255` is a broadcast address for all computers in the network.

A host ID cannot have all bits set to either `1` or `0`, as these addresses would be interpreted to mean either a broadcast address or "this network only." Thus the number of valid addresses will be $(2^n)-2$, where n is the number of bits used for the host ID.

> Common law dictates that address bits cannot be all ones or zeroes. In reality, if—and only if—the routers on the network support extended prefixing addressing, addresses of all ones or zeroes are possible. Both the software and the routers must support RIP V2, and you must disallow the possibility of traffic over any older—incompatible—routers.
>
> Cisco routers, NetWare 4.*x*, and Windows NT support the extended prefixing address (though they often call it a "zero network"). Contrary to the principles of RFC 950, these products permit the use of all-zero and all-one subnets. However, even one NetWare 3.*x* system anywhere on your network, or any older router, means that you cannot use the zero-network option. Therefore, for all practical purposes, you should consider zeroes and ones off limits.

2

You may also notice that compared to the first scheme the second scheme allows for fewer combinations of network IDs. Although the second sample scenario might seem preferable for most networks, you may often not have the freedom to use such a scheme. For example, if the hosts are on the Internet, you must assign a certain set of IP addresses by the Internet address assignment authority, InterNIC. As the number of IP addresses available today is limited, you usually do not have the luxury to choose a scheme that gives so many combinations of available host addresses. Suppose you were assigned the network ID 192.20.5 and had a total of 1,000 hosts on three remote networks. A class C network using the default subnet mask of 255.255.255.0 only has one network (192.20.5) and 254 hosts (192.20.5.1 through 192.20.5.254).

Now look at how a subnet mask is used to determine which part of the IP address is the network ID and which part is the host ID. TCP/IP does a binary calculation using the IP address and the subnet mask to determine the network ID portion of the IP address.

The computation TCP/IP performs is a logical bitwise AND of the IP address and the subnet mask. The calculation sounds complicated, but all it means is that the octets are converted to binary numbers and a logical AND is performed whose result is the network ID. Recall that in the preceding example the network ID is the portion of the IP address corresponding to a bit value of 1 in the subnet mask.

Performing a bitwise AND on two bits results in 1 (or TRUE) if the two values are both 1. If either or both of the values are not 1, then the result is 0 (or FALSE).

Any logical AND with a 0 will result in 0.

For example:

1 AND 1 results in 1.

1 AND 0 results in 0.

0 AND 1 results in 0.

0 AND 0 results in 0.

In the first example of this section, the IP address 192.20.16.5 is ANDed with the subnet mask 255.255.255.0 to give a network ID of 192.20.16. The following minitable shows the calculation:

Decimal Notation	Binary Notation	
IP address:	192 20 16 5	11000000 00010100 00010000 00000101
Subnet mask:	255 255 255 0	11111111 11111111 11111111 00000000
IP address AND subnet mask:	192 20 16 0	11000000 00010100 00010000 00000000

Determining the network ID is very easy if the subnet mask is made up of only 255 and 0 values. Simply *mask,* or cover up, the part of the IP address corresponding to the 0 octet of the subnet mask. For example, if the IP address is 15.6.100.1 and the subnet mask is 255.255.0.0, then the resulting network ID is 15.6. You cannot use a subnet mask with only 255 and 0 values if you need to subdivide your network ID into individual subnets.

2.9.3   Default Subnet Masks

Default masks are usually assigned by the vendor, based on the class network in question. The following table shows the subnet mask that appears in the Subnet Mask field when an IP address is selected:

Default Subnet Masks

Class	IP Address	Default Subnet Mask
A	001.y.z.w to 126.y.z.w	255.0.0.0
B	128.y.z.w to 191.y.z.w	255.255.0.0
C	192.y.z.w to 223.y.z.w	255.255.255.0

Thus using the default mask, the emphasis is on the number of hosts available, and nothing more, as the following table illustrates:

Maximum Number of Networks and Hosts per Network in TCP/IP

Class	Using Default Subnet Mask	Number of Networks	Number of Hosts per Network
A	255.0.0.0	126	16,777,214
B	255.255.0.0	16,384	65,534
C	255.255.255.0	2,097,152	254

If the hosts on your internetwork are not directly on the Internet, then you are free to choose the network IDs that you use. For the hosts and subnets that are a part of the Internet, however, the network IDs you use must be assigned by InterNIC (the Internet Network Information Center).

If you are using network IDs assigned by InterNIC, then you cannot choose the address class you use (and you can bet you will be given class C addresses). In this case, the number of subnets you use is normally limited by the number of network IDs assigned by InterNIC, and the number of hosts per subnet is determined by the class of address. Fortunately, by choosing the proper subnet mask, you can subdivide your network into a greater number of subnets with fewer possible hosts per subnet.

Many companies today with Internet requirements are avoiding the addressing constraints and security risks of having hosts directly on the Internet by setting up private networks with gateway access to the Internet. Having a private network means that only the Internet gateway host needs to have an Internet address. For security, a firewall can be set up to prevent Internet hosts from directly accessing the company's network.

2.9.4   Subdividing a Network

Internetworks are networks made up of individual segments connected by routers. The reasons for having distinct segments are as follows:

- They permit physically remote local networks to be connected.

- They permit a mix of network technologies to be connected, such as Ethernet on one segment and token ring on another.

- They allow an unlimited number of hosts to communicate, whereas the number of hosts on each segment is limited by the type of network used.

- They reduce network congestion, as broadcasts and local network traffic are limited to the local segment.

Each segment is a subnet of the internetwork and requires a unique network ID. If you have only one network ID—for example, if you have an InterNIC-assigned Internet network ID—then you have to subdivide this network ID into other network IDs— a process known as subnetting or subnetworking.

The steps involved in subnetting a network are

1. Determine the number of network IDs required, making sure to allow for future growth.

2. Determine the maximum number of host addresses tat are on each subnet, again allowing for future growth.

3. Define one subnet mask for the entire internetwork that gives the desired number of subnets and allows enough hosts per subnet.

4. Determine the resulting subnet network IDs that are used.

5. Determine the valid host IDs and assign IP addresses to the hosts.

The following sections explain these steps in detail.

Step 1: Determine the Number of Network IDs Required

The first step in subnetting a network is to determine the number of subnets required, making sure to plan for future growth. A unique network ID is required for

- Each subnet
- Each WAN connection

Step 2: Determine the Number of Host IDs per Subnet Required

Determine the maximum number of hosts IDs that are required on each subnet. A host ID is required for

- Each TCP/IP computer network interface card.
- Each TCP/IP printer network interface card.
- Each router interface on each subnet. For example, if a router is connected to two subnets, then it would require two host IDs and therefore two IP addresses.

Items Requiring Host IDs

When determining the number of subnets and hosts per subnet for your internetwork, it is very important to plan for growth! The entire internetwork should have the same subnet mask; therefore, the maximum number of subnets and hosts per subnet is set when the subnet mask is chosen.

To illustrate the need for growth planning, consider an internetwork with two subnets with 50 hosts on each subnet connected by a router. The network administrator is authorized by InterNIC to use the network ID 192.20.16 to put all the hosts on the Internet. As explained in the following sections, a subnet mask of 255.255.255.192 would create two logical subnets on the internetwork, each allowing a maximum of 62 valid host IDs. In the future, if another segment is added or more than 62 hosts are needed on one segment, then the network administrator needs to choose a new subnet mask, shut down every computer on the network to reconfigure the subnet mask, reconfigure a lot of the network software, and probably look for another job.

Step 3: Define the Subnet Mask

The next step is to define for the entire internetwork one subnet mask that gives the desired number of subnets and allows enough hosts per subnet.

As shown previously, the network ID of an IP address is determined by the 1 bits of the subnet mask shown in binary notation. To increase the number of network IDs, you need to add more bits to the subnet mask.

For example, you are assigned a class B network ID of 129.20 by InterNIC. Using the default class B subnet mask 255.255.0.0, you have one network ID (129.20) and about 65,000 valid host

IDs (`129.20.1.1` through `129.20.255.254`). Suppose you wanted to subdivide the network into four subnets.

First, consider the host `129.20.16.1` using the subnet mask `255.255.0.0`. In binary notation, it is represented as:

IP address	10000001	00010100	00010000	00000001
Subnet mask	11111111	11111111	00000000	00000000
Network ID	11000000	00010100		

Remember that the 1 bits in the subnet mask correspond to the network ID bit in the IP address.

By adding bits to the subnet mask, you increase the bits available for the network ID and thus create a few more combinations of network IDs.

Suppose in the preceding example we added 3 bits to the subnet mask. The result increases the number of bits defining the network ID and decreases the number of bits that define the host ID. Thus, you have more network IDs but fewer hosts on each subnet. The new subnet mask is

Subnet mask	11111111	11111111	11100000	00000000
Decimal	255	255	224	0

The three extra bits in the network ID give you six different network IDs. You cannot use all zeroes or all ones because they are reserved for the broadcast address. The former implies "this network only," and the latter would be the same as the subnet mask. Examples of network IDs include

```
11000000 00010100 001

11000000 00010100 010

11000000 00010100 011

11000000 00010100 100

11000000 00010100 101

11000000 00010100 110
```

To summarize the preceding example using decimal notation: By applying the new subnet mask of `255.255.224.0` to the network ID `129.20`, you create six new network IDs: `129.20.32`, `129.20.64`, `129.20.96`, `129.20.128`, `129.20.160`, `129.20.192`.

Note that if you used only two additional bits in the subnet mask, you would only be able to have two subnets. The network IDs that result in the preceding example are

```
10000001      00010100      01      (129.20.64)

10000001      00010100      10      (129.20.128)
```

Therefore, you must use enough additional bits in the new subnet mask to create the desired number of subnets, though still allowing for enough hosts on each subnet.

After you determine the number of subnets you need to create, you can calculate the subnet mask as follows:

1. Convert the number of subnets to binary format. You may want to use the Windows Calculator in Scientific view.

2. The number of bits required to represent the number of subnets in binary is the number of additional bits that you need to add to the default subnet mask.

3. Convert the subnet mask back to decimal format.

For example, you are assigned a class B network ID of 192.20 and you need to create five subnets.

Converting 5 into binary format gives 00000101, or simply 101. By ignoring the 0 bits to the left of the left-most 1, the required number of bits is three.

Therefore, you need to add three bits to the default subnet mask. The default subnet mask for a class B network is 255.255.0.0.

In binary notation, this is

Default subnet mask   11111111   11111111   00000000   00000000

Adding three bits gives the following subnet mask:

                           11111111   11111111   11100000   00000000

or 255.255.224.0 in decimal notation.

Step 4: Determine the Network IDs to Use

The next step is to determine the subnet network IDs that are created by applying the new subnet mask to the original assigned network ID. Any or all of the resulting subnet network IDs are used in the internetwork.

This discussion gives three methods for determining the network IDs. The first is a manual computation, the second is a shortcut for the first method, and the third uses tables with the values already calculated. As noted previously, you should become familiar with the manual calculations in order to understand the fundamentals of subnetting.

Defining the Network IDs Manually

The network ID for each subnet is determined using the same number of bits as were added to default subnet mask in the previous step. To define each subnet network ID:

1. List all possible binary combinations of the bits added to the default subnet mask.

2. Discard the combinations with all ones or all zeroes. All ones or all zeroes are not valid as network IDs; all ones are the same as the subnet mask, and all zeroes imply "this network only" as a destination.

3. Convert the remaining values to decimal notation.

4. Append each value to the original assigned network ID to produce a subnet network ID.

Using the previous example, you were assigned a class B network ID of 129.20 and created at least five subnets. You needed to add 3 bits to the default subnet mask to create the subnets. The new subnet mask was then 255.255.224.0, or in binary:

Subnet mask: 11111111   11111111   11100000   00000000

Listing all combinations of the additional bits gives the following:

000	100
001	101
010	110
011	111

Discarding the values 000 and 111 and converting the remaining combinations to decimal format, you have:

.32	.128
.64	.160
.96	.192

Appending the preceding values to the original assigned network ID gives the following new subnet network IDs:

129.20.32

129.20.64

129.20.96

129.20.128

129.20.160

129.20.192

All the new subnet network IDs use the subnet mask of 255.255.224.0.

A Shortcut for Defining the Network IDs

Using the preceding method becomes tedious when more than 3 bits are added to the default subnet mask because the technique requires listing and converting many bit combinations. You can use the following shortcut for defining the subnet network IDs:

1. List the octet added to the default subnet mask in binary notation.

2. Convert the right-most 1 bit of this value to decimal notation, which is the incremental value between each subnet value, known as delta (D).

3. The number of subnet network IDs that are created is two less than two to the power of n, where n is the number of bits used in step 1 (# of subnets = $(2^n)-2$).

4. Append delta to the original network ID to give the first subnet network ID.

5. Repeat step 4 for each subnet network ID, incrementing each successive value by delta.

Using the previous example, you were assigned a class B network ID of 129.20 and created at least five subnets. You needed to add 3 bits the default subnet mask to create the subnets.

The bits you added to the default subnet mask are 11100000.

The right-most bit converted to decimal (00100000) is 32. Thus the incremental value, delta, is 32.

There are $(2^3)-2 = 6$ subnets created.

The subnets created are

129.20   and delta = 129.20.32

129.20.32   and delta = 129.20.64

129.20.64   and delta = 129.20.96

129.20.96   and delta = 129.20.128

129.20.128   and delta = 129.20.160

129.20.32   and delta = 129.20.192

If you increment the last subnet network ID once more, the last octet matches the last octet of the subnet mask (224) and thus is an invalid network ID.

Step 5: Determine the Host IDs to Use

The final step in subnetting a network is to determine the valid host IDs and assign IP addresses to the hosts.

The host IDs for each subnet start with the value .001 in the last octet and continue up to one less than the subnet ID of the next subnet. Keep in mind that the last octet cannot be .000 or .255, as these are reserved for broadcast addresses.

Finally, the valid IP addresses for each subnet are created by combining the subnet network ID with the host ID.

Using the subnets in the previous example, the range of IP addresses for each subnet would be

Subnet	First IP Address	Last IP Address
129.20.32.0	129.20.32.1	129.20.63.254
129.20.64.0	129.20.64.1	129.20.95.254
129.20.96.0	129.20.96.1	129.20.127.254
129.20.128.0	129.20.128.1	129.20.159.254
129.20.160.0	129.20.160.1	129.20.191.254
129.20.192.0	129.20.192.1	129.20.223.254

2.9.5   Bringing It All into Focus

Having looked at each component of a subnet, you can now go back and attempt to clear up some of the unfinished business by looking at components of the process once more. For simplicity, this explanation looks only at a class C network. In such a network, all but the last 8 bits are used by the network ID. With only 8 bits remaining for the host ID, there are 254 possibilities for host IDs when 0 and 255 are removed.

If you subnet the network, you divide those remaining 8 bits that were all host IDs into host IDs and subnet IDs. If you use the first 3 bits for the subnet ID, then you are using a value of 128+64+32, or 224. This now leaves only 5 bits that can be used for unique host IDs. Those remaining bits add to 16+8+4+2+1, or 31. An address of all ones cannot be used, so there are 30 possible unique host IDs.

The subnet IDs can be mixed and matched into six unique subnet IDs: 128, 64, 32, 32+64 (96), 32+128 (160), or 128+64 (192). Once again, a seventh combination adding them altogether is not allowed.

2.9.6   Practice Problems

1. An IP address of 192 belongs to what class of network?

    A.   Class A

    B.   Class B

    C.   Class C

    D.   Reserved

2. An IP address of 127 belongs to what class of network?

    A.   Class A

    B.   Class B

    C.   Class C

    D.   Reserved

3. An IP address of 92 belongs to what class of network?

   A. Class A

   B. Class B

   C. Class C

   D. Reserved

4. An IP address of 150 belongs to what class of network?

   A. Class A

   B. Class B

   C. Class C

   D. Reserved

5. The default subnet mask for a class B network is

   A. 0.0.0.0

   B. 255.255.255.0

   C. 255.0.0.0

   D. 255.255.0.0

6. With an IP address starting at 200, you currently have 10 subnets and want to maximize the number of hosts you can have at each. What subnet mask should you use to maximize the number of available hosts?

   A. 192

   B. 224

   C. 240

   D. 248

   E. 252

7. The default subnet mask for a class A network is

   A. 0.0.0.0

   B. 255.255.255.0

   C. 255.0.0.0

   D. 255.255.0.0

8. With an IP address of 100, you currently have 80 subnets and want to maximize the number of hosts you can have at each. What subnet mask should you use to maximize the number of available hosts?

   A. 192

   B. 224

   C. 240

   D. 248

   E. 254

9. The default subnet mask for a class C network is

   A. 0.0.0.0

   B. 255.255.255.0

   C. 255.0.0.0

   D. 255.255.0.0

10. With an IP address of 100, you currently have only eight subnets but anticipate adding two more subnets next year. You want to maximize the number of hosts you can have at each. What subnet mask should you use to maximize the number of available hosts?

   A. 192

   B. 224

   C. 240

   D. 248

   E. 252

2.9.7 Practice Problems: Answers and Explanations

1. **C** An IP address of 192 identifies a class C network.

2. **D** An IP address of 127 signifies a reserved address.

3. **A** An IP address of 92 identifies a class A network.

4. **B** An IP address of 150 identifies a class D network.

5. **D** The default subnet mask for a class B network is 255.255.0.0.

6. **C** A subnet mask of 240 will make 14 hosts available on each subnet of a class C network.

7. **C** The default subnet mask for a class A network is 255.0.0.0.

8. **E** A subnet mask of 254 will make 262,142 hosts available on each subnet of a class A network.

9. **B** The default subnet mask for a class C network is 255.255.255.0.

10. **C** A subnet mask of 240 will make over one million hosts available on each subnet of a class A network.

2.9.8 Keywords

subnet A smaller division of a network

subnet mask A number subtracted from an IP address to obtain the subnet

2.10 Configuring Windows NT to Function as an IP Router

Routers use built-in tables to determine where to send a packet destined for a particular network. By default, routers know only about networks to which they are physically attached and depend on tables to inform them about networks to which they are not physically attached—either through manual configuration or dynamic configuration.

Static routers are not capable of discovering networks other than those to which they have a physical interface. If this type of router is to route packets to any other network, it has to be told manually what to do, either through the assignment of a default gateway on the router or by manually editing the route table. Microsoft Windows NT enables the user to build a static router, or multihomed router, using multiple network cards and IP addresses. In a static router environment, new changes are not reflected in the routing tables on these routers.

Dynamic routers, on the other hand, use interrouting protocols. These protocols simply provide a language for routers to communicate changes to their route tables to other routers in their environment. In this way, routing tables are built dynamically, and the administrator does not have to manually edit route tables to bring up a new network segment.

Dynamic routers cannot provide this function without routing protocols, though. The most popular routing protocols are the Routing Information Protocol (RIP) and Open Shortest Path First protocol (OSPF). RIP is a broadcast-based protocol used primarily on small to medium-size networks. The more sophisticated OSPF protocol is used for medium to large networks.

Microsoft Windows NT 4.0 supports the installation and use of RIP to provide dynamic routing for multihomed computers using Windows NT as the operating system. In this way, routing tables can be updated whenever any additions to a network occur. Using RIP or OSPF in a routed environment should help eliminate the need to manually edit route tables in your environment.

2.10.1 The Static Routing Environment

A typical small network environment can have two routers dividing three subnets. Each router has a standard routing table consisting of the networks to which they are attached. Router A would be connected to subnet 1 and 2 and have a routing table that reflects this information. Router B would be connected to subnet 2 and 3, and its routing table would reflect the networks on which it is currently configured.

Assume a ping (echo request) packet is initiated by a machine on subnet 1. From the command prompt, or possibly a specific application on subnet 1, a `ping` command is issued to an IP address on subnet 3; perhaps from IP address 131.107.32.10 to 131.107.96.20. First, IP takes the destination address and compares it to the source address using the subnet mask of that machine. After the comparison is done, IP determines that this destination address is on a remote network. IP checks its internal route table to determine where it's supposed to send packets destined for a remote network. Whenever a destination address is remote, IP knows to ask ARP (Address Resolution Protocol) for the physical address of the default gateway specified in the internal route table. ARP then either returns the physical address from the ARP cache or does a local ARP broadcast for the router's physical address.

At this point, the ping request has not yet left the sending machine. IP gathers the physical address of the router, inserts the destination address into the ping packet and finally transmits the packet onto the wire of subnet 1.

Because IP sends the packet on the wire in such a way that only the router would not discard the packet, the packet safely arrives at the router. The network interface on the router passes the data up its network stack to IP, where IP discovers that this packet is not destined for it.

Normally, IP on a machine would discard the packet. But this machine, a router, is a special kind of machine, which has additional responsibilities including trying to forward packets it receives to the necessary network. Router A reads the IP address of the destination and compares this destination to its own source address using its subnet mask. At this point, IP determines the network to which this packet is supposed to be sent and checks its internal route table to see what to do with packets destined for the 131.107.96.0 network. Unfortunately, this router has no entries for this network and therefore drops this packet. ICMP (Internet Control Messaging Protocol) reports an error to the machine on subnet 1, indicating that the destination address cannot be reached.

This whole process seems like a lot of work just to get an error message, especially if you know that the destination machine is working. There are two ways to get around this kind of scenario:

- Add a default gateway to the router's configuration
- Add a manual entry in the router's internal table

See what happens if you use one or both of these solutions on router A, picking up right where router A decided to drop the packet. Router A has just figured out that the packet's destination address does not match its own IP address. It therefore checks its route table, looking for either a path to the 131.107.96.0 network or for the IP address of its default gateway.

By configuring a default gateway, an administrator indicates to the router that if it handles a packet destined for a network it has no idea about, the router should send it to the default gateway specified and hope for the best. This can be useful if you don't want to configure 37 route table entries on a network. Merely specifying default gateways can minimize the size of your route tables and minimize the number of manual entries you have to maintain. This approach, of course, comes with the possibility of making your network a little more inefficient. Configuring a network always involves trade-offs.

Router A now figures out that it needs to send the ping request to the IP address of the other router based on its route table, in this case 131.107.64.2. Here is yet another conceptual gap. Router A really doesn't know whether the IP address represents a router or just another machine on the network. For that matter, it might be sending this packet into "bit space." Router A trusts that the administrator was wise enough to specify an IP address of a device that will help get the packet to its final destination. As an aside, if you enter a route table entry incorrectly, the router just merrily starts sending packets to wherever you specified.

IP on router A now asks ARP to find the physical address of the next router in line. Just as on another machine, ARP either already has the physical address in cache or initiates an ARP broadcast to get it. After IP has the physical address, it reformulates the packet, addressing it to router B's physical address but leaving the original source address intact. It does not insert its own IP address as the source. If IP did this, the destination address would never respond back to the original machine. The packet is transmitted onto the wire destined for router B.

Router B hears the transmission, goes through basically the same process, determines the destination address, and discovers that it can send the packet directly to the destination machine. Utilizing the same ARP and IP procedures, the packet finally arrives at the destination machine on subnet 3. The ICMP echo request is acknowledged, and ICMP formulates the ICMP echo response packet that must be sent back. Remember that up to this point, the original sending machine is just patiently waiting for a response. The destination machine looks at the source address (131.107.32.10), figures out that it's remote, finds the physical address of router B to send the message back, and transmits it onto the wire.

> **For routing to work in a static routing environment, be sure that each router is aware of all relevant networks. Otherwise, packets will be dropped unexpectedly on their return to a destination.**

Router B receives the packet, breaks it down, and tries to figure out what to do with a packet destined for the 131.107.32.0 subnet. And after all this work, router B drops the packet. Why? We made all our changes to router A in terms of a default gateway and route table entries, but we didn't do anything to router B.

To make static routing work, each router has to be updated and configured to know about other networks in the environment. Only after a default gateway or manual entry in router B's route table is configured will the packets successfully be transmitted between these two networks.

Default Gateways

The two easiest ways to identify default gateways for a machine or multihomed router are through manual configuration through the IP properties sheet or as a DHCP option. You can specify more than one default gateway on a machine. Remember, however, that dead gateway detection will work only for machines initiating a TCP connection. In a routing table, the entry `0.0.0.0` identifies the default gateway(s).

Route Tables

Both machines/hosts on the network and routers use route tables to determine where packets should be sent to reach their final destination. Each router builds an internal route table every time IP is loaded during system initialization. Take a closer look at a route table.

Five columns of information are provided within the route table:

- The network address—This column represents all networks that this machine or router knows about, including entries for the default gateway, subnet and network broadcasts, universal loopback address, and default multicast address. In a route table, you can use names instead of IP addresses to identify networks. If you use names instead of IP addresses, the names are resolved using the networks file found in the `\%system drive%\system32\drivers\etc` directory.

- The netmask—This column simply identifies the subnet mask used for a particular network entry.

- The gateway address—This column is the IP address to which packets should be sent in order to route packets to their final destination. Each network address may specify a different gateway address in which to send packets, particularly if more than one router is connected to one network segment. This column may also have self-referential entries indicating the IP address to which broadcasts should be sent, as well as the local loopback entries. You can also use names to identify these IP addresses. Any names used here will be resolved using the local hosts file on the machine.

- Interface—This IP address primarily identifies the IP address of the machine and identifies this IP address as the interface to the network. On a machine with one network card, only two entries appear. For any network address that is self-referential, the interface is `127.0.0.1`, meaning that packets are not even sent onto the network. For all other communications, the IP address represents the network card interface used to communicate out onto the network. For multihomed machines, the interface IP address changes depending on which network address is configured on each network card. In this case, the interface identifies the IP address of the card connected to a particular network segment.

- The metric—The metric indicates the cost or hops associated with a particular network route. The router's job is to find the path representing the least cost or effort to get the packet to its destination. The lower the cost or hop count, the better or more efficient a particular route. On a static router, the metric for any network address will be 1, indicating that the router thinks every network is only one router hop away. This information is obviously not true, indicating that on static routers, this column is fairly meaningless. On dynamic routers, however, this column tells a router the best possible route for sending packets.

Viewing the Route Table

To view the route table of a Windows NT machine/router, you can use two utilities: the NETSTAT utility and the Route utility. To view the route table through NETSTAT, go to the command prompt and type:

```
netstat -r
```

This command brings up the route table on your machine. However, all you can do is view the table. To view and manage the route table, including adding or changing entries, use the Route utility. To view the route table using the route command, type:

```
route print
```

When you type **route print** from the command prompt, the same table that displays with netstat -r is shown.

The default entries in a Windows NT 4.0 Route table include the following items:

- **0.0.0.0**—This entry identifies the IP address of the default gateway or the IP address to which packets will be sent if no other specific route table entry exists for a destination network. If multiple gateways are defined on a Windows NT machine, you may notice more than one entry that looks like this, specifying each default gateway that is defined.

- **127.0.0.1**—This entry is the local loopback address used for diagnostics, to make sure that the IP stack on a machine is properly installed and running.

- Local network—This entry identifies the local network address. It indicates the gateway and interface machine's IP address that is used whenever a packet needs to be transmitted to a local destination.

- Local host—This entry is used for self-referential purposes and points to the local loopback address as the gateway and interface.

- Subnet broadcast—This entry is a directed broadcast and is treated as a directed packet by routers. Routers support the transmission of directed broadcasts to the network that is defined by the broadcast. The packet is forwarded to the network where it is broadcast to the machines on that network. In this case, the default entry specifies the IP address of the current machine for sending out subnet broadcasts to this machine's network.

- **224.0.0.0**—This entry is the default multicast address. If this machine is a member of any multicast groups, this and other multicast entries indicate to IP the interface used to communicate with the multicast network.

- **255.255.255.255**—This entry is a limited broadcast address for broadcasts destined for any machine on the local network. Routers that receive packets destined for this address may listen to the packet as a normal host, but do not support transmission of these types of broadcasts to other networks.

When a router looks for a destination for a particular packet, the router searches through the route table from first to last entry. After a route has been determined, meaning that a destination IP address has been found for the data, IP asks ARP for the physical address of that IP address. As soon as ARP replies, the frame can be constructed and transmitted onto the wire.

Building a Static Routing Table

The route command has a number of other switches that you can use to manage a route table statically. Up to this point, the print command is the only parameter that has been used. To manage a route table, however, an administrator must be able to add, delete, change, and clear route table entries. The commands are shown in the following table:

To Add or Modify a Static Route	Function
`route add [net id] mask [netmask][gateway]`	Adds a route
`route -p add [net id] mask [netmask][gateway]`	Adds a persistent route
`route delete [net id][gateway]`	Deletes a route
`route change [net id][gateway]`	Modifies a route
`route print`	Displays route table
`route -f`	Clears all routes and rebuilds routes to the physically attached networks, but does not reenter the default gateway

Notice the entry that utilizes a `-p` (persistent) before the `add` parameter. By default, route table entries are kept only in memory. After a machine is rebooted, any entries that were manually added are gone and must be reentered. You can use batch files, startup scripts—or the persistent switch—to reenter static routes. The persistent-entry switch writes route entries into the Registry so they survive a reboot of the machine. Naturally, this method means that you don't have to create batch files or scripts, but it requires manual deletion of the routes if they should change.

Route table entries are kept only in memory and will not survive a reboot unless the -p switch is used.

The TRACERT Utility

Windows NT includes the TRACERT utility, which verifies the route a packet takes to reach its destination. To use this utility, simply go to the command prompt and type:

```
tracert <IP address>
```

The result of running this utility for a destination address will probably look similar to the following output:

```
C:\>tracert www.learnix.com

Tracing route to www.learnix.com [199.45.92.97]over a maximum of 30 hops:

  1   156 ms    156 ms    141 ms   annex.intranet.ca [206.51.251.5]
  2   157 ms    156 ms    156 ms   cisco2.intranet.ca [206.51.251.10]
  3   172 ms    156 ms    172 ms   spc-tor-6-Serial3-3.Sprint-Canada.Net [206.186.248.85]
  4   156 ms    172 ms    187 ms   204.50.128.17
  5   171 ms    172 ms    157 ms   205.150.206.97
  6   172 ms    172 ms    297 ms   h5.bb1.tor2.h4.bb1.ott1.uunet.ca [205.150.242.70]
  7   172 ms    171 ms    172 ms   max1.ott1.uunet.ca [205.150.233.2]
  8   188 ms    203 ms    218 ms   router.learnix.ca [199.71.122.193]
  9   203 ms    218 ms    235 ms   sparky [199.45.92.97]

Trace complete.
```

The result shows each router traversed to get to a destination as well as how long it took to get through each particular router. The time it takes to get through a particular router is calculated using three algorithms, which are displayed for each router hop. The IP address of each router traversed also displays. If a FQDN is available, this displays as well.

The TRACERT utility is useful for two primary diagnostic purposes:

- It detects whether a particular router is not functioning along a known path. For instance, suppose a user knows that packets on a network always go through Texas to get from Florida to California, but communication seems to be dead. A TRACERT to a California address shows all the hops up to the point where the router in Texas should respond. If it does not respond, the time values are marked with asterisks (*), indicating a nonfunctioning path.

- This utility also determines whether a router is slow and possibly needs to be upgraded or helped by adding routes on the network. You can make this determination simply by looking at the time it takes for a packet to get through a particular router. If a particular router is deluged by packets, its return time may be significantly higher than that of any of the other hops, indicating it should be upgraded or helped in some way.

2.10.2 Dynamic Routing

Discussion to this point has focused on manually editing the route table to notify routers of the existence of networks to which they are not physically connected. This task would be enormously difficult on large networks on which routes and networks may change on a frequent basis. Manual editing also makes redundant pathways horribly complex to manage because you have to rely on each host to manage multiple default gateways and utilize dead gateway detection. Even utilizing these features on the client side does not guarantee timely reactions to failure of links between routers.

These problems led to the development of routing protocols, used specifically by routers to dynamically update each other's tables. Two of the most common protocols used by dynamic routers are RIP and OSPF. These protocols notify other routers that support these protocols of the networks they are attached to and of any changes that occur because of links being disconnected or becoming too congested to efficiently pass traffic.

The standard rule of thumb when considering the use of either protocol is that RIP works well for small to medium-size networks and OSPF works well for medium to large networks. The characteristics of RIP are discussed here because Windows NT supports RIP on its multihomed routers, but the characteristics of OSPF are left to other reference sources. Windows NT multihomed routers do not support the OSPF protocol out of the box.

Routing Internet Protocol

To understand RIP better on routers, first consider static routing, where routing tables had to be built manually. To pass packets from one network to another, each router had to be told where to send packets destined for a specific network (route table entry) or where to send packets without a specific destination (default gateway).

By default, routers know about the networks to which they are physically attached because their IP addresses on each of those networks give them the necessary information. The problem of remote networks is encountered almost immediately, though. For this reason, it became apparent that as networks grew in size, a more sophisticated way to update route tables would be necessary. From this need arose routing protocols, which enable routers to communicate with each other. The protocols enable one router to send information about the networks it knows about to any other router physically connected to the wire and also enable the router to receive information about other networks dynamically from other routers that also are able to communicate.

The RIP procedure for communicating between routers is through broadcasts over User Datagram Protocol (UDP) port 520. RIP routers broadcast their route tables over this port and listen on this port for broadcasts from other routers that may be connected to the network. In this way, eventually all routers that are physically connected have up-to-date route tables and know where to send data for any network in the environment.

Routers broadcast both the networks to which they are attached and the distance of remote networks from their particular location. This distance to another network is called a *hop*, or metric, and each router keeps track of this value within the route table. Each router along the path to a destination network represents a hop. For this reason, RIP is considered a distance-vector routing protocol. In this fashion, RIP can determine the route with the least number of hops necessary to get a packet to its final destination.

As RIP was being developed, it was decided that routers would need to keep track of a maximum of 15 hops between networks. Therefore, any network address that had a hop count of 16 is considered unreachable. If a router's route table has two different hop counts for a particular network, the router sends the data to the route that has the least number of hops to the destination network.

Initially, it doesn't seem to make sense to limit the number of hops to a destination address, but this limitation is based primarily on how the RIP protocol works. Because RIP routers broadcast the networks they know about and how far away they are from those networks, certain precautions must be made in case any of these connections fail. After a router determines that a connection has failed, it must find a better route to that network from other route tables. This process could create circular and upward-spiraling loops between routers, and the hop count could continue to increase ad infinitum.

If a redundant connection to that network exists with a higher hop count, eventually each router's tables increase to the point that the redundant route is chosen over the connection that died. But if no redundant route is available, the hop count could continue to increase indefinitely. To reduce this risk, several algorithms have been written to successfully react to connection failures, including the maximum hop count of 16, indicating an unreachable network. Administrators also have the ability to alter the hop count between routers, to encourage the use of some network routers over others that may be used purely for redundancy. Broadcasts between routers always occur every 30 seconds, whether the route table has changed or not.

Because RIP is the oldest routing protocol on the block and is widely used throughout the industry, several well-known problems exist when trying to implement this protocol in larger networks. These protocol deficiencies result in RIP being useful only in small to medium-size networks. RIP falls short in the following basic categories:

- Because RIP keeps track of every route table entry, including multiple paths to a particular network, routing tables can become large rather quickly. This condition can result in the broadcasting of multiple RIP packets to send a complete route table to other routers.

- Because RIP can allow hop counts only up to 15, with 16 representing an unreachable network, the size of networks on which RIP can be successfully implemented is necessarily restricted. Any large enterprise may need to achieve hop counts beyond this value.

- Broadcasts are sent by default every 30 seconds, which causes two fundamental problems:

  - Significant time delays occur between the times when a route goes down and all routers in the environment are notified of this change in the network. If a network goes down nine routers (hops) away, it can take up to $4^{1}/_{2}$ minutes for that change to reach the other end of the network. Meanwhile, packets sent in that direction can be lost and connections dropped.

  - On a LAN, these broadcasts may not be significant in terms of bandwidth, but on an expensive WAN connection, these broadcasts may become bothersome, especially if the network is stable and the route tables are large. These broadcasts consistently transmit redundant route table entries every 30 seconds, even when not necessary.

But these problems should not discourage the administrator of a small to medium-size network from using RIP. As long as you understand the benefits and limitations of the protocol, you should be able to use it quite successfully.

2.10.3   Building a Multihomed Router

Windows NT enables an administrator to convert a machine into either a static or dynamic IP router. Static routers work well for extending a small network segment, and dynamic routers using RIP work well on small to medium-size networks. A multihomed computer would probably not work well on large networks, however, based on RIP's limitations and the significant overhead associated with maintaining large route tables. Other considerations aside, however, building a Windows NT router is fairly simple and easy to do.

But before continuing, a definition of the term *multihomed computer,* or *multihomed router,* is in order. A multihomed router is simply a computer with more than one network card that has been configured to route packets from one network segment to another. On a multihomed router the operating system performs the routing; in contrast, a hardware router is a device that is specifically manufactured and designed exclusively for routing. In simpler terms, you can run any Windows application, including Freecell, on a multihomed router, but you can't run applications on a hardware router.

The first step in building a Windows NT router is to install two or more network cards in the machine. Anyone who has ever tried to do so will tell you that this job can often sound much easier than it is. Each network card has to have its own IRQ and I/O address to use on the machine. These must be independent of other hardware cards you may be using in your machine, including video cards, sound cards, modems, hard-disk controller cards, and so on. Basically, the machine needs to be stripped of any bells and whistles and other functions so that enough resources are available. Any resource conflicts result in significant headaches as your network cards don't appear and protocol drivers fail to load.

The typical machine built for Windows NT seminars and classes uses a Windows NT router with three network cards and little else. After the machine successfully identifies the network cards, be careful of installing additional third-party utilities. Sometimes they decide to steal the I/O addresses that your network cards are using. The bottom line is that after this machine is built, try to leave it alone. Stabilizing your machine will be the toughest part of the job. Afterward, everything else is easy.

After you install your network cards, make sure to assign separate IP addresses to each card. Follow this procedure:

1. In the network section of Control Panel under the Protocol tab, select TCP/IP and choose Properties. Notice that where the network card is identified, the drop-down box reveals all the network cards you have installed, enabling you to choose a different IP address scheme for each network card.

2. After you give each network card its own IP address, indicating which network it is on, the machine can respond to packets coming from the networks to which it is attached. However, the machine is still not a router.

3. To turn the machine into a router, go back to TCP/IP properties and choose the Routing tab. Select the Enable IP Forwarding check box. After you select this box and have chosen OK to exit this configuration and the network configuration, you are asked to reboot your machine.

4. Reboot the machine. Now the machine is officially a router that can pass packets from one network to another.

The administrator then needs to decide whether the router will be static or dynamic. After IP forwarding is enabled, the router is a static router. If a static router is desired, no more configuration is necessary. If the administrator wants to have a dynamic router instead, then RIP needs to be installed.

RIP can be installed in the Services tab through the Network icon. After RIP is installed, this router listens for other RIP broadcasts and broadcasts its own route table entries.

Although Windows NT supports the capability to create a static or dynamic router, the most important consideration for an administrator is probably whether to upgrade a machine for occasional routing of packets or to purchase a hardware router. If the administrator plans to spend more than $1,000 for a machine to route packets on a network, he or she may be better off spending it on hardware optimized for that purpose. Think of Windows NT routing versus hardware routing in much the same way as you would think about Windows NT RAID versus hardware RAID. Hardware implementation is usually a little more expensive, but it is optimized for that specific task; on the other hand, Windows NT implementations work well and are cheaper, but are not designed for constant pounding by a large network.

2.10.4 Exercises

Exercise 1: Viewing the Route Table

Follow these steps to view your Windows NT machine's route table:

1. From the start menu, select Command Prompt.

2. Type **route print** at the command prompt.

Exercise 2: Adding an Entry to Your Route Table

Follow these steps to add a network to your route table:

1. From the Start menu, select Command Prompt.

2. Type **route add 131.107.64.0 mask 255.255.224.0** *IP address of your current gateway*.

3. Type **route print** to observe the addition.

Exercise 3: Using the TRACERT Utility

1. From the Start menu, select Command Prompt.

2. Type **tracert** *IP_address* at the command prompt. For *IP_address*, you'll want to choose a site that doesn't mind you hitting its server. Most sites won't mind an occasional hit, but it's bad form to continually do so.

3. Observe the results.

2.10.5 Practice Problems

1. In your environment, you have a Windows NT machine that seems to not be responding to ping requests using an IP address. You want to make sure that the machine's configuration is appropriate for the network. Which of the following options would you need to check?

    A. IP address

    B. Subnet mask

    C. Default gateway

    D. DNS

2. You've noticed a significant increase in the amount of time it takes to reach your remote offices. You think one of your routers may not be functioning. Which utility would you use to find the pathway a packet takes to reach its destination?

    A. WINS

    B. DNS

    C. TRACERT

    D. Network Monitor

3. You have a machine that seems to be able to communicate with other machines on its same local subnet, but whenever you try to reach destinations on a remote network, the communications fail. What is the most likely cause of the problem?

    A. IP address

    B. Subnet mask

    C. Default gateway

    D. WINS

4. You've set up a simple routed environment in which one router is central to three subnets, meaning that the router can see each of the three segments. No default gateway has been assigned because there doesn't seem to be any reason to do so. If a router doesn't know where to send a packet and no default gateway has been assigned, what will the router do with the packet?

    A. Drop the packet

    B. Store the packet for later processing

    C. Broadcast on the local network

    D. Use ARP to locate another pathway

5. You want your Windows NT routers to share information on the network so that you don't have to continually update the route tables manually. What protocol do you need to install to allow this to happen?

    A. DNS

    B. RIP

C. OSPF

D. WINS

6. Ten machines on your network have stopped communicating with other machines on remote network segments. The router seems to be working properly, but you want to make sure the route table has not been modified. What utilities can you use to view the route table on your Windows NT router?

A. Route

B. NETSTAT

C. PING

D. RTTABLE

7. Your environment consists of both LAN and WAN connections spread out over five continents. You've begun an expansion that has added a number of routers to your already large organization. Your network currently uses RIP as the routing protocol, but as new network segments are being added, routers on either end of your network insist that they can't see each other and that they are unreachable. What seems to be the problem?

A. The routers aren't made by Microsoft.

B. RIP can't share route table information.

C. RIP can't support more than 15 hops.

D. Routers aren't designed for WAN connections.

8. When installing and testing a brand new Windows NT router, you notice that the router routes packets to any network to which it is physically attached but drops packets to networks (seven of them) to which it is not attached. What would be the easiest way to make sure the router performs its function for those other networks.

A. Disable IP routing

B. Enable IP filtering on all ports

C. Change the IP address bindings

D. Add a default gateway

9. After adding a network segment (131.107.7.0) for a new wing, you discover that your route tables need to be altered. In this case, you simply need to add a new entry for this segment, but you want to make sure that the entry survives a reboot. Which of the following commands would you choose for the addition?

A. `route change 131.107.2.0`
    `➡131.107.7.0`

B. `route add 131.107.7.0 mask`
    `➡255.255.255.0 131.107.2.1`

C. `route -p add 131.107.2.1 mask`
    `➡255.255.255.0 131.107.7.0`

D. `route -p add 131.107.7.0 mask`
    `➡255.255.255.0 131.107.2.1`

10. Last year one of the big problems you encountered was connectivity problems associated with only having one router in your environment that could route packets between subnets. This year your budget enabled you to add a second router to provide some backup for your primary router. Windows NT is smart enough to utilize dead gateway detection, but during your test of this feature, it didn't work at all. What might you have forgotten to configure for dead gateway detection to work?

A. Dead gateway detection must use RIP, so RIP must be installed on each router.

B. Each host machine must be configured with the IP addresses of both routers before dead gateway detection is used.

C. Static route table entries must be configured on the routers so that they can communicate with each other.

D. Every application must be individually tailored to perform dead gateway detection because they are initiating the communication.

11. After checking a route table, you notice that it is missing a very important route to one of your network segments. Before you can add the route to your router's table however, you need to know what pieces of information to use the Route utility?

    A. Network ID

    B. Netmask

    C. MAC address

    D. Gateway address

2.10.6   Practice Problems: Answers and Explanations

1. **A, B, C**   The three components of TCP/IP configuration are the IP address, the subnet mask, and the default gateway.

2. **C**   TRACERT is used to find the pathway a packet takes to reach its destination.

3. **C**   The default gateway is the pathway to the remote network.

4. **A**   The router will drop the packet.

5. **B, C**   RIP is used to share router information, as is OSPF.

6. **A, B**   Route and NETSTAT are used to view the routing table(s).

7. **C**   RIP's support is limited to 15 hops.

8. **D**   Adding a default gateway is the easiest solution to the problem.

9. **D**   Choices B and D are both correct in syntax, but only D makes the connection persistent—surviving a reboot.

10. **B**   Each host machine must be configured with the IP addresses of both routers before dead gateway detection is used.

11. **A, B, D**   The network ID, netmask, and gateway address must be known to use the Route utility.

2.10.7   Keywords

dynamic routers   Use interrouting protocols

OSPF   Open Shortest Path First protocol

RIP   The Routing Information Protocol

static routers   Are not able to discover networks other than those to which they have a physical interface

2.11   Installing and Configuring the DHCP Relay Agent

Essentially, the job of the DHCP relay agent is to forward DHCP broadcast messages between DHCP-enabled clients and DHCP servers, across IP routers. The relay agent can be configured on any Windows NT Server computer and adds very little load.

> **The DCHP relay agent that comes with Windows NT 4.0 is a new service that will listen for DHCP broadcasts and forward them to one or more configured DHCP servers. This process is different from an RFC1542-compliant router in that the system running the relay agent is not a router.**

1. Open the Network Configuration dialog box and select the Services tab.

2. Select Add | DHCP Relay Agent. Click OK; when prompted, enter the path to the distribution files.

3. Click the Protocols tab and double-click the TCP/IP protocol.

4. On the DHCP Relay tab, enter the IP address of a DHCP server and the maximum number of hops and seconds that the relay can take.

5. Close the TCP/IP Configuration dialog box and the Network Configuration dialog box.

6. Restart the computer when prompted.

2.11.1 Practice Problems

1. Which statements about the function of the DHCP relay agent are false?

   A. Forwards DHCP broadcast messages between DHCP-enabled clients and DHCP servers

   B. Goes across IP routers

   C. Forwards DHCP broadcasts between non-DHCP–enabled clients and DHCP servers

   D. Updates routing tables

2. On which computers can a DHCP relay agent be configured?

   A. Windows 3.1x or greater

   B. Windows 95 or greater

   C. Windows NT Workstation or greater

   D. Windows NT Server

2.11.2 Practice Problems: Answers and Explanations

1. **C, D** The job of the DHCP relay agent is to forward DHCP broadcast messages between DHCP-enabled clients and DHCP servers across IP routers.

2. **D** The relay agent can be configured on any Windows NT Server computer.

2.12 Installing and Configuring DNS

The system on which you install the DNS service must be running Windows NT Server and needs to have a static IP configuration. Installing the DNS server is the same as installing any other network service. The steps are as follows:

1. Open the Network Settings dialog box (right-click Network Neighborhood and choose Properties).

2. On the Services tab, click Add and then select Microsoft DNS Server.

3. Click OK to add the service. When prompted, enter the directory in which your Windows NT source files are located.

4. Choose Close from the Network Settings dialog box and, when prompted, restart your system.

You have now installed the DNS server. To verify that the service is correctly installed, check the Services icon in Control Panel to ensure the Microsoft DNS server is listed and has started.

2.12.1 Enabling DNS on the Client

Now that you have a DNS server, your clients need to use it. To enable Windows clients to use the DNS server, you can add the address of the DNS server to each station (manually), or you can set the DNS server option on the DHCP server.

For Windows NT (and Windows 95), you can use the following procedure to set the DNS server address:

1. Open the TCP/IP Settings dialog box. (Open the Network Settings dialog box; from the Protocol tab, double-click TCP/IP.)

2. On the DNS tab, enter the required information. As a minimum, you need to enter the IP address of a DNS server. Descriptions of the other options on this tab follow:

   - Host Name—The name of the local host. This entry is the same as the NetBIOS name by default; however, you can change it. (If you select a different name, you are warned that if the NetBIOS name is ever changed, the host name is set to the new NetBIOS name. If you use WINS to create a dynamic DNS, the NetBIOS name and the host name must be the same.)

   - Domain—The Internet domain to which the system belongs. This entry is combined with the host name to create the FQDN name or this system.

   - DNS Service Search Order—The IP address of one or more DNS servers that you use. They are tried in the order given.

   - Domain Suffix Search Order—When you search for another host—for example, if you enter `FTP sparky`—the system first looks for `sparky` as the name in the DNS server. If `sparky` is not in your current domain, then that system will not be found and you would have to enter `FTP sparky.scrimtech.com`. If you work with servers at `scrimtech.com` frequently, you can add the domain `scrimtech.com` into this area, and if the address is not resolved from `sparky`, a second query for `sparky.scrimtech.com` is automatically sent.

3. Click OK to close the TCP/IP settings. (If you are installing TCP/IP, you will need to enter the path to the Windows NT source files.)

4. Choose Close from the Network Settings dialog box and restart your system. (This step is not absolutely required, but generally it is recommended to ensure that the values are correctly set.)

You can also use the DNS server in place of the WINS server for resolving NetBIOS names. To do so, you need to change the settings on the WINS tab in the TCP/IP configuration. Specifically, you need to select the option to use DNS to resolve host names.

2.12.2   Using Existing BIND Files

If you already have a series of BIND files set up on an existing DNS server, you can use these files to configure the Microsoft DNS server. Follow these steps to configure Microsoft DNS server to use existing BIND files:

1. Install the Microsoft DNS service (see the preceding section for instructions).

2. Stop the DNS service (from the Control Panel, choose the Services icon, click Microsoft DNS, and click Stop).

3. Copy the BIND files to the `%winroot%\System32\DNS` directory.

4. Start the DNS service (from the Control Panel, choose the Services icon, click Microsoft DNS, and click Start).

5. Use DNS Manager to verify that your entries are there.

2.12.3   Reinstalling Microsoft DNS Server

A quick note should be made here in case you need to reinstall the DNS server. When you start adding zones to a Microsoft DNS server, by default it switches to starting from the Registry rather than from the DNS files. It makes a note of this in the boot file. Removing the server (before you reinstall) does not remove the existing file; therefore, when you reinstall the DNS server, it assumes the boot file is valid and tries to read it. This procedure causes several errors in the Event Log and causes the DNS not to start.

Therefore, if you need to remove the DNS server, you should remove the boot file from the DNS directory. The original file is in the directory `%winroot%\system32\dns\backup`, and you can copy the files back from there; however, the server continues to boot from the Registry.

If you need to enable the system to boot from files, you must use the Registry editor to open `HKEY_LOCAL_MACHINE\SYSTEM\CurrentControlSet\Services\DNS\Parameters` and delete the value `EnableRegistryBoot`.

2.12.4   The DNS Administration Tool

Adding the DNS server also adds the DNS administration tool. This tool makes configuring and maintaining the DNS server very simple. It also provides single-seat administration as you can add several DNS servers.

First, you need to add the DNS server that you wish to manage. Follow these simple steps:

1.   Start DNS Manager by choosing Start | Programs | Administrative Tools | DNS Manager.

2.   In the left pane of DNS Manager, right-click Server List.

3.   Choose New Server from the menu.

4.   In the DNS server box, enter the name or IP address of the server you wish to add.

Now that you have added the server, you can configure it and add entries. The DNS server needs to be configured for the role that it plays in the overall system, and you should know what the server you are configuring will be used for. Roles are examined and discussed in section 2.15.

2.12.5   Creating a Subdomain

Many organizations are broken down into smaller groups that focus on one area of the business. Other organizations are dispersed geographically. In either case, the company may decide that it wants to break down its main domain into subdomains. This task is simple in Microsoft's DNS server. Choose the parent domain (`scrimtech.com`, for example) and then right-click. Choose New Domain and enter the subdomain name in the dialog box.

If the subdomain is handled on another server, enter NS records for each of the other servers. If it is handled locally, simply add the records that are required.

2.12.6   Updating DNS Startup Files

After you have added several records to the DNS server, you need to update the information in the files on the system. Even if the server boots from the Registry, the database (zone) files are stored. To do so, choose DNS from the menu and then choose Update Server Data Files. The files update automatically when the server is shut down or when you exit DNS Manager.

2.12.7   DNS Manager Preferences

As a final note, you can set the following three options under Options | Preferences that affect the behavior of DNS Manager:

- Auto Refresh Statistics—Enables you to configure the statistics screen to automatically update information.

- Show Automatically Created Zones—Shows the zones that are automatically created. These are used for internal purposes only.

- Expose TTL—Enables you to expose the TTL for entries in your cache. (You can view these by double-clicking Cache and then double-clicking the subfolders.)

2.12.8   NSLOOKUP

In addition to a DNS server, Windows NT 4.0 also has a tool that uses the DNS and enables you to verify that it is working. The NSLOOKUP command line is

```
NSLOOKUP [-option ...] [computer-to-find ¦ - [server]]
```

You can use NSLOOKUP to query the DNS server from the command line (see Table 2.12.1 for a list of switches), or you can start an interactive session with the server to enable you to query the database. For our purposes, only look at the command line.

Table 2.12.1   Command-Line Switches for the NSLOOKUP **Command**

Switch	Description
-option	Allows you to enter one or more commands from the command line. A list of the commands follows. For each option you wish to add, enter a hyphen (-) followed immediately by the command name. Note that the command-line length needs to be less than 256 characters.
Computer to find	This is the host or IP address about which you want to find information. It is processed using the default server or, if given, using the server that is specified.

The following list provides the options that are available with the NSLOOKUP command.

- -t querytype—Lists all records of a given type. The record types are listed under querytype.

- -a—Lists all the CNAME entries from the DNS server.

- -d—Dumps all records that are in the DNS server.

- -h—Returns information on the DNS server's CPU and operating system.

- -s—Returns the well-known services for hosts in the DNS domain.

2.12.9   Exercises

Exercise 1: Installing the Microsoft DNS Server

First, you need to install the DNS server. This exercise assumes you have a network card in your system. If you do not, install the MS loopback adapter so that you can perform the following exercises. If the system you are working on is running DNS, back up the files before you proceed, just in case.

1. Open the Network Settings dialog box. Choose the Protocols tab and double-click the TCP/IP protocol.

2. On the DNS tab, enter your IP address as the DNS server and click Add. Also add the domain **SunnyDays.com** into the domain field.

3. Click the Services tab and choose Add. From the list that appears, choose the Microsoft DNS server and click OK.

4. Enter the directory for the Windows NT source files.

5. Close the Network Settings dialog box and restart your computer.

Exercise 2: Testing the DNS Server

This exercise gives you a chance to test the information you entered and to check that everything is working correctly.

1. Start a command prompt.

2. Type the command **NSLOOKUP 160.106.101.80** and press the Enter key. What response did you get? (The response should show that 160.106.101.80 is mail2.SunnyDays.com. Here you have done a reverse lookup on the IP address.)

3. Using the NSLOOKUP command, find out what responses the following entries give you:

    160.106.66.7

    160.106.99.99

    www.SunnyDays.com

    www.dev.SunnyDays.com

    ftp.SunnyDays.com

    The results should be

160.106.66.7	rob.SunnyDays.com
160.106.99.99	ftp_pub1.SunnyDays.com
www.SunnyDays.com	160.106.65.7 (web1.SunnyDays.com)
www.dev.SunnyDays.com	148.55.72.14 (web2.SunnyDays.com)
ftp.SunnyDays.com	160.106.99.99 (ftp_pub1.SunnyDays.com)

4. Start an interactive session with the name server by typing **NSLOOKUP** and pressing the Enter key.

5. Try the following commands:

```
ls SunnyDays.com

ls -t mx SunnyDays.com

ls -d

q=soa

SunnyDays.com

q=mx

SunnyDays.com

Where is the third mail server?

dev.SunnyDays.com
```

6. Press Ctrl+C to exit the interactive query.

7. Close the command prompt.

2.12.10   Practice Problems

1. You have installed and tested the Microsoft DNS server configuration. Later you remove and reinstall the service in preparation for configuring the DNS server with the real information. What must you do to make sure the DNS server starts cleanly?

   A. Remove the files from the `%winroot%\system32\dns` directory.

   B. Reinstall Windows NT.

   C. Also remove and reinstall the WINS server.

   D. Nothing, the configuration will work fine.

2. Which of the following NSLOOKUP commands will provide a list of all the mail servers for the domain nt.com?

   A. `NSLOOKUP -t MX nt.com`

   B. `NSLOOKUP -a MX nt.com`

   C. `NSLOOKUP -h nt.com`

   D. `NSLOOKUP -m nt.com`

3. What is the purpose of the Domain Suffix Search Order?

   A. When you look for a host name, entries here can be used to complete the FQDN.

   B. When you look for a NetBIOS name, entries here can be used as the NetBIOS Scope ID.

   C. It allows your computer to be in more than one domain at a time.

   D. It tells your systems which Windows NT domains to search when looking for a logon server.

4. Which of the following best describes the order in which you should configure the DNS server?

   A. Install the server, create the zone, enter all the records, create the reverse lookup zone, and add the WINS records

   B. Install the server, create the reverse lookup zone, add the zone information, add the WINS lookup records, and add the other hosts

   C. Create the DNS server database files using a text editor, install the server, and verify the information

   D. Install the DNS server and then

transfer the zone from the WINS server

5. If you do not specify the host name and domain in the TCP/IP configuration before installing DNS, what happens during the DNS installation?

   A. An NS record is not created on the server.

   B. DNS doesn't install.

   C. Default values are used to create NS and SOA records.

   D. You cannot create any zones on the server.

2.12.11   Practice Problems: Answers and Explanations

1. **A**   Remove the files from the %winroot%\system32\dns directory.

2. **A**   NSLOOKUP -t MX nt.com is the correct answer.

3. **A**   When you look for a host name, entries in the Domain Suffix Search Order can be used to complete the FQDN.

4. **B**   The correct sequence is install the server, create the reverse lookup zone, add the zone information, add the WINS lookup records, and add the other hosts.

5. **A**   The host name and domain values are used to create default records when the server is installed. You may have to create these records later so the DNS server can communicate with its clients and other servers, but you can still install DNS and create zones. If the values aren't specified, only the SOA record is created automatically.

2.12.12   Keywords

host name   Name of the host computer

DNS   Domain Name System

NSLOOKUP   Utility used to access DNS tables

2.13   Integrating DNS with Other Name Servers

The other name server that DNS can integrate with is WINS. During the installation process, the last tab in the zone configuration dialog box is the WINS tab. You can use WINS to resolve DNS queries by telling the server to use the WINS server. Remember, for this process to work, the hosts must use the same name for both their NetBIOS name and the host name, and they must register with the WINS server.

The following options are available:

- Use WINS Resolution—Check this box to enable the DNS server to query the WINS server for queries it receives that it cannot resolve from its own database.

- Settings Only Affect Local Server—Normally a temporary entry is added to the domain when this resolution method is used. Selecting this option allows only the current server to see these entries.

- WINS servers—Here you need to enter the address of at least one WINS server. This server is queried in the order entered.

From the WINS tab, you can also open the Advanced Options dialog box. You may need to use a few other settings in this dialog box.

The options available are described in the following list:

- Submit DNS Domain as NetBIOS Scope—Some organizations use the NetBIOS scope ID to limit the number of hosts you can see using NetBIOS. The WINS server responds with the address only if matching scope IDs are used. Therefore, this option enables you to use the domain name as the NetBIOS scope.

- Cache Timeout Value—Length of time the DNS server keeps the information that it gets from the WINS server.

- Lookup Timeout Value—Length of time the DNS server waits for a resolution from the WINS server.

2.13.1 Adding HOSTS

Now that the domain has been created and the WINS resolution is set up, you need to add the records that the WINS resolution cannot handle. Essentially, this is any non-WINS client that you have on your network, as well as any host that has an alias (discussed in the next section).

Adding a host record (or any record) is simple. All you need to do is right-click the domain (or subdomain) to which you want to add the record. A menu appears from which you can choose New Host.

When you choose New Host, you see a dialog box. Enter the host name and the IP address in this dialog box. You need only the host name because the domain or subdomain you clicked is assumed.

An option to Create Associated PTR Record also exists. This option enters the required information for the reverse lookup zone for this host. You need to create the reverse lookup zone before you can use it.

2.13.2 Adding Other Records

The main purpose of a DNS server is to resolve a host name to an IP address. However, organizations may also want other types of information, such as the address of your mail server. You can add several types of records to the DNS server. The following list describes these other records:

- A—A host entry, exactly the same as was entered in the previous section.

- AAAA—Also a host entry; however, with AAAA you can enter an IPng address (the new version of TCP/IP that will use 128-bit addresses rather than 32-bit).

- AFSDB—Gives the address of an Andrew File System (AFS) database server or a Distributed Computing Environment (DCE) authenticated name server.

- CNAME—The canonical name is an alias that points one name such as WWW to another such as web. CNAME is one of the most common records that you need to enter.

- HINFO—Enters machine information about a host, which allows other hosts on the network to find out central processing unit (CPU) type and operating system information.

- ISDN—Enables you to map an entry to an Integrated Services Digital Network (ISDN) phone number rather than to an IP address. This record is used with a Route Through (RT) record (see below) to automate routing over dial-up ISDN.

- MB—An experimental record type used to associate an email ID with a particular host ID.

- MG—Like an MB record, the MG is experimental; it associates an MB record with a mail group that could be used for mailing lists.

- MINFO—Another experimental record, MINFO enables you to enter the mail information about the person responsible for a given mail record.

- MR—Another experimental record that provides for the mail records the same service that CNAME entries provide for host names—aliases.

- MX—You need to enter at least one MX record. The MX record directs incoming connections for mail to a mail server. You may enter more than one MX record. If you do, the system uses the preference number to determine the order in which to try them (lowest first).

- NS—A name server record. It is used to find the other name servers in the domain.

- PTR—The pointer record is part of the reverse lookup zone and is used to point the IP address at the host name.

- RP—Where you enter the name (or names) of the people responsible for the domain for which the server provides resolution. You may enter more than one. There can be multiple RP record entries of this type.

- RT—Route through points at another record in the DNS database. The RT record provides information on how to get to a host using dial-up ISDN or X.25.

- SOA—As already discussed, the start of authority record provides the basic configuration for a zone.

- TXT—The text record is a way of associating text information with a host. This record can provide information about the computer (in addition to the information in an HINFO entry) or other information such as the location.

- WKS—Provides the capability to indicate which well known services are running on a particular host. These match the service and protocols that are listed in the services file (%winroot%\ System32\drivers\etc) below port 256.

- X25—Similar to the ISDN entry, X25provides the capability to map a name to an X.121 name.

Adding these records is similar to adding a host record. Right-click the domain or subdomain and choose New Record.

2.13.3   Exercise

Exercise 1: Adding Records

Now that you have created the reverse lookup domain and the SunnyDays.com domain, add some records to the database.

1. Right-click the SunnyDays.com domain and choose Add Host.

2. In the New Host dialog box, add **Rob** as the host name and **160.106.66.7** as the host IP address.

3. Check Create Associated PTR Record to create the reverse lookup record at the same time.

4. Choose Add Host. Now enter **Judy** as the host name and **160.106.66.9** as the host IP address.

5. Click Add Host. Then click the Done button to close the dialog box. You should see the two new records in DNS Manager.

6. Click the 106.160.in-addr.arpa domain and press F5 to refresh. Notice there is now a 66 subdomain.

7. Double-click the 66 subdomain. You should see PTR records for the two hosts you just added.

8. Select the SunnyDays.com domain again. Add the following hosts and the associated PTR records:

Mail1	160.106.92.14
Mail2	160.106.101.80
Mail3	160.106.127.14
Web1	160.106.65.7
Web2	160.106.72.14
FTP_Pub1	160.106.99.99
FTP_Pub2	160.106.104.255
DEV	160.106.82.7

9. Close the New Host dialog box. Verify that the records were added to SunnyDays.com and the reverse lookup domains.

10. Highlight SunnyDays.com and choose DNS | New Domain from the menu.

11. Enter **DEV** as the name for the new domain and choose OK.

12. Right-click the DEV subdomain. Choose New Record. Select CNAME as the record type.

13. Enter **WWW** as the alias and **web2.SunnyDays.com** as the host. (This entry sets up WWW.DEV.SUNNYDAYS.COM to point to WEB2.SUNNYDAYS.COM).

14. Click OK to add the record. (It should appear in the Zone Info window.)

15. Create the following CNAME entries in the SunnyDays.com domain. Right-click SunnyDays.com, each time choosing New Record.

Alias	Host
WWW	web1.SunnyDays.com
FTP	FTP_PUB1.SunnyDays.com
DEV_FTP	FTP_PUB2.SunnyDays.com

16. Create a new record in the SunnyDays.com domain. This time, choose MX as the record type.

17. Leave the Host blank for this record and enter **mail1.SunnyDays.com** as the mail exchange server DNS name. Enter **10** as the preference.

18. Click OK to add the record. Add a second MX record for the SunnyDays.com using **mail2.SunnyDays.com** as the mail server and **20** as the preference.

19. Add the MX record for dev.SunnyDays.com. To do so, right-click SunnyDays.com and choose New Record; again, this is an MX record. The difference is that you include the host name.

20. Enter **DEV** as the host, add **mail3.SunnyDays.com** as the mail exchange server DNS name, and add **10** as the preference.

21. Ensure that all the records appear to be in place and then close DNS Manager.

2.13.4   Practice Problems

1. You have a computer called WEBSERVER with a TPC/IP address of 148.53.66.45 running Microsoft Internet Information Server. This system provides the HTTP and FTP services for your organization on the Internet. Which of the following sets of entries are correct for your database file?

   A. www IN A 148.53.66.45

      ftp IN A 148.53.66.45

   B. www IN A 148.53.66.45

      ftp IN A 148.53.66.45

      webserver CNAME www

   C. webserver IN A 148.53.66.45

      www CNAME webserver

      ftp CNAME webserver

   D. 45.66.53.148 IN PTR webserver

2. When you are configuring your DNS server, where do you configure the length of time that an entry will be cached on your server?

   A. Set the TTL in the DNS Manager properties on your server

   B. Set the TTL in the cache file on the remote server

   C. Set the TTL in the Registry under HKEY_LOCAL_MACHINE\ SYSTEM\CurrentControlSet\ Services\TCPIP\Parameters

   D. Set the TTL in the remote server in the SOA record

3. Your user is at a computer called prod172. The IP address of the computer is 152.63.85.5, and the computer is used to publish to the World Wide Web for the domain gowest.com. Which entries should you find in the database file?

   A. prod172 IN MX 152.63.85.5

   B. www cname 152.63.85.5

   C. prod172 IN A 152.63.85.5

      www CNAME 152.63.85.5

   D. prod172 IN A 152.63.85.5

      www CNAME prod172

4. What is the purpose of a HINFO record?

   A. Provides host information including the user name

   B. Provides host information including CPU type

   C. Provides host information including BIOS version

   D. Provides host information including hard disk size

5. What information is contained in an MX record? (Choose all that apply.)

   A. A preference entry.

   B. The mail server name.

   C. The WWW server name.

   D. There is no such record.

2.13.5   Practice Problems: Answers and Explanations

1. **C**   The correct syntax is

   webserver IN A 148.53.66.45

   www CNAME webserver

   ftp CNAME webserver

2. **D**   Set the TTL in the remote server in the SOA record.

3. **D**   The correct syntax is

   prod172 IN A 152.63.85.5

   www CNAME prod172

4. **B**   HINFO provides host information including CPU type.

5. **A, B**   An MX record contains a preference entry and the mail server name.

2.14   Connecting a DNS Server to a DNS Root Server

DNS includes a cache file that has entries for top-level servers of the Internet domains. If a host name cannot be resolved from local zone files, DNS uses the cache file to look for a higher-level DNS server to resolve the name. If your organization has only an intranet without any Internet access, you should replace this file with one that lists the top-level DNS servers in your organization. This file is called `cache.dns` and is located at `\winnt\system32\dns`.

The latest version of this file can be downloaded from InterNIC at `ftp://rs.internic.net/domain/named.cache`.

2.15   Configuring DNS Server Roles

The roles that a server can take include that of a primary and secondary DNS server, an IP forwarder, or a caching only server. The latter can resolve addresses, but does not host any domains or subdomains (zones).

The next few sections examine each of these roles, starting with the simplest and ending with the most complicated.

2.15.1   Configuring for Caching Only

There is just about nothing you need to do to run a server as a caching only server. The caching only server does not host any zones. If this is all you need, stop here.

2.15.2   Configuring as an IP Forwarder

An IP forwarder is also a caching only server; however, you need to configure it with the address of another DNS server (another Microsoft DNS server or any other DNS—for example, the one from your ISP). This configuration is fairly simple, and the only information you require is the IP address of the server to use. Follow these steps:

1. Right-click the server in the Server list and select Properties.

2. On the Forwarders tab, check the Use Forwarders box.

3. If the server is to only use the services of the other system, select Operate as Slave Server. (If you don't select this option, the server attempts to resolve through the forwarder; however, it then uses an iterative query if that fails.)

4. Enter the address or addresses of the DNS servers to which this one should forward queries.

5. If desired, set a time-out for the request.

6. Click OK to close the dialog box.

2.15.3   Creating a Primary DNS Server

The purpose of DNS is to resolve names to IP addresses. Therefore, you need to enter the addresses into the DNS server so other users can find your hosts. You do this by creating a zone in the DNS server and entering the information that you want to make available to the world. Here's how to create a zone:

1. Right-click the server that hosts the zone in the Server list.

2. Choose New Zone.

3. From the dialog box that appears, choose Primary. Then choose Next.

4. Enter the name of the domain (or subdomain) for which you are creating a zone on the next screen. Then press the Tab key. (This step automatically enters a zone filename; if you are adding an existing zone file, enter the name of the file that has the information—it must be in the `%winroot%\System32\DNS` directory.) When the information is in, click Next.

5. Choose Finish.

That is all there is to creating a zone. Now you can configure the zone and add the host (and other) records.

Setting Up and Reviewing the SOA Record

Configuring a zone is straightforward. Essentially, the information that you are entering here includes details for the Start of Authority (SOA) record and information about using WINS. The following steps show you how to set up the information:

1. Right-click the zone you want to configure. Choose Properties from the menu. The Properties dialog box should appear and present the basic zone information.

2. Click the SOA Record tab to bring up the information about the SOA.

3. Edit the information in the SOA record. You can change the following fields:

    *   Primary Name Server DNS Name—The name of the primary name server that contains the files for the domain. Note that only the host name is entered and then a period (.) that means this domain (for example, `NS1` is `NS1.ScrimTech.com`).

    *   Responsible Person Mailbox DNS Name—The email address of the person who is in charge of the DNS. (As with the primary name server, you need to enter only the email address—followed by a period—if the email address is within this domain.)

    *   Serial Number—A version ID that is assigned to the zone. The number is updated whenever you make changes to the database so that the secondary servers know that changes were made and can retrieve the new information.

    *   Refresh Interval—Tells the secondary servers how often they should check their version number with the primary servers to see whether they need to transfer the zone information again.

    *   Retry Interval—Tells how long the secondary server should wait before retrying the primary server if the secondary server could not connect at the time given in Refresh Interval.

    *   Expire Time—Sets how long a secondary server continues to give out information on this zone after not being able to connect with the primary server.

    *   Minimum Default TTL—When a DNS server performs an iterative query to resolve a name, the name is cached. This value sets the duration that other DNS servers are allowed to keep the information about records that your DNS server resolves for them.

4. Click the Notify tab. (This is not really part of the SOA; however, it is added here because it deals with the secondary servers.)

5. Enter the IP addresses of all secondary servers that should be notified when a change is made.

6. If desired, you can choose Only Allow Access from Secondaries Included on Notify List, which restricts which servers can retrieve your zone information.

7. Click OK to accept the changes you have made. (The WINS tab is covered in the next section.)

2.15.4   Setting Up the Secondary DNS Server

After you configure your server, you need to add a secondary server. Adding this server provides redundancy and also splits the workload among the servers. (You can have several secondary servers if you wish.) Follow these steps:

1. In DNS Manager, right-click the server to be configured as a secondary server.

2. Choose New Zone from the context menu. From the New Zone dialog box, choose Secondary.

> **This screen asks for the zone name and the server from which to get zone files. A handy option is the capability (as seen here) to drag the hand over another server listed in DNS Manager to automatically pick up the information.**
>
> **If the Primary DNS server is not a Microsoft DNS server, you will need to enter the information manually.**

3. Click the Next button, and you can enter the information for the file. This information should already be entered, and you should click Next to accept the defaults.

4. The next screen asks you to identify the IP master for the zone. This information should already be filled in for you.

5. The last screen tells you that you are finished. Click Finish to close this screen.

2.15.5   Exercises

Exercise 1: Configuring a DNS Domain

Now that the server is up and running, you need to create the domains that you will use. The first domain to be created is the reverse lookup domain. After that is in place, you create the SunnyDays.com domain.

1. From the Start menu, choose Programs | Administrative Tools | DNS Manager.

2. From the menu, choose DNS | New Server. Enter your IP address and click OK.

3. To create the reverse lookup domain, click your system's address. Choose DNS | New Zone.

4. Choose Primary and click Next.

5. For the zone, enter **106.160.in-addr.arpa** and press the Tab key (the filename is filled in for you).

6. Click Next to continue; then choose Finish.

7. Ensure that 106.160.in-addr.arpa is highlighted; choose DNS | Properties from the menu.

8. On the WINS Reverse Lookup tab, check the box to Use WINS Reverse Lookup. Enter **SUNNYDAYS.COM** as the host domain and then click OK. A new host record should now exist.

9. Select your DNS server's address and select DNS | New Zone from the menu.

10. Select Primary and choose Next. Enter **SUNNYDAYS.COM** as the zone name. Press the Tab key to have the system fill in the filename; then choose Next. Finally, click the Finish button.

11. Right-click the SunnyDays.com domain name. From the context menu that appears, select Properties.

12. Select the WINS Lookup tab.

13. Check the Use WINS Resolution box. Enter your IP address in the WINS server space and choose Add.

14. Click OK to close the dialog box. A WINS record should be in the SunnyDays.com domain.

2.15.6 Practice Problems

1. Which of the following are roles for which you can configure your DNS server? (Choose all that apply.)

   A. Primary

   B. Tertiary

   C. Backup

   D. IP forwarder

2. How do you create a primary DNS server?

   A. Install DNS on a primary Domain Controller.

   B. Configure the DNS server to be a primary server in the Server Properties.

   C. During DNS installation, specify that it is to be a primary server.

   D. Create a primary zone.

3. Where can a secondary server receive a copy of the zone file?

   A. Only from the primary server for the zone

   B. From any server that has a copy of the zone file

   C. Only from the master server for the zone

   D. Only from the top-level DNS server for the domain

2.15.7 Practice Problems: Answers and Explanations

1. **A, D** Primary and IP forwarder are both DNS roles, as are caching only and secondary.

2. **D** The designation primary server means that the DNS server is the primary server for a zone file. It can also be the secondary server for another zone file. In other words, the role of a DNS server is determined on a zone-by-zone basis.

3. **B** A secondary server can receive a copy of the zone file from a primary server or from a secondary server that has a copy of the zone file. The server from which the secondary server receives the copy is its master server. However, zones do not have master servers. A zone may have five secondary servers, each receiving a copy of the zone file from another secondary server in the zone. A zone file can have any number of master servers.

2.16   Configuring HOSTS and LMHOSTS Files

The HOSTS file is used for static host name mapping to IP addresses (in place of DNS); LMHOSTS provides static mapping to NetBIOS names (in place of WINS).

2.16.1   Configure HOSTS Files

The HOSTS file is an ASCII text file that statically maps local and remote host names and IP addresses. It is located in \systemroot\System32\Drivers\etc.

The HOSTS file is case sensitive in Windows NT versions prior to 4.0 and on other operating systems. It is limited to 255 characters per entry. It is used by PING and other utilities to resolve host names locally and remotely. One HOSTS file must reside on each host, and the file is read from top to bottom. As soon as a match is found for a host name, the reading stops. For that reason, when the file contains duplicate entries, the latter ones are always ignored and the most commonly used names should be near the top of the file.

An example of the default HOSTS file follows:

```
# Copyright (c) 1993-1995 Microsoft Corp.
#
# This is a sample HOSTS file used by Microsoft TCP/IP for Windows NT.
#
# This file contains the mappings of IP addresses to host names. Each
# entry should be kept on an individual line. The IP address should
# be placed in the first column followed by the corresponding host name.
# The IP address and the host name should be separated by at least one
# space.
#
# Additionally, comments (such as these) may be inserted on individual
# lines or following the machine name denoted by a '#' symbol.
#
# For example:
#
#     102.54.94.97     rhino.acme.com          # source server
#      38.25.63.10     x.acme.com              # x client host

127.0.0.1       localhost
```

The first thing to notice in this file is that the pound sign (#) indicates a comment. When the system reads the file, the system ignores every line beginning with a comment. When a # appears in the middle of a line, the line is only read up to the sign. To use this example on a live system, the first 17 lines should be deleted or moved to the end of the file to keep them from being read every time the file is referenced.

The second thing to note is the entry:

```
127.0.0.1       localhost
```

This is a loopback address in every host. It references the internal card, regardless of the actual host address, and can be used to verify that things are working properly internally before testing that they are working properly down the wire.

Within the HOSTS file, fields are separated by whitespace that can be either tabs or spaces. As mentioned earlier, a host can be referred to by more than one name; to do so, separate the entries on the same line with whitespace, as shown in the following example:

```
127.0.0.1       me loopback localhost
199.9.200.7     SALES7 victor
199.9.200.4     SALES4 nikki
199.9.200.3     SALES3 cole
199.9.200.2     SALES2 victoria
199.9.200.1     SALES1 nicholas
199.9.200.5     SALES5 jack
199.9.200.11    ACCT1
199.9.200.12    ACCT2
199.9.200.13    ACCT3
199.9.200.14    ACCT4
199.9.200.15    ACCT5
199.9.200.17    ACCT7
```

The aliases are other names by which the system can be referenced. Here, me and loopback do the same as localhost, whereas nicholas is the same as SALES1. If an alias is used more than once, the search stops at the first match because the file is searched sequentially.

2.16.2 Configure LMHOSTS Files

Whereas the HOSTS file contains the mappings of IP addresses to host names, the LMHOSTS file contains the mappings of IP addresses to Windows NT computer names. When speaking of Windows NT computer names, the inference is to NetBIOS names, or the names that would be used in conjunction with NET USE statements.

An example of the default version of this file follows:

```
# Copyright (c) 1993-1995 Microsoft Corp.
#
# This is a sample LMHOSTS file used by the Microsoft TCP/IP for Windows
# NT.
#
# This file contains the mappings of IP addresses to NT computer
# (NetBIOS) names.  Each entry should be kept on an individual line.
# The IP address should be placed in the first column followed by the
# corresponding computer name. The address and the computer name
# should be separated by at least one space or tab. The "#" character
# is generally used to denote the start of a comment (see the exceptions
# below).
#
# This file is compatible with Microsoft LAN Manager 2.x TCP/IP lmhosts
# files and offers the following extensions:
#
```

2

```
#       #PRE
#       #DOM:<domain>
#       #INCLUDE <filename>
#       #BEGIN_ALTERNATE
#       #END_ALTERNATE
#       \0xnn (non-printing character support)
#
# Following any entry in the file with the characters "#PRE" will cause
# the entry to be preloaded into the name cache. By default, entries are
# not preloaded, but are parsed only after dynamic name resolution fails.
#
# Following an entry with the "#DOM:<domain>" tag will associate the
# entry with the domain specified by <domain>. This affects how the
# browser and logon services behave in TCP/IP environments. To preload
# the host name associated with #DOM entry, it is necessary to also add a
# #PRE to the line. The <domain> is always preloaded although it will not
# be shown when the name cache is viewed.
#
# Specifying "#INCLUDE <filename>" will force the RFC NetBIOS (NBT)
# software to seek the specified <filename> and parse it as if it were
# local. <filename> is generally a UNC-based name, allowing a
# centralized lmhosts file to be maintained on a server.
# It is ALWAYS necessary to provide a mapping for the IP address of the
# server prior to the #INCLUDE. This mapping must use the #PRE directive.
# In addition the share "public" in the example below must be in the
# LanManServer list of "NullSessionShares" in order for client machines to
# be able to read the lmhosts file successfully. This key is under \machine\
# system\currentcontrolset\services\lanmanserver\parameters\nullsessionshares
# in the registry. Simply add "public" to the list found there.
#
# The #BEGIN_ and #END_ALTERNATE keywords allow multiple #INCLUDE
# statements to be grouped together. Any single successful include
# will cause the group to succeed.
#
# Finally, nonprinting characters can be embedded in mappings by
# first surrounding the NetBIOS name in quotations, then using the
# \0xnn notation to specify a hex value for a nonprinting character.
#
# The following example illustrates all of these extensions:
#
# 102.54.94.97    rhino        #PRE #DOM:networking #net group's DC
# 102.54.94.102   "appname  \0x14"                  #special app server
# 102.54.94.123   popular      #PRE                 #source server
# 102.54.94.117   localsrv     #PRE                 #needed for the include
#
# #BEGIN_ALTERNATE
# #INCLUDE \\localsrv\public\lmhosts
# #INCLUDE \\rhino\public\lmhosts
# #END_ALTERNATE
```

```
#
# In the above example, the "appname" server contains a special
# character in its name, the "popular" and "localsrv" server names are
# preloaded, and the "rhino" server name is specified so it can be used
# to later #INCLUDE a centrally maintained lmhosts file if the "localsrv"
# system is unavailable.
#
# Note that the whole file is parsed including comments on each lookup,
# so keeping the number of comments to a minimum will improve performance.
# Therefore, it is not advisable to simply add lmhosts file entries onto the
# end of this file.
```

Once more, the pound sign (#) indicates comments, and the file is read sequentially on each lookup, so limiting the size of the comment lines at the beginning of the file is highly recommended.

A number of special commands can be used in the file to load entries into a name cache, which is scanned on each lookup prior to referencing the file. (By default, entries are not preloaded, but are parsed only after dynamic name resolution fails.) Using these commands will decrease your lookup time and increase system efficiency.

2.16.3   Exercise

Exercise 1: Edit the HOSTS File

The following exercise shows you how to find and edit the HOSTS file.

1. From the Start menu, choose Programs | MS-DOS Prompt.

2. Change to the appropriate location by typing **cd\systemroot\System32\Drivers\etc** where **systemroot** is your Windows NT directory.

3. Type **PING ME** and notice the error that comes back because the host is not found.

4. Type **EDIT HOSTS**.

5. The last line of the file should read:

    ```
    127.0.0.1         localhost
    ```

6. Move one space to the right of last character and enter

    ME

    so the line now reads:

    ```
    127.0.0.1         localhost ME
    ```

7. Exit the editor and save the changes.

8. Type **PING ME** and notice the successful results.

2.16.4   Practice Problems

1. HOSTS file entries are limited to how many characters?

   A. 8

   B. 255

   C. 500

   D. Unlimited

2. The number of entries in the HOSTS file is limited to:

   A. 8

   B. 255

   C. 500

   D. Unlimited

3. Which of the following files in Windows NT, prior to 4.0, is case sensitive?

   A. HOSTS

   B. LMHOSTS

   C. ARP

   D. FQDN

4. Which of the following files is used for NetBIOS name resolution?

   A. HOSTS

   B. LMHOSTS

   C. ARP

   D. FQDN

5. Which address is the loopback address?

   A. 0.0.0.1

   B. 127.0.0.0

   C. 127.0.0.1

   D. 255.255.255.255

2.16.5   Practice Problems: Answers and Explanations

1. **B** HOSTS file lines are limited to 255 characters.

2. **D** The HOSTS file can contain unlimited entries.

3. **A** Prior to Windows NT 4.0, the HOSTS file was case sensitive.

4. **B** The LMHOSTS file is used for NetBIOS-to-IP resolution.

5. **C** The loopback address is 127.0.0.1.

2.17   Configuring a Windows NT Server to Support TCP/IP Printing

Printing within Windows NT is a remarkably complex process. The same is true of remote host systems, such as UNIX platforms. The Windows NT and host system print models can interact to a large extent. The following sections describe how clients and servers on Windows NT and remote host systems can interact.

2.17.1   Windows NT Client Printing to a Remote Host System

You can use two methods to print to a remote host from a Windows NT client: using the LPR command from the Windows NT client computer or creating an LPR printer on a Windows NT client computer.

Using the LPR Command-Line Utility

One of the utilities included with Microsoft TCP/IP Printing is the LPR utility. This program allows a Windows NT computer to send a print job to a remote host printer. The remote host system must be running the LPD daemon, and you must know the name of the remote host and the printer. This utility has the following command-line options:

```
Sends a print job to a network printerUsage: lpr -S server -P printer [-C class] [-J job]
[-o option] [-x] [-d] filename


Options:
    -S server    Name or IP address of the host providing LPD service
    -P printer   Name of the print queue
    -C class     Job classification for use on the first page
    -J job       Job name to print on the first page
    -o option    Indicates the type of file (by default assumes a text
                 file). Use "-o l" for binary (for example, postscript)
                 files
    -x           Compatibility with SunOS 4.1.x and prior versions
    -d           Sends data file first
```

Creating an LPR Printer on a Windows NT Computer

Creating an LPR printer on the Windows NT client computer provides a higher degree of transparency. If the printer is shared, the Windows NT client can act as a print gateway for other Windows NT computers.

To create an LPR printer under Windows NT after Microsoft TCP/IP Printing has been installed, simply follow this procedure:

1. Select Settings | Printers and then click Add Printer. Select My Computer because you need to add a new printer port.

2. At this point, select Add Port and select LPR port.

3. You are then prompted to provide the host name (or IP address) of the remote host system as well as the printer name.

4. If you choose to share the printer, any client computer that can print to your Windows NT computer can also print to the LPR printer on the remote host system.

2.17.2   Remote Host Client Printing to a Windows NT Server

Remote hosts also can print to a Windows NT printer because Windows NT can provide an LPD service. The LPD service (lpdsvc) provides the same service that an LPD daemon provides on a UNIX host. Because LPD is implemented as a service, it is controlled through Control Panel | Services. This service automatically installs when you opt to install TCP/IP print services.

Remote host systems use different commands for printing. One command that works on most systems is the LPR command. A sample command line that would work on most systems is

```
LPR -s NTSYSTEM -p NTPRINTER filename
```

For the LPR command on the remote system, specify the DNS name (or IP address) of your Windows NT system along with the printer name. Windows NT internally directs the print job to the specified printer.

2.17.3 Practice Problems

1. A user at a Windows NT computer running the TCP/IP protocol wants to send a print job to an LPR printer on a remote host system. Which methods enable the user to send the print job to the remote host?

   A. Using the LPD command-line utility from the Windows NT system, and specifying the host name, printer name, and filename

   B. Using the LPR command-line utility from the Windows NT system, and specifying the host name, printer name, and filename

   C. Creating an LPR printer in Control Panel | Printers, and specifying the host name and printer name required for the creation of an LPR report

   D. Creating an LPR printer in Control Panel | Printers, and specifying the host name and printer name required for the creation of an LPD server on the Windows NT computer

2. Which procedure enables a remote computer to send a print job to a Windows NT printer in the fewest steps?

   A. Creating an LPR printer on the Windows NT computer, sharing the printer, and running the LPR command from the remote host system specifying the required information

   B. Creating the LPD printer on the Windows NT computer and running the LPR command from the remote host system specifying the required information

   C. Running the LPR command on the remote system—Windows NT automatically routes the print job to the printer with no further configuration on the Windows NT computer

   D. Running the LPD command from the remote host because the LPD command spawns a copy of the LPDSVC command on the Windows NT computer whether or not TCP/IP printing support is installed

3. Which of the following configurations allows a Windows NT computer to act as a print gateway to an LPR printer on a remote host?

   A. Creating an LPR printer on the Windows NT computer, sharing the printer, and connecting to the newly created printer from any other computer on the network

   B. Creating an LPR printer on the Windows NT computer and installing an LPR printer on every other computer on the network because Windows NT computers cannot act as print gateways to LPR printers

   C. Creating an LPR printer on the Windows NT computer and installing the LPDSVC service on every other computer on the network

   D. None of the above—Windows NT automatically routes print jobs to any printer, including LPR, without any configuration

4. Which parameters are required when using the LPR command on a Windows NT computer to send a print job to a remote host?

A. The remote host name

B. User name and password for the remote system

C. The remote printer name

D. The name of the file to be printed

E. The remote system's SMB server name

5. By creating an LPR printer on a Windows NT computer and sharing the newly created printer, which of the following statements describes the added functions?

    A. Remote host systems can print to the LPR printer, and Windows NT client computers can print to the LPR printer, but only by using the LPR command.

    B. Remote host systems can print to the LPR printer, and Windows NT computers can print to the LPR printer using Windows NT printing, but other Windows NT computers cannot print to the LPR printer.

    C. Remote host systems can print to the LPR printer, Windows NT computers can print to the LPR printer using Windows NT printing, and other Windows NT computers can print to the LPR printer.

    D. Remote host systems cannot print to the LPR printer, Windows NT computers can print to the LPR

printer using Windows NT printing, and other Windows NT computers can print to the LPR printer.

2.17.4 Practice Problems: Answers and Explanations

1. **B, C** Using the LPR command-line utility from the Windows NT system; specifying the host name, printer name and filename; and creating an LPR printer in Control Panel | Printers, specifying the host name and printer name required for the creation of an LPR port.

2. **B** Creating the LPD printer on the Windows NT computer and running the LPR command from the remote host system specifying the required information.

3. **A** Creating an LPR printer on the Windows NT computer, sharing the printer, and connecting to the newly created printer from any other computer on the network.

4. **A, C, D** The remote host name, the remote printer name, and the name of the file to be printed.

5. **C** Remote host systems can print to the LPR printer, Windows NT computers can print to the LPR printer using Windows NT printing, and other Windows NT computers can print to the LPR printer.

2.18 Configuring SNMP

Simple Network Management Protocol (SNMP) is part of the TCP/IP protocol suite. It corresponds to the application layer in the Internet protocol suite.

SNMP enables network administrators to remotely troubleshoot and monitor hubs and routers. Much of SNMP is defined within RFCs 1157 and 1212, although other RFCs are relevant. SNMP can be found, along with other RFCs, on various Web sites, including http://ds.internic.net. You can also do a search on SNMP or RFC and find more specific information related to a specific part of SNMP—for example, on just Ethernet and SNMP.

SNMP enables you to get information about remote devices without having to be at the device itself. SNMP can be a very useful tool if understood and used properly. You can find a wide variety of information about these devices, depending on the device itself, of course. Some examples include

- IP address of a router

- Number of open files

- Amount of hard drive space available

- Version number of a Windows NT host

Before you set up SNMP, you need the IP address or host names of the systems that will either be the initiators or those that will respond to the requests. Microsoft's SNMP service uses the regular Windows NT host name resolution, such as HOSTS, DNS, WINS, and LMHOSTS. Therefore, if you are using one of these resolution methods, add the correct host name to IP address resolution for the computers that you are setting up with SNMP.

The types of systems on which you can find data include

- Mainframes

- Gateways and routers

- Hubs and bridges

- Windows NT Servers

- LAN Manager servers

- SNMP agents

SNMP uses a distributed architecture design to facilitate its properties. That is, various parts of SNMP are spread throughout the network to complete the task of collecting and processing data to provide remote management.

Because SNMP is a distributed system, you can spread out the management of it in different locations so as not to overtax any one PC and for multiple management functionality.

An SNMP service by Microsoft enables a machine running Windows NT to transfer its current condition to a computer running an SNMP management system. However, this is only the agent side, not the management tools. Various third-party management utilities are available, including the following:

- IBM NetView

- Sun Net Manager

- Hewlett-Packard OpenView

> The management utilities are not included on the Microsoft exam.

2.18.1 SNMP Agents and Management

SNMP has two main parts: the agent and the management system.

- The management station is the centralized location from which you can manage SNMP.

- The agent station is the piece of equipment from which you are trying to extract data.

Each part is discussed in the following sections.

The SNMP Management System

The management system is the key component for obtaining information from the client. You need at least one management system to even be able to use the SNMP service. The management system is responsible for "asking the questions." As mentioned earlier, there are a certain number of questions it can ask each device, depending upon the type of device. The management system is a computer running one of the various software components mentioned earlier.

In addition, certain commands can be given specifically at the management system. These are generic commands not specific to any type of management system directly:

- get—Requests a specific value. For example, it can query how many active sessions are open.

- get-next—Requests the next object's value. For example, you can query a client's ARP cache and then ask for each subsequent value.

- set—Changes the value on an object that has the properties of read/write. For security reasons, this command is not often used; in addition, most objects have a read-only attribute.

Usually, you have only one management system running the SNMP service per group of hosts. This group is known as a *community*. Sometimes, however, you may want to have multiple management systems. Some of these reasons are discussed in the following list:

- You may want multiple management systems to send different queries to the same agents.

- There might be different management sites for one community.

- As the network grows and becomes more complex, you may need to help differentiate certain aspects of your community.

The SNMP Agent

You have seen so far what the SNMP management side is responsible for and can specifically do. For the most part, the management side is the active component for getting information. The SNMP agent, on the other hand, is responsible for complying with the requests and responding to the SNMP manager accordingly. Generally, the agent is a router, server, or hub. The agent is usually a passive component only responding to a direct query.

In one particular instance, however, the agent is the initiator, acting on its own without a direct query. This special case is called a *trap*. A trap is set up from the management side on the agent. But the management does not need to go to the agent to find out if the trap information has been tripped. The agent sends an alert to the management system telling it that the event has occurred. Except in this instance, the agent is usually passive. A trap is similar to a father and son fishing with a net on a stream. The dad sets up the net on the stream. The holes in the net are just the right size for catching a certain type and size of fish. The dad then goes downstream to set up more, leaving his son to tend to the net. When the fish comes along, it gets caught in the net and the son runs to tell his father.

The stream is the traffic going through the router. The net is the trap set by the management system. The son is the one responding to the trap and running to tell his father that a fish has been caught without the father having to go back and check on his trap. The special fish that is caught might be an alert that a particular server's hard drive is full or that there is a duplicate IP address. Although this analogy is rough, it gets the basic idea across. What happens, however, if a spare tire comes down the stream and gets caught in the trap? Sometimes invalid packets can set off the trap without it being what you are looking for. These are rare events, and the traps are very specific in what they are looking for.

2.18.2   Management Information Base

Now that you've learned a little about the management system and agents, you can delve into the different types of query databases.

The data that the management system requests from an agent is contained in a *Management Information Base* (MIB), which is a list of questions that the management system can ask. The list of questions depends on what type of device it is asking. The MIB is the database of information that can be queried against. The specific queries that can be asked (or queried against) depend on what type of system it is. The MIB defines what type of objects can be used and what type of information is available about the network device.

A variety of MIB databases can be established. The MIB is stored on the SNMP agent and is similar to the Windows NT Registry in its hierarchical structure. These MIBs are available to both the agents and management system as a reference that both can pull information from.

The Microsoft SNMP service supports the following MIB databases:

- Internet MIB II
- LAN Manager MIB II
- DHCP MIB
- WINS MIB

These databases are discussed in the following sections.

Internet MIB II

Internet MIB II defines 171 objects for fault troubleshooting on the network and configuration analysis. It is defined in RFC 1212, which adds to and overwrites, the previous version, Internet MIB I.

LAN Manager MIB II

LAN Manager MIB II defines about 90 objects associated with Microsoft Networking, such as

- Shares
- Users
- Logon
- Sessions
- Statistical

Most of LAN Manager MIB II's objects are set to read-only mode due to the limited security function of SNMP.

DHCP MIB

The DHCP MIB identifies objects that can monitor the DHCP server's actions. It is set up automatically when a DHCP server service is installed and is called DHCPMIB.DLL. It has 14 objects that can be used for monitoring the DHCP server activity, including items such as the following:

- The number of active leases
- The number of failures
- The number of DHCP discover requests received

WINS MIB

WINS MIB (WINSMIB.DLL) is a Microsoft-specific MIB relating directly to the WINS server service. It is automatically installed when WINS is set up. It monitors WINS server activity and has approximately 70 objects. It checks such items as the number of resolution requests, success and failure, and the date and time of last database replication.

MIB Structure

As mentioned previously, the name space for MIB objects is hierarchical. It is structured in this manner so that each manageable object can be assigned a globally unique name. Certain organizations have the authority to assign the name space for parts of the tree design.

The MIB structure is similar to TCP/IP addresses. You get only one address from the InterNIC and then subnet it according to your needs. You do not have to contact InterNIC to inquire about each address assignment. The same applies here. Organizations can assign names without consulting an Internet authority for every specific assignment. For example, the name space assigned to Microsoft's LAN Manager is 1.3.6.1.4.1.77. More recently, the Microsoft corporation has been assigned 1.3.6.1.4.1.311; any new MIB would then be identified under that branch.

The object identifier in the hierarchy is written as a sequence of labels beginning at the root and ending at the object. It flows down the chart, starting with the International Standards Organization (ISO) and ending with the object MIB II. Labels are separated by periods. The following is an example of this labeling technique.

The object identifier for an MIB II is

Object Name	Object Number
`iso.org.dod.internet.management.mibii`	1.3.6.2.2.1

The object identifier for LAN Manager MIB II is

Object Name	Object Number
`iso.org.dod.internet.private.` `enterprise.lanmanager`	1.3.6.1.4.77

> **The name space used here for the object identifiers is completely separate from that used with UNIX domain names.**

2.18.3   Microsoft SNMP Service

The SNMP service is an additional component of Windows NT TCP/IP software. It includes the four supported MIBs; each is a dynamic link library and can be loaded and unloaded as needed. It provides SNMP agent services to any TCP/IP host running SNMP management software. It also performs the following:

- Reports special happenings, such as traps, to multiple hosts

- Responds to requests for information from multiple hosts

- Can be set up on any system running Windows NT and TCP/IP

- Sets up special counters in Performance Monitor that can be used to monitor the TCP/IP performance related to SNMP

- Uses host names and IP addresses to recognize which hosts it receives; requests information

2.18.4   SNMP Architecture

The MIB architecture can be extended to enable developers to create their own MIB libraries, called *extension agents*. Extension agents expand the list of objects that an MIB can report on, making it not only more expansive but also specifically related to network setup and devices.

Although the Microsoft SNMP service doesn't include management software, it does have a Microsoft Win32 SNMP Manager Application Programming Interface (API) that works with the Windows Sockets. The API can then be used by developers to create third-party SNMP management utilities.

SNMP uses User Datagram Protocol (UDP) port 161 to send and receive messages and IP to route messages.

SNMP Communities

A *community* is a group of hosts running the SNMP service to which they all belong. These usually consist of at least one management system and multiple agents. The idea is to logically organize systems into organizational units for better network management.

Communities are called by a *community name*. This name is case sensitive. The default community name is public and generally all hosts belong to it. Also by default, all SNMP agents respond to any request using the community public name. By using unique community names, however, you can provide limited security and segregation of hosts.

Agents do not accept requests nor respond to hosts that are not from their configured community. Agents can be members of multiple communities at the same time, but they must be explicitly configured as such. This feature enables them to respond to different SNMP managers from various communities.

Security

There really is no established security with SNMP. The data is not encrypted, and there is no setup to stop someone from accessing the network, discovering the community names and addresses used, and sending fake requests to agents.

A major reason most MIBs are read-only is to prevent unauthorized changes. The best security you can have is to use unique community names. Choose Send Authentication Trap and specify a trap destination; you can also stipulate Only Accept SNMP Packets from These Hosts.

You might also set up traps that let you know whether the agents receive requests from communities or addresses not specified. This way, you can track down unauthorized SNMP activity.

2.18.5   Installing and Configuring SNMP

The SNMP service can be installed for the following reasons:

- You want to monitor TCP/IP with Performance Monitor.
- You want to monitor a Windows NT–based system with a third-party application.
- You want to set up your computer as an SNMP agent.

The following steps install the SNMP service, assuming you already have TCP/IP installed and set up. These steps also assume you have administrative privileges to install and utilize SNMP.

1. Click on Start | Settings | Control Panel.
2. Double-click on Network to bring up the Network properties dialog box.
3. On the Network Settings dialog box, click Add.
4. Click the Services tab and click Add. The Select Network Service dialog box appears.
5. Click SNMP Service and then click OK.
6. Specify the location of the Windows NT distribution files.
7. After the files are copied, the SNMP Service Configuration dialog box appears. The parameters that need to be configured are shown in Table 2.18.1.

Table 2.18.1   SNMP Configuration Options

Parameter	Definition
Community Name	The community name to which traps are sent. Remember, it is public by default. There must be a management system in that community to receive and request information.
Trap Destination	The IP addresses of hosts to which you want the SNMP service to send traps. Note that you can use IP addresses, host names (as long as they are resolved properly), and IPX addresses.

8. Now choose OK to close the SNMP Properties dialog box. Then choose Close to exit the Network Properties dialog box. When prompted, restart your computer.

2.18.6   SNMP Security Parameters

There are Several options that you can set that affect the security of the SNMP agent. By default, the agent will respond to any manager using community name public. Because this name can be inside or outside your organization, you should at the very least change the community name.

Table 2.18.2 describes the options that are available.

Table 2.18.2   Security Options for the SNMP Agent

Parameter	Description
Send Authentication Trap	Sends information back to the trap initiator, responding that the trap failed. This failure could occur because of an incorrect community name or because the host is not specified for service.
Accepted Community Names	When a manager sends a query, a community name is included (this is a list of community names that the agent will respond to).
Accept SNMP Packets from Any Host	Responds to any query from any management system in any community.
Only Accept SNMP Packets from These Hosts	Responds to only the hosts listed.

2.18.7   SNMP Agent

In some cases, you will configure other aspects of the SNMP agent. These set the type of devices that you will monitor and who is responsible for the system.

The options available on this screen are as follows:.

- The contact name of the person you want to be alerted about conditions on this station—generally, this person is the user of the computer.

- The location is a descriptive field for the computer to help keep track of the system sending the alert.

- The last part of the screen identifies the types of connections/devices this agent will monitor. These include:

    - Physical—You are managing physical devices such as repeaters or hubs.

    - Applications—Set if the Windows NT computer uses an application that uses TCP/IP. You should place a check mark in this box every time, as just by using SNMP you should have TCP/IP set up.

    - Datalink/Subnetwork—For managing a bridge.

    - Internet—When Enable IP Forwarding is turned on, this monitors the Windows NT computer's acting as an IP gateway, or router.

    - End-to-End—Causes the Windows NT computer to act as an IP host. You should check this box every time, as you are most likely an IP host.

Any errors with SNMP will be recorded in the System Log. The log records any SNMP activity. Use Event Viewer to look at the errors and to find the problem and possible solutions.

2.18.8   Using the SNMP Utility

The SNMP utility does not come with Windows NT. It is included in the Windows NT Resource Kit and called SNMPUTIL.EXE. Basically, it is a command-line management system utility. It checks that the SNMP service has been set up and is working correctly. You can also use it to make command calls. You cannot do full SNMP management from this utility, but, as you will see, you would not want to because of the complex syntax.

The following is the general syntax structure:

```
snmputil command gent community object_identifier_(OID)
```

The following are the commands you can use:

- walk—Moves through the MIB branch identified by what you have placed in the object_identifer

- get—Returns the value of the item specified by the object_identifier

- getnext—Returns the value of the next object after the one specified by the get command

To find out the time the WINS server service began, for example, providing WINS is installed and the SNMP agent is running, you query the WINS MIB with the following command:

```
c:\>snmputil getnext localhost public .1.3.6.1.4.1.311.1.1.1.1
```

In this example, the first part refers to the Microsoft branch: .1.3.6.1.4.1.311 (or iso.org.dod.internet.private.enterprise.microsoft). The last part of the example refers to the specific MIB and object you are querying: `.1.1.1.1` (or `.software.Wins.Par.ParWinsStartTime`). A returned value might appear like the following:

```
Value = OCTET STRING - 01:17:22 on 11:23:1997.<0xa>
```

2.18.9 What SNMP Is Really Doing

The following example tracks a sample of SNMP traffic between a manager and an agent. Remember that in real life you will use management software (such as HP's Openview, which will allow you to see the MIB's and query without knowing all the numbers).

1. The SNMP management system makes a request of an agent using the agent's IP address or host name.

    a. Request sent by the application to UDP port 161.

    b. Host name resolved to an IP address, if host name was used, using host name resolution methods: localhost, HOSTS file, DNS, WINS, broadcast, LMHOSTS file.

2. SNMP packet gets set up with the listed information inside, and routes the packet on the agent's UDP port 161:

    a. The command for the objects: `get`, `get-next`, `set`.

    b. The community name and any other specified data.

3. An SNMP agent gets the packet and puts it into its buffer.

    a. The community name is checked for validity. If it is not correct or is corrupted, the packet is rejected.

    b. If the community name checks out, the agent checks to see whether the originating host name or IP address is correct as well. If not, it is thrown out.

    c. The inquiry is then passed to the correct DLL as described in the preceding section on MIBs.

    d. The object identifier is mapped to the specific API and that call is made.

    e. The DLL sends the data to the agent.

4. The SNMP packet is given to the SNMP manager with the requested information.

2.18.9 Exercises

Exercise 1: Exploring Performance Monitor Counters

After you have installed SNMP, you may want to look at the Performance Monitor utility and notice the TCP/IP objects available for monitoring. To do this, use the following steps:

1. Choose Start | Programs | Administrative Tools and select Performance Monitor.

2. Click the Edit menu and click Add to Chart.

3. Look at the list of available TCP/IP objects.

A sample exercise monitoring SNMP, using one of the TCP/IP-related objects, is as follows:

1. Follow the preceding exercise.

2. Select the ICMP object from the list.

3. Click on Messages/sec in the Counter box.

4. Set the scale to 1, and then click Add.

5. Select another object IP.

6. From the Counter list, click Datagrams Sent/sec.

7. Set the scale to 1 and then click Add.

8. Select Done.

9. Make certain you are using the Chart view.

10. Change Vertical Maximum to 10 and click OK.

11. Go to a command prompt and ping another computer.

12. Go back to Performance Monitor and notice what happened.

13. There should be two messages for ICMP and one IP datagram (two ICMP messages—one request, one reply).

14. Shut down Performance Monitor and go to the next exercise.

Exercise 2: Using SNMPUTIL to Access MIB Objects

This exercise is dependent on DHCP, WINS, TCP/IP, and SNMP being set up and your performing these exercises from that host machine. You may want to use the F3 key to bring up similar commands and check your number sequence carefully.

1. Copy the SNMPUtil.exe to winnt_root.

2. Go to a command prompt.

3. Type the following to find out the number of IP addresses leased by your DHCP server by querying the DHCP MIB:

   ```
   snmputil getnext your_ip_address community_name
   .1.3.6.1.4.1.311.1.3.2.1.1.1
   ```

4. Type the following to find out how many failed queries have been done by your WINS server by querying the WINS MIB:

   ```
   snmputil getnext your_ip_address community_name
   .1.3.6.1.4.1.311.1.2.1.18
   ```

5. Type the following to find out how many successful queries have been done by your WINS server by querying the WINS MIB:

   ```
   snmputil getnext your_ip_address community_name
   .1.3.6.1.4.1.311.1.2.1.17
   ```

6. Type the following to find out the version of Windows NT server that you are using. Notice that this step requires two queries; you combine the results to get your full response. Notice that here you are querying the LAN Manager MIB, as noted by the change in the hierarchical format.

```
snmputil getnext your_ip_address community_name
  .1.3.6.1.4.1.77.1.1.1
snmputil getnext your_ip_address community_name
  .1.3.6.1.4.1.77.1.1.2
```

2.18.11 Practice Problems

1. When using an SNMP management system to query an agent, you can find out which of the following when querying the WINS MIB?

   A. The number of WINS servers available on your network

   B. The number of successful queries made on the WINS proxy server

   C. The number of unsuccessful queries processed by the WINS server

   D. The number of unsuccessful queries processed by DNS

2. Through the use of SNMP, you can find out remote management information on which of the following items?

   A. Hub

   B. Router

   C. Bridge

   D. Windows NT Server

   E. Windows NT Workstation

3. When using SNMP in a TCP/IP network across a router with UNIX hosts, Windows NT Servers and LAN Manager stations, how would SNMP be able to resolve a host name?

   A. HOSTS file

   B. LMHOSTS file

   C. DNS

   D. DHCP

   E. WINS

4. The commands that you are able to implement on the management system side when making requests to the agents consist of which of the following?

   A. `get, set, go`

   B. `walk, get, get-next`

   C. `get, get-next, walk`

   D. `set, get-next, get`

5. The active component of the SNMP system that performs the trap is which of the following?

   A. Management system

   B. Agent

   C. Alert

   D. Monitor

6. The part of SNMP that has specific objects related to the type of item that the management system is able to make queries against and is stored on the agent is called what?

   A. MIIB

   B. Management Information Base

   C. MHB

   D. Management Internet Information Base

7. Which of the following statements regarding the activity of SNMP and its actions are false?

   A. Reports traps to multiple hosts

   B. Responds to requests from multiple hosts

C. Sets up counters in Performance Monitor for SNMP

D. Uses host names and IP addresses to identify source and destination

8. A community is a group of hosts running SNMP, to which they all belong and respond to requests from a management system to agents. The default community name for all communities is

    A. punic

    B. comm

    C. community

    D. public

9. When setting up security in SNMP, what is the most secure option you can select without limiting the potential for additional communities?

    A. Have a community name other than public, select Only Accept SNMP Packets from These Hosts, and set a trap to alert invalid inquiries

    B. Have a community name of public, select Only Accept SNMP Packets from These Hosts, and set a trap to alert invalid inquiries

    C. Have a community name of public and select Accept SNMP Packets from These Hosts

    D. Have a community name other than public, select Not Only Accept SNMP Packets from These Hosts, and set a trap to ignore invalid inquiries

10. When setting up an SNMP management system on a Windows NT host machine, what MIBs are supported by default under Windows NT 4.0?

    A. Internet MIB I, LAN Manager MIB II, WINS MIB, DHCP MIB

    B. Internet MIB II, LAN Manager MIB I, WINS MIB, DHCP MIB

    C. Internet MIB II, LAN Manager MIB II, WINS MIB, DHCP MIB

    D. Internet MIB II, LAN Manager MIB II, WINS MIB I, DHCP MIB

11. For SNMP agents and management systems to communicate with each other, they need to be set up with the same _____ name.

    A. Public

    B. Unity

    C. Group

    D. Community

12. If you are having problems with SNMP, where in Windows NT should you look?

    A. Event Viewer in Windows NT Administrative Tools

    B. Performance Monitor

    C. The SNMP log

    D. The System Log

13. Which agent services are enabled by default when setting up the Windows NT SNMP agent?

    A. Internet

    B. Physical

    C. End-to-End

    D. Application

14. Which SNMP operation is instituted by the agent instead of the management system?

    A. walk

    B. set

    C. trap

    D. get

15. The message sent by an SNMP agent to warn an SNMP management system of an error or specific event is known as a _____.

A. Net

B. Trap

C. Get

D. Warning event

16. Which utility in the Windows NT Resource Kit enables you to check whether the SNMP service is configured correctly and working with the SNMP management system?

    A. SNMPCHECK

    B. SNMPSTAT

    C. SNMPUTIL

    D. SNMPMANG

17. What is the object identifier for an MIB II?

    A. `iso.org.dod.internet.`
       `management.mib2`

    B. `iso.org.dod.internet.`
       `management.mibii`

    C. `1.3.6.2.2`

    D. `2.2.6.3.1`

18. The MIB architecture can be extended to enable developers to create their own MIB libraries by using _____:

    A. Extension agents

    B. Extendor agents

    C. Additional dynamic link libraries

    D. Relay agents

19. Why would you install the SNMP service?

    A. You want to monitor TCP/IP with Performance Monitor.

    B. You want to remotely manage a proxy agent.

    C. You want to monitor a Windows NT–based system with a third-party application.

    D. You want to set up your computer as an SNMP agent.

2.18.12 Practice Problems: Answers and Explanations

1. **C** The WINS MIB reports the number of unsuccessful queries processed by the WINS server.

2. **A, B, C, D, E** All choices are correct.

3. **A, B, C, E** SNMP would not use DHCP to resolve a host name; all other choices are correct.

4. **D** Agent commands consist of set, get-next, and get.

5. **B** The agent is the active component of SNMP that performs the trap.

6. **B** The Management Information Base, or MIB, is where the queries are stored.

7. **C** SNMP does not set up counters in Performance Monitor; all other statements are true.

8. **D** The public community is the default.

9. **A** The most secure option is to have a community name other than public, select Only Accept SNMP Packets from These Hosts, and set a trap to alert invalid inquiries.

10. **C** Internet MIB II, LAN Manager MIB II, WINS MIB, DHCP MIB is the correct answer.

11. **D** Agents and management systems must have the same community name to communicate with each other.

12. **A** The Windows Event Viewer is used to examine SNMP problems.

13. **A, C, D** Internet, End-to-End, and Application agent services are enabled by default.

14. **C** A trap is instituted by an agent.

15. **B** A trap is a message sent to warn of an error.

16. **C** SNMPUTIL is included in the Windows NT Resource Kit.

2

17. **B** `iso.org.dod.internet.management.mibii` is the correct answer.

18. **A** Extension agents allow developers to create their own MIB libraries.

19. **A, C, D** The SNMP service should be used if you want to monitor TCP/IP with Performance Monitor, monitor a Windows NT–based system with a third-party application, or set up your computer as an SNMP agent.

2.19 Practice Exam

1. Which of the following static files is used to map IP addresses to host names on a Windows NT Server computer?

    A. LMHOSTS
    B. HOSTS
    C. WINS
    D. DNS

2. With an IP address of `201.142.23.12`, what is your default subnet mask?

    A. `0.0.0.0`
    B. `255.0.0.0`
    C. `255.255.0.0`
    D. `255.255.255.0`

3. On a UNIX-based server/host, which file is used to statically map aliases to IP addresses?

    A. LMHOSTS
    B. HOSTS
    C. WINS
    D. DNS

4. With an IP address set starting with 150, you currently have six offices that you are treating as subnets. Plans are in place to open 10 more offices before the end of the

year. What subnet mask should you use to satisfy the needed number of subnets and maximize the number of hosts available at each site?

    A. 192
    B. 224
    C. 240
    D. 248
    E. 252

5. On a class C network with a subnet mask of 192, how many hosts are available?

    A. 254
    B. 62
    C. 30
    D. 14
    E. 2

6. On a class C network with a subnet mask of 192, how many subnets are available?

    A. 254
    B. 62
    C. 30
    D. 14
    E. 2

7. What record must be added to a zone file to alias a host to another name?

    A. An A record
    B. An SOA record
    C. A CNAME record
    D. A PTR record

8. How do you configure a client to use DNS to resolve a HOST name before using other methods?

    A. Query for a host name longer than 15 characters.

B. Move DNS up in the Host Resolution Order dialog box.

C. A client always searches DNS last.

D. Configure the DNS to advertise itself to DNS clients.

9. How does a caching-only DNS server build a database of host records?

A. The caching server downloads a copy of zone files into its cache from master servers when the caching server starts.

B. Entries from the local cache file are read into cache.

C. The server captures the results of queries as they are sent across the network.

D. The server makes queries.

10. What kind of query does a DNS client make to a DNS server?

A. A reverse lookup query

B. An iterative query

C. A recursive query

D. A resolver query

11. Which server can be a master server for a UNIX DNS server that is the secondary server for a zone? (Select all that apply.)

A. Any Windows NT DNS server with a primary zone

B. Any UNIX server with a primary zone

C. Any Windows NT DNS server with a secondary zone

D. Any Windows NT DNS server with a zone that doesn't use WINS lookup

12. How can zone files be modified? (Select all that apply.)

A. With NSLOOKUP

B. By editing the zone files with a text editor

C. With DNS Manager

D. With DNSCNFG

13. What is the use of the cache file on a DNS server?

A. It has records for DNS servers at top-level domains.

B. It provides initial values to the DNS cache.

C. It specifies the TTL for cached entries.

D. It specifies the amount of memory and its location for DNS caching.

14. What would the reverse lookup zone be called for a server with the IP address of `149.56.85.105`?

A. `105.85.56.149.in-addr.arpa`

B. `149.56.85.105.in-addr.arpa`

C. `56.149.in-addr.arpa`

D. `149.56.in-addr.arpa`

15. How can you configure a secondary server to receive changes to zone files as soon as they are made?

A. Decrease the refresh interval on the secondary server.

B. Turn on the Notify feature on the primary server.

C. Configure the primary server with push replication.

D. Make the primary server the master server for the secondary.

16. You have several secondary DNS servers on one side of a slow WAN link. How should you configure the master server for these secondary servers to minimize traffic over this slow WAN link?

A. Have all the secondary servers on one side of the link use one master server on the other side of the link.

B. Have one secondary server use the primary server on the other side of the link as the master. Other secondary servers use the secondary on their side of the link as the master.

C. Use a caching only server as the master.

D. Configure DNS for pull replication scheduled during low traffic times.

17. Where can you find the files needed to install DNS?

A. On the Windows NT 4.0 Server Resource Kit

B. On the Backoffice CD

C. On the Windows NT 4.0 Server CD

D. On the DNS CD

18. On a class B network, how many hosts are available at each site with a subnet mask of 248?

A. 16,382

B. 8,190

C. 4,094

D. 2,046

E. 1,022

19. On a class B network, how many subnets are available with a subnet mask of 248?

A. 2

B. 6

C. 30

D. 62

E. 126

20. Which of the following services dynamically resolves NetBIOS-to-IP resolution?

A. DNS

B. DHCP

C. WINS

D. LMHOSTS

2.19.1 Practice Exam: Answers and Explanations

1. **B** The HOSTS file is used to statically map host names to IP addresses.

2. **D** The default subnet mask on a class C network is 255.255.255.0.

3. **B** The HOSTS file is used on UNIX hosts to statically map IP addresses to host and alias names.

4. **D** On a class B network, a subnet mask of 248 will provide for up to 30 subnets and 2,046 hosts on each.

5. **B** On a class C network, 62 hosts are available at each subnet with a subnet mask of 192.

6. **E** On a class C network, two subnets are available with a subnet mask of 192.

7. **C** A CNAME record is a canonical name record used to create aliases. An A record is used to register the real host name. An SOA record contains the authority information for the zone file. A PTR record exists only in reverse lookup zones and maps the IP address to a host name, not the host name to an IP address.

8. **A** DNS is always tried last in the host resolution methods unless the host name is longer than 15 characters. In that case, DNS is tried first because other methods, like WINS, simply resolve NetBIOS names, which are limited to 15 characters. DNS can resolve Fully Qualified Domain Names that can be much longer than 15 characters. You cannot manually change the order in which the host resolution methods are used.

9. **D** A caching only server starts without any entries in its cache. It builds entries through making queries on behalf of clients to other DNS servers. When the results are returned from other DNS servers, the caching only server adds these entries to its cache.

10. **C** Clients make recursive queries to servers; that is, the server must give the client a positive or negative response, not a referral to another server. Servers make iterative queries of each other, which enable the servers to respond with a pointer to another server. Reverse lookup queries are made by a server that needs to know the host name for a given IP address. The term *resolver query* isn't used in DNS.

11. **B, D** UNIX servers can be primary or secondary servers for Windows NT DNS servers. However, a UNIX server should never be secondary for a zone on a Windows NT Server that has WINS lookup enabled. Enabling WINS lookup adds a record to the file that is not compatible with UNIX implementations of DNS.

12. **B, C** NSLOOKUP enables you to examine the entries in zone files, but not to make any changes. Zone files are simply text files, so they can be edited. DNS Manager is the Windows interface used to modify zone files. There isn't a utility called DNSCNFG.

13. **A** The cache file has entries for the top-level servers for Internet domains. On an intranet, this file must be modified to reflect the top-level servers in the local organization.

14. **C** Only the network portion of the IP address is used to specify reverse lookup zones. Then the IP network address is listed in reverse order to match the specific-to-general naming scheme used by DNS.

15. **B** If the Notify feature is turned on, the primary server notifies the secondary servers as soon as a change is made to the zone file. Decreasing the refresh interval keeps the secondary server more up-to-date, but it doesn't necessarily update the zone file soon after changes are made. Push replication is used for WINS servers. If the primary server is the master, it provides a copy of the zone file to the secondary server. However, the primary server will not provide changes any faster unless the Notify feature is turned on. The Notify feature is the key to quick updates.

16. **B** The best way to reduce traffic is to have the zone file passed once across the link and then distributed to the other servers on that side of the link. Using a caching only server is another strategy that can be used across a slow WAN link, but the caching only server never gets a copy of any zone files. Pull replication is used for WINS, not for DNS.

17. **C** DNS used to be part of the Resource Kit for Windows NT 3.51; it was not included in the Windows NT source files. With Windows NT 4.0, DNS is included in the Windows NT source files.

18. **D** On a class B network, 2,046 hosts are available on each subnet with a subnet mask of 248.

19. **C** On a class B network, 30 subnets are available with a subnet mask of 248.

20. **C** WINS provides dynamic NetBios-to-IP resolution.

2

## CHAPTER 3

Connectivity

This chapter helps you prepare for the exam by covering the following objectives:

- Given a scenario, identify which utility to use to connect to a TCP/IP-based UNIX host

- Configure a Remote Access Service (RAS) server and Dial-Up Networking for use on a TCP/IP network

- Configure and support browsing in a multiple-domain routed network

3.1 Utilities Used to Connect to a TCP/IP-Based UNIX Host

Windows NT includes TCP/IP utilities that provide many options for connecting to foreign systems using the TCP/IP protocol. At times when connecting to remote host systems using Microsoft networking is impossible, these utilities provide a variety of network services.

These utilities allow Microsoft clients to perform remote execution, data transfer, printing services, and much more. The following sections examine these utilities in more detail.

3.1.1 Remote Execution Utilities

Windows NT includes a series of remote execution utilities that enable a user to execute commands on a UNIX host system. These utilities provide varying degrees of security. Note that varying subsets of these utilities are available with Windows NT Server and Workstation, whereas the Windows NT Server Resource Kit includes all of these utilities.

> **Any of these utilities that require passwords transmit the password as plain text. Unlike the Windows NT logon sequence, the logon information is not encrypted before being transmitted. Any unscrupulous user with access to network monitoring software could intercept the user name and password for the remote host. If you use the same user name and password on the remote host and on your Windows NT system, your Windows NT account could be compromised.**

Windows NT provides three remote execution utilities. Each is discussed in more detail in the following sections.

The REXEC Utility

REXEC enables a user to start a process on a remote host system, using a user name and password for authentication. If the host authenticates the user, REXEC starts the specified process and terminates. Command-line options are as follows:

```
D:\>rexec /?
Runs commands on remote hosts running the REXEC service. REXEC
authenticates the user name on the remote host before executing the
specified command.

REXEC host [-l user name] [-n] command

   host            Specifies the remote host on which to run command.
  -l user name     Specifies the user name on the remote host.
  -n               Redirects the input of REXEC to NULL.
   command         Specifies the command to run.
```

You can specify the remote host as an IP address or as a host name. After REXEC connects to the specified host, it prompts for a password. If the host authenticates the user, the specified command is executed, and the REXEC utility exits. REXEC can be used for command-line programs—interactive programs such as text editors would not be usable with REXEC.

This utility provides a reasonable degree of security because the remote host authenticates the user. The down side is that the user name and password are not encrypted prior to transmission.

The RSH Utility

RSH provides much the same function as REXEC, but user authentication is handled differently. In contrast to REXEC, RSH does not require you to specify a user name. The only validation performed by RSH is to verify that the user name is in a hidden file on the UNIX system (the .rhosts file). If the remote host is configured to allow any user to use RSH, a user name is not necessary.

> On UNIX systems, the .rhosts and the hosts.equiv files are used for authentication. Because these files can be used to grant access to either all users on a computer or some users on a computer, you should be careful with their use.

However, because it is extremely unlikely for a system to be configured in this way, the RSH utility provides the logged-on user name if no user name is provided. This can be overridden if desired. RSH has the following command-line options:

```
C:\>rsh /?
rsh: remote terminal session not supported

Runs commands on remote hosts running the RSH service.

RSH host [-l user name] [-n] command

    host              Specifies the remote host on which to run command.
    -l user name      Specifies the user name to use on the remote host. If
                      omitted, the logged on user name is used.
    -n                Redirects the input of RSH to NULL.
    command           Specifies the command to run.
```

After you start RSH, it connects to the remote system's RSH daemon (UNIX-speak for a service). The RSH daemon ensures that the user name is in the .rhosts file on the remote host, and if authentication succeeds, the specified command is executed.

Like REXEC, RSH provides a certain degree of security insofar as the remote host validates the access.

The Telnet Utility

Telnet is defined in RFC 854 as a remote terminal emulation protocol. It provides terminal emulation for DEC VT100, DEC VT52, and TTY terminals. Telnet uses the connection-oriented services of the TCP/IP protocol for communications.

The remote host system must be running a Telnet daemon. After you start Telnet, you can connect to a remote host using the Connect/Remote system option. You are prompted for the information required for a Telnet session:

- Host name—The IP address or host name of the remote host
- Port—One of the ports supported by the Telnet application—Telnet, daytime, echo, quotd, or chargen
- Terminal type—VT100, ANSI (TTY), or VT52

As with REXEC and RSH, Telnet provides some security, insofar as access to the remote system requires a user name and password.

> **Telnet does not encrypt any information whatsoever. The password and user name are sent as clear text, as is your entire terminal session. If you are using Telnet to perform remote administration on a UNIX system, your root password could be intercepted by an unscrupulous user.**

3.1.2 Data Transfer Utilities

The following sections describe several utilities that enable you to transfer files between Windows NT systems and remote hosts. As with remote execution utilities, you must use care when dealing with user names and passwords.

RCP

The RCP command copies files from a Windows NT system to a remote host and handles authentication in much the same way as RSH does. To communicate with the RCP daemon on the remote system, the user name provided must be in the remote host's .rhosts file. The following command-line options are available:

```
C:\>rcp ?

Copies files to and from computer running the RCP service.

RCP [-a ¦ -b] [-h] [-r] [host][.user:]source [host][.user:] path\destination

   -a                   Specifies ASCII transfer mode. This mode converts the
                        EOL characters to a carriage return for UNIX and a
                        carriage return/line feed for personal computers.This is
                        the default transfer mode.
   -b                   Specifies binary image transfer mode.
   -h                   Transfers hidden files.
   -r                   Copies the contents of all subdirectories;
                        destination must be a directory.
   host                 Specifies the local or remote host. If host is
                        specified as an IP address, you must specify the
                        user.
   .user:               Specifies a user name to use, rather than the
                        current user name.
   source               Specifies the files to copy.
   path\destination     Specifies the path relative to the logon directory
                        on the remote host. Use the escape characters
                        (\ , ", or ') in remote paths to use wildcard
                        characters on the remote host.
```

As with RSH, RCP provides security by matching the user name provided with a user name in the .rhosts file. Unlike RSH, RCP does not prompt for a password.

FTP

File Transfer Protocol, or FTP, provides a simple but robust mechanism for copying files to or from remote hosts using the connection-oriented services of TCP/IP. FTP is a component of the TCP/IP protocol and is defined in RFC 959. To use FTP to send or receive files, the following requirements must be met:

- The client computer must have FTP client software, such as the FTP client included with Windows NT.

- The user must have a user name and password on the remote system. In some cases, a user name of *anonymous* with no password suffices.

- The remote system must be running an FTP daemon or service (depending upon whether it is UNIX or NT).

- Your system and the remote system must be running the TCP/IP protocol.

You can use FTP in either a command-line mode or in a command-interpreter mode. The following options are available from the command line:

```
C:\>ftp ?
Transfers files to and from a computer running an FTP server service
(sometimes called a daemon). FTP can be used interactively.


FTP [-v] [-d][-i] [-n] [-g] [-s:filename] [-a] [-w:windowsize] [host]


   -v           Suppresses display of remote server responses.
   -n           Suppresses auto-login upon initial connection.
   -i           Turns off interactive prompting during multiple file
                transfers.
   -d           Enables debugging.
   -g           Disables filename globbing (see GLOB command).
   -s:filename  Specifies a text file containing FTP commands; the
                commands will automatically run after FTP starts.
   -a           Use any local interface when binding data connection.
   -w:buffersize Overrides the default transfer buffer size of 4096.
   host         Specifies the host name or IP address of the remote
                host to connect to.
```

If you use FTP in a command-interpreter mode, some of the more frequently used options are as follows:

- open—Specifies the remote system to which you connect.

- close—Disconnects from a remote system.

- ls—Obtains a directory listing on a remote system, much like the dir command in DOS. Note that the ls -1 command provides file size and time stamps.

- cd—Changes directories on the remote system. This command functions in much the same way as the DOS cd command.

- lcd—Changes directories on the local system. This command also functions in much the same way as the DOS cd command.

- binary—Instructs FTP to treat all files transferred as binary.

- ascii—Instructs FTP to treat all files transferred as text. You have to choose a transfer type because certain files cannot be read correctly as binary, whereas ASCII is universally accepted.

- get—Copies a file from the remote host to your local computer.

- put—Copies a file from your local computer to the remote host.

- debug—Turns on debugging commands that can be useful in diagnosing problems.

Because remote host systems are typically based on UNIX, you will encounter a number of nuances relating to UNIX, such as the following:

- The UNIX operating system uses the forward slash in path references, not the backward slash. In Windows NT, the filename \WINNT40\README.TXT would be /WINNT40/README.TXT.

- UNIX is case sensitive at all times—the command get MyFile and the command get MYFILE are not the same. User names and passwords are also case sensitive.

- UNIX treats wildcard characters, such as the asterisk and the question mark, differently. The glob command within FTP controls the way that wildcard characters in local filenames are treated.

You can also install a Windows NT FTP server, which can provide FTP file transfer services to other systems. This approach allows the server to serve clients in the manner that has been traditional on UNIX machines. The FTP service is a component of Internet Information Server (IIS).

TFTP

TFTP and FTP provide similar functions. Unlike FTP, however, TFTP uses the connectionless communication features of TCP/IP. Consequently, you can equate TFTP to FTP in the same way that you can equate UDP to TCP. Both TCP and FTP require connections to be established, whereas UDP and TFTP work without requiring an established connection.

The features available in FTP are complex; those in TFTP are simpler. Unlike FTP, TFTP can be used only in a command-line mode—no command-interpreter mode is available. For command-line mode, the following options are available:

```
C:\>tftp /?

Transfers files to and from a remote computer running the TFTP service.

TFTP [-i] host [GET ¦ PUT] source [destination]

    -i              Specifies binary image transfer mode (also called
                    octet). In binary image mode the file is moved
                    literally, byte by byte. Use this mode when
                    transferring binary files.
    host            Specifies the local or remote host.
    GET             Transfers the file destination on the remote host to
                    the file source on the local host.
    PUT             Transfers the file source on the local host to
                    the file destination on the remote host.
    source          Specifies the file to transfer.
    destination     Specifies where to transfer the file.
```

Windows NT does not include a TFTP server, but third-party TFTP servers are available.

Why use TFTP instead of FTP? Some platforms, notably devices that require firmware updates, don't support FTP. Routers typically require the use of TFTP to update firmware information, such as microkernels.

> Many network devices, such as routers and concentrators, use an operating system stored in firmware. As such, upgrades are usually handled using TFTP—the process is known as a firmware update.

HTTP and Web Browsers

The explosive growth of the Internet in recent years is largely due to its flexibility. One of the Internet's building blocks is the Hypertext Transfer Protocol (HTTP). It defines a way of transferring hypertext data across TCP/IP networks. The hypertext data is formatted in Hypertext Markup Language (HTML). An HTML document can have a link to any other HTML document. This feature enables Web page designers to include text, audio files, graphics, and video in the same page.

HTTP and HTML are comprehensive standards, and a full discussion is outside the scope of this book. However, a discussion of Web browsers is in order. You can use Web-browsing software to download and view HTML documents using the HTTP protocol, as well as to download documents using FTP, Gopher, or other protocols.

Unlike the other file-transfer utilities mentioned in this section, HTTP does not use a user name or password by default. Information on the World Wide Web is typically destined for access by any user and therefore usually does not require authentication, although that function can be enabled.

Many Web browsers are available; however, they all function in much the same way.

3.1.3 Practice Problems

1. Remote execution utilities transmit passwords as

   A. Encrypted text

   B. Plain text

   C. LAN Manager–compatible text

   D. RS232 strings

2. Three execution utilities available with Windows NT are

   A. REXEC

   B. Telnet

   C. FTP

   D. RSH

3. REXEC can specify a host by which two methods?

   A. Host name

   B. ARP address

   C. MAC address

   D. IP address

4. Which parameter is used with REXEC to specify a different user name on the remote host?

   A. -n

   B. -l

   C. -u

   D. -name

5. Which parameter is used with REXEC to specify that the input should be null?

    A. -n

    B. -l

    C. -u

    D. -name

6. For which of the following applications would REXEC not be appropriate?

    A. Obtaining a directory listing with the command ls

    B. Checking which processes are running with the command ps

    C. Starting a text editor with the command vi

    D. Checking the amount of free space on a drive with the command df

7. Which method does the REXEC command use to authenticate the user?

    A. User name

    B. Password

    C. User name and password

    D. .rhosts file

8. The biggest difference between RSH and REXEC is in which area?

    A. Availability to system resources

    B. System overhead

    C. Permissions

    D. Authentication

9. If no user name is given, what user name does RSH use to establish a connection to the remote host?

    A. Root

    B. Anonymous

    C. Current user name

    D. Guest

10. Which method does the RSH command use to authenticate the user?

    A. User name

    B. Password

    C. User name and password

    D. .rhosts file

11. Which two files can be used on a UNIX system to grant access to all users or some users for remote authentication?

    A. /passwd

    B. /dialup

    C. .rhosts

    D. hosts.equiv

12. In the UNIX world, which of the following is comparable to a service in the NT world?

    A. Command

    B. Daemon

    C. Setting

    D. Environment

13. Which Telnet option is used to connect to a remote host?

    A. Connect/Remote

    B. Get

    C. Establish

    D. Call

14. Which of the following items are required for a Telnet session?

    A. Port

    B. Service

    C. Terminal type

    D. Host name

15. Ports supported by Telnet applications include all of the following except:

    A. vt100

    B. daytime

    C. echo

    D. quotd

16. Which method does the `telnet` command use to authenticate the user?

    A. User name

    B. Password

    C. User name and password

    D. `.rhosts` file

17. Which of the following utilities does Windows NT *not* support for data file transfer?

    A. Telnet

    B. RCP

    C. FTP

    D. TFTP

18. Which method does the RCP command use to authenticate the user?

    A. User name

    B. Password

    C. User name and password

    D. `.rhosts` file

19. The parameter used with RCP to transfer hidden files is

    A. -b

    B. -r

    C. -a

    D. -h

20. The parameter used with RCP to copy subdirectories and files beneath a specified directory is

    A. -b

    B. -r

    C. -a

    D. -h

21. The parameter used with RCP to convert EOL characters to a carriage return is

    A. -b

    B. -r

    C. -a

    D. -h

22. The parameter used with RCP to specify binary transfer mode is

    A. -b

    B. -r

    C. -a

    D. -h

23. FTP stands for

    A. Fast Transfer Protocol

    B. File Transfer Protocol

    C. Fixed Transfer Protocol

    D. Flash Timing Protocol

24. To establish an FTP session, which of the following criteria must be met? (Select all correct answers.)

    A. Both systems must be running TCP/IP.

    B. NetBEUI must be used to broadcast service availability.

    C. The remote system must be running an FTP host service.

    D. The client system must be running FTP client software.

    E. A user name and password (or anonymous) must be on the remote.

25. Which parameter is used with FTP (in command-line mode) to suppress the display of remote server responses?

    A. -i
    B. -v
    C. -n
    D. -d

26. Which parameter is used with FTP (in command-line mode) to enable debugging?

    A. -i
    B. -v
    C. -n
    D. -d

27. Which parameter is used with FTP (in command-line mode) to suppress the auto-login?

    A. -i
    B. -v
    C. -n
    D. -d

28. Which parameter is used with FTP (in command-line mode) to turn off interactive prompting?

    A. -i
    B. -v
    C. -n
    D. -d

29. How many modes are available with FTP?

    A. 1
    B. 2
    C. 3
    D. 4

30. Which FTP command changes directories on the local system?

    A. cd
    B. lcd
    C. open
    D. get
    E. put

31. Which FTP command starts a file transfer from the remote host?

    A. cd
    B. lcd
    C. open
    D. get
    E. put

32. Which FTP command starts a file transfer from the local host?

    A. cd
    B. lcd
    C. open
    D. get
    E. put

33. Which FTP command specifies a remote system to connect to?

    A. cd
    B. lcd
    C. open
    D. get
    E. put

34. Which of the following represents the differences between FTP and TFTP?

    A. FTP is connection oriented.
    B. TFTP is connection oriented.
    C. FTP is connectionless oriented.
    D. TFTP is connectionless oriented.

35. How many modes are available with TFTP?

    A. 1

    B. 2

    C. 3

    D. 4

36. Which type of support for TFTP is available from third parties, but is not included in Windows NT?

    A. As a client

    B. As a server

    C. As a server or a client

    D. Windows NT includes full TFTP support

3.1.4 Practice Problems: Answers and Explanations

1. **B** Remote execution utilities transmit passwords as plain text, creating a security weakness.

2. **A, B, D** REXEC, RSH, and Telnet are remote execution utilities. FTP is also supported, but it is a file-transfer utility, and the question was only asking for remote execution utilities.

3. **A, D** REXEC can specify a host by its IP address or host name.

4. **B** REXEC -1 *username* is the syntax used to specify a different user name on the remote host.

5. **A** REXEC -n is the syntax used to specify the input should be NULL.

6. **C** REXEC should be used for commands that do not require interactive input. This makes the vi text editor a bad choice.

7. **C** REXEC authenticates a user by user name and password.

8. **D** RSH works like REXEC but is not as stringent on authentication.

9. **C** If no user name is specified, RSH uses the current user name.

10. **D** The .rhosts file is used to authenticate users with RSH.

11. **C, D** The .rhosts and hosts.equiv files can be used on UNIX systems for authentication of (or the lack thereof) remote users.

12. **B** A daemon is to the UNIX world what a service is to the NT world.

13. **A** The Connect/Remote system option of Telnet is used to connect to a remote host.

14. **A, C, D** Terminal type, port, and host name or IP address are required information for a Telnet session.

15. **A** VT100 is a supported terminal type, not a port.

16. **C** Telnet authenticates users by user name and password.

17. **A** Telnet is a remote execution utility; it isn't used for data file transfer.

18. **D** RCP authenticates users by the .rhosts file.

19. **D** RCP -h is the syntax used to transfer hidden files.

20. **B** RCP -r is the syntax used to recursively copy subdirectories and files.

21. **C** RCP -a is the syntax used to convert files to ASCII format.

22. **A** RCP -b is the syntax used to specify binary transfer mode.

23. **B** FTP stands for File Transfer Protocol.

24. **A, C, D, E** NetBEUI is not used with FTP, whereas all other choices are correct.

25. **B** The -v parameter suppresses the display of remote server responses.

26. **D** The -d parameter enables debugging.

27. **C** The -n parameter suppresses auto-login.

28. **A** The -i parameter turns off interactive prompting during multiple file transfers.

29. **B**　FTP supports two modes: command line and command interpreter.

30. **B**　The `lcd` command changes directories on the local host.

31. **D**　The `get` command starts a file transfer from a remote host.

32. **E**　The `put` command starts a file transfer from the local host.

33. **C**　The `open` command specifies a remote host to connect to.

34. **A, D**　FTP is connection oriented, whereas TFTP is connectionless.

35. **A**　TFTP has only the command-line mode.

36. **B**　Windows NT does not include support for TFTP server services.

3.1.5　Keywords

daemon　Background process or service running in UNIX

data transfer　The ability provided by a utility to transfer a file from a remote host to a local host

local host　The system you are currently sitting at

plain text　Unencrypted text, subject to interception by third parties

remote execution　The ability provided by a utility to run a process on another host over the network

remote host　A system other than the system you are currently sitting at

service　Background process running in NT

3.2　RAS Servers and Dial-Up Networking

Essentially, RAS allows users to connect to your network and act as if they are directly connected to it. There are two main components to RAS; the server (Remote Access Service) and the client (Dial-Up Networking). The RAS server can be Windows NT Server, Windows NT Workstation, or Windows 95 (either with Service Pack 1 or OEM Service Release 2) and will enable users to connect to the network from a remote location. The Microsoft RAS Server always uses the Point to Point Protocol (PPP) as the line protocol when users are dialing in to the network.

In addition to connecting to a Microsoft RAS server, Windows Dial-Up Networking can connect with other forms of RAS (other dial-in servers such as UNIX terminal servers), using either Serial Line Internet Protocol (SLIP) or PPP. All that is required is a communications device.

3.2.1　PPP versus SLIP

When clients connect to a server using a modem, they must do so through something other than the frames that normally traverse a network (such as IEEE802.3). Some other transport method is needed. In the case of dial-up servers (or terminal servers), two popular line protocols are available. SLIP, the older of the two, is used frequently in UNIX implementations and is geared directly toward TCP/IP communications. Windows NT can use the services of a SLIP server, but does not provide a SLIP server. Microsoft's RAS server uses PPP because SLIP requires a static IP address and does not provide a facility for secured logon (passwords are sent as clear text).

PPP was developed as a replacement for SLIP and provides several advantages over the earlier protocol. PPP can automatically provide the client computer with an IP address and other configuration. It provides a secure logon and can transport protocols other than TCP/IP (such as AppleTalk, IPX, and NetBEUI).

Two important extensions to PPP are the Multilink Protocol (MP) and Point to Point Tunneling Protocol (PPTP). Windows NT supports both extensions.

MP allows a client station to connect to a remote server using more than one physical connection. This capability provides better throughput over standard modems. You will, however, need multiple phone lines and modems to enable this protocol. MP can be an easy interim solution if you need to temporarily connect to offices and don't have the time or the budget to set up a leased line or other similar connection.

PPTP facilitates secure connections across the Internet. Using PPTP, users can connect to any Internet service provider (ISP) and will be able to use the ISP's network as a gateway to connect to the office network. During the session initialization, the client and server negotiate a 40-bit session key. This key is then used to encrypt all packets that are sent back and forth over the Internet. The packets are encapsulated into PPP packets as the data.

3.2.2   Modems

Modems have been around for years and provide a cheap and relatively reliable method of communications over the Public Switched Telephone Network (PSTN). Installing a modem in a computer is a straightforward process. This section covers the configuring and testing of modems and what can go wrong with them.

The two main types of modems are internal and external. Internal modems cost a little less than external modems do, but you have to open the computer to install them; in addition, internal modems require a free interrupt (IRQ). If you elect to go with an external modem, you should check that you have a communications (COM) port available and that it will be able to handle the speed of the modem.

Ports

Regardless of whether you have an internal or external modem, you will need to install the modem as a communications port. Normally doing so is no problem; however, sometimes (notably with internal modems) you will need to change the settings for the port. Changing port settings can also cause problems with an external modem. If you cannot talk to the modem, you should also check the port settings.

To check the port settings, open the Control Panel (Start | Settings | Control Panel) and double-click on the Ports icon. This will bring up the Ports dialog box.

Select the port that you want to inspect and click Settings. Another dialog box shows the settings for the port.

Five settings are available. These are general settings, however, and deal only with applications that don't set these parameters. The following list briefly describes the settings:

- Baud Rate—This setting controls the rate at which the data will flow. Serial communications move your data 1 bit at a time. In addition, for every byte that is sent there are (normally) 4 bits of overhead. To find the transfer rate in bytes, divide this number by 12.

- Data Bits—Not all systems will use 8 bits to store one character. Some systems use only 7. This setting enables the computer to adjust the number of bits used in the transfer.

- Parity—Parity is used to verify that information that is being transferred is getting across the line successfully. The parity can be Even, Odd, Mark, or Space, or you can use No Parity (which is the normal setting).

- Stop Bits—In some systems, these are used to mark the end of the transmission.

- Flow Control—This option can be set to Xon/Xoff, Hardware, or None. Flow control, as the name implies, controls the movement of the data between the modem and your computer. Hardware flow control uses Request to Send (RTS) and Clear to Send (CTS). The system will send a signal through the RTS wire in the cable, telling the modem it wants to send. When the modem has finished transmitting the contents of its buffer and has space, it will signal the computer that it can send the data using the CTS wire. Xon/Xoff is a software form of flow control in which the modem will send Xon (ASCII character 17) when it is ready for data from the computer and Xoff (ASCII character 19) when it has too much data. (This type of flow control does not work well with binary transfers as the Xon and Xoff characters can be part of a file.)

In most cases, you can ignore these settings. They will be set and reset by the application that you will use. However, if you click the Advanced button, you will find some settings that you need to be aware of.

> **If you make changes in the Advanced dialog box, the system will no longer be a standard system. Many applications can be affected if you make changes here.**

The options that you can set in here will affect all applications that use the communications port. The following list provides an overview of the options that you can set.

- COM Port Number—Here you will select the port that you want to configure.

- Base I/O Port Address—When information is received from a hardware (physical) device, the BIOS places that information in RAM. This setting changes the place in RAM where you will place the information. Unless your hardware requires a different address, do not change this setting.

- Interrupt Request Line (IRQ)—After the BIOS places the information in RAM, it will use a hardware interrupt to alert the CPU to the presence of the data. Interrupts are a prime source for conflicts and one of the main causes of system failures. Unless your hardware requires you to do so, do not change this option.

- FIFO Enabled—This setting enables the on-chip buffering available in 16550 UARTs. Note that on some of the older revisions of the 16550, there were problems with random data loss when using

FIFO. If you are experiencing unexplained problems, try disabling FIFO. Enabling FIFO might provide a slight increase in throughput.

When you are attempting to troubleshoot a serial problem, you should always check that these settings are correct. Making sure that the port options are correct will allow you to communicate with the modem.

Configuring Modems

The most common method of connecting to an office network or to the Internet is to connect using a modem. This section deals with installing and troubleshooting modems.

Installing a Modem

Installing a modem is simple in Windows NT. After the hardware is connected, go to the Control Panel and double-click the Modems icon. If no modem is installed, the modem installer will start automatically. This wizard will step you through the installation of the modem. If you have a modem already, then you will need to click Add.

If the installer is unable to detect the modem, you probably have one of two problems. Either the modem cannot be detected and you will have to install it manually, or the system can't see the modem, in which case you should check the port. If you need to install the modem manually, place a check in the Don't Detect My Modem, I Will Select It from a List check box. You can select the modem from the following screen.

After you have the modem installed, you can check modem properties using the Modems icon in the Control Panel. When you open the icon, you will see a dialog box that lists the available modems.

From here you will be able to check and set the properties for the modems that are installed in the computer. Several options are of interest. Select Modem | Properties to display the General properties for the modem.

The General tab contains only a few settings that you need to set. The following list describes the properties on the General tab and explains the elements you should check for.

- Port—Displays the port on which the modem was installed. You should check the port if the hardware has been changed; also check the port settings if the modem is not working.

- Speaker Volume—Determines the volume of the speaker during the connection phase. This should be turned up to allow you to verify that you are getting dial tone and that the other end is in fact a modem.

- Maximum Speed—Sets the fastest rate that the system will attempt to communicate with the modem. If this setting is too high, some modems will not be able to respond to the system. In this case, try lowering the rate.

- Only Connect at This Speed—Instruct the modem that it must connect to the remote site at the same speed you set for communications with the modem. If the other site is unable to support this speed, you will not be able to communicate.

The other tab in the Modem Properties dialog box is the Connections tab. It deals with the way that the modem will connect and has two sections: connection preferences and call preferences. The connection preferences are the communications settings (which were discussed in the Ports section). These settings will override the port settings. The three items from the call preferences section are described next.

- Wait for Tone Before Dialing—Normally this item should be selected. However, some phone systems in the world do not have a dial tone. Make sure that this setting is correct for your area.

- Cancel the Call If Not Connected Within—This option sets the maximum length of time that it will take for the call to be established. If the line conditions are very bad, you may have to bump up this number to allow the modem more time to establish a connection and negotiate the line speed that will be used.

- Disconnect a Call If Idle for More Than—This option enables you to set the maximum length of time that a call can sit idle. Windows NT 4 provides an autodial service that automatically calls back a server if you are disconnected and attempt to use a network service. This feature reduces the amount of time a user will tie up a line and can prevent massive long-distance charges. However, users need to know about the time limit. If they are required to enter information for a terminal logon, they should be told, because the terminal screen will appear unexpectedly when the system tries to autoconnect.

  If the user is not aware that autoconnect is being used and you are employing an ISP for email, the user needs to be warned that setting the email program to check for new mail at regular intervals will cause the system to automatically dial the server—possibly using up the allowed number of hours with the ISP.

The final thing to check when configuring modems and troubleshooting is the Advanced Connection information. These settings can adversely affect communications.

You will want to verify several of the Advanced options. The following list describes the options and the things that you should look for.

- Use Error Control—Turns on or off some common settings that affect the way the system deals with the modem. The specific options follow.

  - Required to Connect—Forces the modem to establish that an error-correcting protocol (such as MNP class 5) be used before the connection is made. This option should not be used by default. If the modem on the other end of the connection does not support the same class of error detection, the connection will fail.

  - Compress Data—Tells the modem to use data compression. Microsoft RAS will automatically implement software compression between the client and workstation if both are Microsoft servers. This option should be turned on only if you will be talking to a non-Microsoft server; otherwise the modem will try to compress data that is already compressed.

  - Use Cellular Protocol—Tells the system that the modem is a cellular modem.

- User Flow Control—Overrides the flow control setting for the port. Both types of flow control are available. In most cases, you should choose to use hardware flow control. Using flow control enables you to set the speed of the transmission between the computer and the modem. The choices are Xon/Xoff and hardware.

- Modulation Type—Enables users to set the type of frequency modulation for the modem to that of the phone system they are using. The modulation is either standard or Bell and deals with the sound frequency that is used for the send and receive channels for the communicating hosts.

- Extra Settings—Enables you to enter extra modem initialization strings that you wish to send to the modem whenever you place a call.

- Record a Log File—This setting is probably is the most important setting from the perspective of troubleshooting. The log file is a record of the communications that take place between the modem and the computer during the connection phase of the communications.

Dialing Properties

From the Modem Properties dialog box, you can also click on the Dialing Properties button, which enables you to configure the system so that it knows where you are dialing from. This information will be used in conjunction with Dial-Up Networking to allow the system to determine whether your call is long distance, if it should use a calling card, how to disable the call waiting feature, and so on.

When you click on the Dialing Properties dialog box, a dialog box will appear. You can create either a single location or multiple locations.

Several items are available in the Dialing Properties dialog box, and if this information is not set correctly, the client computer may attempt to connect to a local server as a long-distance call (or vice versa). The following list describes the Dialing Properties entries.

- I Am Dialing From—This entry is the name of the location. To create a new entry, click the New button and enter a name in this box. The user will need to know which entry to use when dialing.

- The Area Code Is—The computer uses this information to determine whether to dial the call as a long-distance call or a local call.

- I Am In—Sets the country code for dialing purposes so the system will be able to connect to international numbers.

- To Access an Outside Line, First Dial—Sets the access code for dialing out from a location. There is an entry for local calls and one for long distance.

- Dial Using Calling Card—Enables you to have the computer enter the calling-card information to make the connection with the remote host. Click the Change button to review or change your calling-card information.

- This Location Has Call Waiting—The call waiting tone will often cause a connection to be dropped. You can tell the computer to disable call waiting for the location that you are dialing from.

- The Phone System at This Location Uses—Specifies whether the system that you are calling from uses tone or pulse dialing.

If you encounter any connection problems, you should always verify the information in the Dialing Properties dialog box.

3.2.3   Other Communications Technologies

As stated earlier, there are other ways in which you will be able to connect to the Windows NT Server. There are two principal ways that you will be able to connect: by using the Integrated Services Digital Network (ISDN), or X.25 (which is a wide area networking standard).

ISDN

ISDN is one of the most common choices for connecting remote sites or even for individuals or small organizations to connect to the Internet. Indeed, ISDN is becoming a very common method of communications.

Whereas a standard phone line can handle transmission speeds of up to 9,600 bits per second (compression makes up the rest of the transmission speed in most modems such as those that transfer data at 33.6Kbps), ISDN transmits at speeds of 64Kbps or 128Kbps, depending on whether it is one or two channel.

ISDN is a point-to-point communications technology, and special equipment must be installed at both the server and the remote site. You will need to install an ISDN card (which will act as a network card) in place of a modem in both computers. As you will have guessed by now, ISDN connections are more expensive than modems. However, if your site has a requirement for higher speed, the cost will most likely be justified. Be aware though that in some parts of the world, ISDN is a metered service—the more you use, the more you pay.

X.25

The X.25 protocol is not an actual device, but rather a standard for connections. It is a packet-switching communication protocol that was designed for WAN connectivity.

RAS suppports X.25 connections using Packet Assemblers/Disassemblers (PADs) and X.25 smart cards. These will be installed as network cards, just as ISDN is.

3.2.4   Dial-in Permissions

As with all other aspects of Windows NT, security is built into the RAS server. At a minimum, a user will require an account in Windows NT, and that account will need to have dial-in permissions set.

You can grant users dial-in permission using the User Manager (or User Manager for Domains) or through the Remote Access Admin program. If you are having problems connecting to the RAS server, permissions is one of the first things you should check. Follow these steps to set or check dial-in permissions:

1. Open the User Manager for Domains utility (Start | Programs | Administrative Tools | User Manager for Domains).

2. Select the account that you are using and choose User | Properties. You will see the User Properties sheet.

3. Click the Dialin button to open the Dialin Information permissions dialog box.

4. Check the Grant Dialin Permission to User box to allow the user to dial in.

You can also check the permissions from the Remote Access Admin utility by following these steps:

1. Start the Remote Access Admin (Start | Programs | Administrative tools | RAS Admin).

2. From the menu, choose Users | Permissions.

3. In the Permissions dialog box, select the user and ensure that Dialin premission is granted.

Callback Security

You probably noticed a setting named Call Back in both of the preceding methods. *Call back* means that the server will return the user's call. This feature can be set to one of three options.

- No Call Back—This option is the default and means that the callback feature is disabled.

- Set by Caller—This option enables the user to set the number that should be used when the server calls back. This option is useful if you have many users who will be traveling and wish to centralize long distance calls.

- Preset To—This option enhances the security of the network by forcing the user to be at a set phone number. If set, the user can place a call only from that one location.

3.2.5 PPP Problems

As was mentioned earlier, Windows NT acts as a PPP server. Consequently, the client station and the server will undergo a negotiation during the initial phase of the call.

During the negotiation, the client and server decide on the protocol to be used and the parameters for the protocol. If there are problems attempting to connect, you may want to set up PPP logging to actually watch the negotiation between the server and client.

PPP logging is set up on the server by changing the Logging option under the following:

```
HKEY_LOCAL_MACHINE\SYSTEM\CurrentControlSet\Services\RASMAN\PPP\Parameters
```

The log file is in the system32\RAS directory and, like the modem log, can be viewed using any text editor.

Some of the most common problems that you may encounter with PPP follow.

- You must ensure that the protocol that you are requesting from the RAS client is available on the RAS server. If no common protocol is available, the connection will fail.

- If you are using NetBEUI, ensure that the name you are using on the RAS client is not in use on the network that you are attempting to connect to.

- If you are attempting to connect using TCP/IP, then the RAS server must be configured to provide you with an address.

3.2.6   Dial-Up Networking

This section describes the configuration of the client computer and points out the important features. Dial-Up Networking is the component that is used to connect to the RAS server. Before you can configure Dial-Up Networking, you must install a modem or other means of communications.

Using Dial-Up Networking, you will create a phonebook entry for each location that you will call. Follow these steps to create an entry:

1. Open the My Computer icon and then open Dial-Up Networking. (If you do not have an entry, a wizard will step you through creating a phonebook entry.)

2. Click the New button to create an entry. You can also select an entry in the list, click More, and choose Edit the Entry.

   If you choose New, the New Entry wizard will appear. You can choose to enter the information manually, as explained in this section.

3. The New (or Edit) Phonebook Entry dialog box opens. By default it will open to the Basic tab; enter or verify the following information:

   • Entry Name—The name of the entry.

   • Comment—Any comment you wish to make about the entry.

   • Phone Number—The phone number for the entry, which you should verify. You can enter multiple phone numbers by selecting the Alternates button. The numbers will be tried in the sequence in which they are entered, and you have the option of moving the successful number to the top of the list.

   • Use Telephony-Dialing Properties—Tells the system to use the properties that you set for your location when dialing the number. When you are troubleshooting, you should try turning off this option.

   • Dial Using—Tells the system which modem you wish to use when dialing. Verify that the modem exists. In addition, if Multilink is selected, choose Configure and verify the phone numbers for each modem on the list.

   • Use Another Port If Busy—Tells the system to use another modem if the modem specified is busy.

4. Select the Server tab and enter or verify the following information:

   • Dial-Up Server Type—Tells the system what type of server you are trying to connect to. You can use three types of servers: PPP (such as Windows NT), SLIP, and Windows NT 3.1 RAS. If the correct type is not selected, your computer will attempt to use the wrong line protocol.

   • Network Protocols—Tells the computer which protocols you want to use. If the client computer will be using the Internet, you must select TCP/IP. If the client is going to use the services of a remote NetWare server, you must select IPX/SPX. If you will be using only the services from a Windows NT network, then you can choose any of the protocols (remembering that the server must also use this protocol).

- Enable Software Compression—If you are working with a Windows NT server, you can select this to turn on the software compression feature. For troubleshooting purposes, you should turn off software compression.

- Enable PPP LCP Extensions—Tells the system that the PPP server will be able to set up the client station and will be able to verify the user name and password. This option also should be turned off when you are troubleshooting.

5. If you are using TCP/IP for this connection, you should also set or verify the TCP/IP settings. The TCP/IP setting screen will appear; the selections depend on the type of server you selected. The following list describes the TCP/IP setting options.

- Server Assigned IP Address—Tells the computer that the server will assign the IP address for this station. The server must have some means of assigning IP addresses to use this option.

- Specify an IP Address—Enables you to give the station an IP address. The address needs to be unique and must be correct for the server's network. The server must also allow the client to request an IP address.

- Server Assigned Name Server Addresses—Tells the system that the server will assign the IP addresses for DNS and Windows Internet Naming Service (WINS) servers.

- Specify Name Server Addresses—Enables you to set the addresses for DNS and WINS servers. This setting enables you to see whether the server is giving you correct addresses.

- Use IP Header Compression—Using IP header compression reduces the overhead that is transmitted over the modem. For troubleshooting, you should disable this setting.

- Use Default Gateway on the Remote Network—If you are connected to a network and dialed into a service provider, this setting tells NT to send information that is bound for a remote network to the gateway on the dial-in server.

6. Set the script options on the Script tab.

- After Dialing (login)— Three settings are available here; make sure the correct one is used. For NT-to-NT communications, you can select None. For other connections, you may have to enter information. For troubleshooting, you should try the terminal window. This setting enables you to enter the information manually rather than using the script. If this works, then you should verify the script.

- Before Dialing—If you click this button, you will see the same basic options that were presented in the After Dialing dialog box. This setting can be used to bring up a window or to run a script before you dial the remote host.

7. Check or enter the security information on the Security tab. This should be set to the same level as the security on the server, or the connection will probably fail.

- Authentication and Encryption Policy—Here you can set the level of security that you want to use. For troubleshooting, you can try Accept any Authentication Including Clear Text. This setting should be set to match the setting on the server.

- Require Data Encryption—If you are using Microsoft encrypted authentication, you will have the option to encrypt all data that is being sent over the connection. This should be set the same as the server.

- User Current Name and Password—Allows Windows to send the current user name and password as your logon information. If you are not using the same name and password on the client as you do on the network, do not check this box. You will be prompted for the user name and password to log on as when you attempt to connect.

- Unsave Password—If you told the system to save the logon password for a connection, you can clear it by clicking this button. You should unsave the password in the case of a logon problem.

8. Enter or check the information for X.25 connections.

There are a lot of different options that you can configure, and therefore the potential for errors is great. Client errors tend to be either validation problems or errors in the network protocols. Remember that you may need to check the configuration of the server.

3.2.7   The RAS Server

This section covers the RAS server and its configuration. After a short description of the installation, this section moves on to the configuration of the server.

Installing the RAS Server

Follow these steps to install RAS:

1. Open the Network Setting dialog box (Start | Settings | Control Panel | Network).

2. From the Services tab, choose Add.

3. Choose Remote Access Service and then click OK.

4. When prompted, enter the path to the Windows NT source files.

5. RAS asks you for the device that it should use at that point. (This will include ISDN and X.25.)

6. When the Remote Access Setup dialog box opens, click continue. (The options for this dialog box are described in the following section.)

7. From the Network settings dialog box, click Close.

8. When prompted, shut down and restart your system.

Configuring the RAS Server

If several users are having problems connecting to your RAS server, check the modem first and then check the configuration of the server. This section covers the basic configuration for a RAS server. This configuration is done when you install RAS or when you verify it after installation by going to the Network Settings dialog box and double-clicking on Remote Access Service from the Services tab.

A dialog box enables you to configure each port and set the overall network preferences. The following four buttons relate to port settings.

- Add—Enables you to add another port to the RAS server. This could be a modem, X.25 PAD or a PPTP Virtual Private Network.

- Remove—Removes the port from RAS.

- Configure—Opens a dialog box that enables you to configure how this port is to be used. You should inspect this setting if no users are able to dial in.

- Clone—Enables you to copy a port. Windows NT Server has been tested with up to 256 ports.

> **Windows NT Workstation and Windows 95 (with Service Pack 1 or the OSR2 release) allow only one client to dial in.**

After the ports are configured, you need to configure the network settings. These will affect what users will be able to see, how they are authenticated, and what protocols they will be able to use when they dial in to the network. When you click the Network button, you will see a dialog box.

This dialog box has three main sections. The dial-out protocols specify the protocols you can use to dial into another server. The dial-in protocols set the protocols with which users can connect to you. The third section specifies encryption settings. The level of security that you choose must also be set on the client computer. If the client and the server do not use the same level of security, the server will not be able to validate the client.

Each server-side protocol has a configuration button. The following sections explain these configurations. Before you can use a protocol with RAS, it has to be installed on the server.

Configuring TCP/IP on the RAS Server

If you run a mixed network that includes UNIX-like hosts, then you should enable the TCP/IP protocol on the RAS server. Doing so will also enable your clients to use an Internet connection on your network. The TCP/IP configuration dialog box again includes the capability to restrict network access to the RAS server.

The other options all deal with the assignment of TCP/IP addresses to the clients that are dialing in. By default, the RAS server will use the services of a Dynamic Host Configuration Protocol (DHCP) server to assign the addresses. If your DHCP server has a long lease period, you may want to assign the numbers from a pool of addresses that are given on the server. If you allow the client to request an address, you will need to configure the client stations for all other parameters.

If your clients are having problems connecting, assign a range of addresses to the RAS server. This approach will eliminate any problems that are related to the DHCP server and still allow you to prevent clients from requesting specific IP addresses.

3.2.8 Monitoring the RAS Connection

After you make the RAS connection, you will be able to monitor the connection. There is a tool for both the client side and the server side. This section looks at both of them, as they can be used to see what is happening with the connection.

Monitoring from the RAS Server

From the server, you can use the Remote Access Admin tool to monitor the ports. From the Start menu, choose Programs | Administrative Tools | RAS Admin to display the Admin tool.

Double-click the server that you want to inspect. A list of the communications ports will appear. For every port that is available on the server, you will see the name of the currently connected user and the time when the connection was made.

From here you can disconnect users, send a message to a single user, or send a message to all the users who are connected to the server. You can also check the port status. This area displays all the connection information for the port.

Dial-Up Networking Monitor

The Dial-Up Networking Monitor application on the client side enables you to check the status of the communications. The monitor has three tabs.

The Status Tab

The Status tab provides basic information about the connection. From here you have the option to hang up the connection or to view details about the connection.

The Details tab provides detailed information about the names of the clients names on the network.

The Summary Tab

The Summary tab summarizes all the connections that the client currently has open. This information is really only useful when you have multiple connections.

The Preferences Tab

The Preferences tab enables you to control the settings for Dial-Up Networking. The options that you can set on this tab break down into two main areas. You can control when a sound is played and how the Dial-Up Networking monitor will look.

3.2.9   Common RAS Problems

This section describes the two common problems that clients will experience with RAS.

Authentication

Authentication can be a problem in two areas. The first is obvious. The client can attempt to connect using the incorrect user name and password. This situation can easily occur if the user is dialing from a home system. The RAS client may be set to attempt the connection using the current user name and password.

The other authentication problem occurs if the security settings on the server and the client do not match. You can get around this problem by using the Allow Any Authentication setting or possibly by using the After Dial terminal window.

Callback Security with Multilink

You cannot currently configure callback security in a Multilink setup. If you attempt to do so, the initial connections will be made, but then the server will hang up. The server has only one number for the client and will therefore call back to only one port.

3.2.10   Exercises

Exercise 1: Adding a Null Modem

In this exercise, you install a Null modem so that anyone without a modem can proceed through some of the remaining exercises.

1. Open the Control Panel and double-click the Modems icon.

2. Click the Add button to open the modem installer.

3. Choose Don't Detect My Modem, I Will Select It from a List and then click Next.

4. The list of manufacturers and models appears. From the Standard Modem Types, choose Dial-Up Networking Serial Cable between 2 PCs; then click Next.

5. Choose any available port and then click Next. NT will install your modem. When the next screen appears, choose Finish.

6. Choose OK to close the modem installer.

Exercise 2: Installing Remote Access Service

In this exercise, you will install the RAS. If you already have this installed, skip to Exercise 3.

1. Open the Network Setting dialog box and then choose Add from the Services tab.

2. Choose the Remote Access Service and click OK; when prompted, enter the source files directory.

3. Choose Close on the Network Settings dialog box. When prompted, select either the Null modem or the modem you already had.

4. From the RAS Setup dialog box, choose Configure, Dial Out. Click OK to return to the RAS Setup dialog box.

5. Click the Continue button.

6. When prompted, restart your system.

Exercise 3: Creating Phonebook Entries

You will now create a new phonebook entry. This exercise covers all the steps for creating a real phonebook entry.

1. Open the My Computer icon and double-click the Dial-Up Networking button.

2. As this is the first time that you have run Dial-Up Networking, you will be informed that the phonebook is empty and be asked to add a new entry.

> **If you have already used Dial-Up Networking, click the New button. You will now be able to follow the sequence of steps.**

3. For the Name, type **Test Entry Number 1**; then click Next.

4. Select the first (I Am Calling the Internet) and third (The non-Windows NT Server) check boxes. Click Next.

5. Enter **555-3840** as the phone number and click Next.

6. Select PPP as the protocol and click Next.

7. Choose Use a Terminal Window from the next screen and then click Next.

8. Assuming the server will provide an address, click Next.

9. Enter `148.53.66.7` as the DNS server and click Next.

10. Click Finish.

Exercise 4: Editing Phonebook Entries

In this exercise, you edit a phonebook entry and its preferences.

1. To create a shortcut to the entry, choose More | Create a Shortcut to the Entry.

2. Accept the default name (`Test Entry Number 1.rnk`).

3. Close the Dial-Up Networking dialog box.

4. On the desktop, right-click the PhoneBook icon; choose Edit Entry and Modem Properties.

5. Add the alternate numbers `555-9930` and `555-6110`. To do so, click the Alternates button, type the first number in the New Phone Number field, and click Add. Do the same for the second number.

6. Click OK to save the changes.

7. You have created a script for this entry and wish to use it. Right-click the PhoneBook icon on the desktop; choose Edit Entry and Modem Properties.

8. Select the Script tab and click Run This Script.

9. From the drop-down list box, choose `PPPMENU.SCP`.

10. Click on the Server tab and check Enable Software Compression.

11. Click OK to save the changes.

Exercise 5: Configuring RAS as a Server

In this exercise, you will set up the Remote Access Service to act as a RAS server, which enables others to dial into your machine.

1. Open the Network Setting dialog box and choose the Services tab.

2. Click Remote Access Service and then click the Properties button.

3. Select the Null modem (or the modem you are using) and select Configure.

4. Click the Dial Out and Receive Calls option; then click OK to close the dialog box.

5. Click the Network button. From here, ensure that TCP/IP is configured in the Server settings.

6. Click the Configure button beside TCP/IP; choose Use Static Address Pool.

7. Enter `148.53.90.0` as the Begin Address and `148.53.90.255` as the End Address. Click OK to close the dialog box; click OK again to close the Server settings.

8. Click Continue to return to the Network Settings dialog box and then choose Close.

9. Restart your computer.

Exercise 6: Assigning Permissions

You will now provide your users with dial-in permissions and review the Remote Access Admin program.

1. Start the User Manager for Domains (User Manager works fine in this case).

2. Choose User | New User and then enter the following information:

   User name   `Bilbo`

   Full name   `Bilbo Baggins`

   Description   `Hobbit (small with fury feet)`

   Password   Blank

3. Click the Dial-in icon and check the Grant Dial-in Permission option.

4. Click OK to close the dial-in screen; click OK to add the user.

5. Close User Manager for Domains.

6. Open the Remote Access Admin program from the Administrative Tools group.

7. Choose Users | Permissions from the menu. Click Bilbo's name in the list. Does he have dial-in permission? (He should.)

8. Choose the account you logged on as; if you do not have dial-in permission, grant it to yourself.

3.2.11 Practice Problems

1. A RAS server can be which of the following? (Choose all correct answers.)

   A. Windows NT Server

   B. Windows NT Workstation

   C. Windows 95

   D. Windows 3.11

2. When users are dialing in to a Microsoft RAS, what line protocol is always used?

   A. SLIP

   B. PPP

   C. TCP/IP

   D. NetBEUI

3. Which of the following is an extension to PPP that enables clients to connect to remote servers over the Internet?

   A. SLIP

   B. POP

   C. PPTP

   D. PPP+

4. Windows NT Workstation 4.0 supports which two line protocols?

   A. SLIP

   B. PPP

   C. PPTP

   D. TCP/IP

5. Which of the following is an industry standard that supports only TCP/IP connections made over serial lines?

   A. SLIP

   B. PPP

   C. PPTP

   D. TCP/IP

6. Which of the following protocols work with SLIP?

   A. TCP/IP

   B. NetBEUI

   C. IPX/SPX

   D. PPTP

7. How does Windows NT Workstation support SLIP functionality?

   A. As a server.

   B. As a client.

   C. As a client and a server.

   D. Windows NT Workstation does not support SLIP.

8. Which of the following protocols works with PPP?

   A. TCP/IP

   B. NetBEUI

   C. IPX/SPX

   D. PPTP

9. Which of the following line protocols supports DHCP addresses?

   A. SLIP

   B. PPP

   C. IPX/SPX

   D. TCP/IP

10. Which of the following protocols creates virtual private networks over the Internet?

    A. SLIP

    B. PPP

    C. POP

    D. PPTP

11. How many RAS sessions can Windows NT Workstation serve at a time?

    A. 1

    B. 2

    C. 5

    D. 255

12. RAS can be configured in which three of the following ways?

    A. Dial out only

    B. Receive calls only

    C. Dial out and Receive calls

    D. Manual

13. Which of the following configuration settings is the default for Workstation RAS?

    A. Dial out only

    B. Receive calls only

    C. Dial out and Receive calls

    D. Manual

14. How are authentication and encryption settings set?

    A. For each workstation

    B. For each domain

    C. For each phonebook entry

    D. For each user

15. The Dialing Properties dialog box is accessed from which Control Panel applet?

    A. System

    B. Services

    C. RAS

    D. Telephony

16. Which of the following are limitations of SLIP for Dial-Up Networking (DUN) clients?

    A. DUN doesn't support use as a SLIP client.

    B. SLIP doesn't support NWLink or NetBEUI.

C. SLIP doesn't support DHCP.

D. SLIP doesn't support encrypted authentication.

17. What methods are supported by Dial-Up Networking to establish sessions with remote networks?

A. ISDN

B. X.25

C. Dial up with modems and ordinary phone lines

D. XNS

3.2.12 Practice Problems: Answers and Explanations

1. **A, B, C** A RAS server can be an NT Server, an NT Workstation, or a Windows 95 machine.

2. **B** PPP will always be used when clients are dialing in to a Microsoft RAS server.

3. **C** The Point-to-Point Tunneling Protocol (PPTP) is an extension to PPP that enables clients to connect to remote servers over the Internet.

4. **A, B** Windows NT Workstation 4.0 supports two different line protocols: SLIP and PPP.

5. **A** SLIP is an industry standard that supports TCP/IP connections made over serial lines.

6. **A** SLIP supports only TCP/IP.

7. **B** Windows NT Workstation supports only SLIP client functionality.

8. **A, B, C** PPP supports TCP/IP, NetBEUI, and IPX/SPX, among others.

9. **B** TCP/IP and IPX/SPX are not line protocols. SLIP does not support DHCP addressing—only static addressing. PPP

supports DHCP addressing.

10. **D** You can use PPTP to create virtual private networks over the Internet.

11. **A** Windows NT Workstation is limited to one RAS session at a time.

12. **A, B, C** Dial out only, Receive calls only, and Dial out and Receive calls are the three settings for RAS.

13. **A** Dial out only is the default RAS setting.

14. **C** Authentication and encryption settings are set individually for each phonebook entry.

15. **D** Telephony is the Control Panel applet that gives access to Dialing Properties.

16. **B, C, D** Windows NT Workstation 4.0 supports use as a SLIP client, but not as a SLIP server.

17. **A, B, C** DUN doesn't support XNS.

3.2.13 Keywords

encryption Maskingvalues sent to avoid capture by unwanted third parties

PPP Point to Point Protocol; a newer Internet protocol that is replacing SLIP and adding functionality

PPTP Point to Point Tunneling Protocol; a secure extension of PPP

protocol A standard for communicating

RAS Remote Access Service; the ability to access your network from a remote location

SLIP Older Internet protocol mostly used with UNIX systems

telephony Telephone services used through a computer

3

3.3 Browsing in a Multiple-Domain Routed Network

The sharing of resources is the key to networking. For what other purpose does networking exist? Therefore, having an easy way of not only sharing a resource but also of knowing what resources on the network are accessible is of utmost importance. Microsoft has made the process of viewing network resources available through so-called browsers.

These browsers actually collect a list (called the browse list) of the resources available on the network and pass this list out to requesting clients. One main computer is designated to collect and update the browse list. Having one computer keep track of the browse list frees the other systems to continue processing without the added overhead of constantly having to find resources. This approach also reduces network traffic by having a single source for this list, rather than a separate copy for all computers.

3.3.1 Browsing Tools

Now you might ask, "How do I browse and what am I browsing for?" The answer is easier than you might think, and you have probably already used this browsing technique. One very simple example of how browsing is employed is the Network Neighborhood icon on your desktop. When you open Network Neighborhood, it provides a list of the network resources availablein your local workgroup or domain. These network resources include, but are not limited to, printers, fax capabilities, CD-ROMs, and other drives or applications available on the network. You should see this default list when you open Network Neighborhood. The top icon, Entire Network, refers to just that: anything else that may be available on your network but not necessarily in your local workgroup or domain. This implies that there may be multiple workgroups and/or domains in your network environment.

When you start opening some of these remote domains or workgroups, you are in the process of browsing. This activity is much like window shopping. You go to the mall not knowing exactly what you need, and so you browse through the shops until you find what you want.

The same process applies to the network, but now you are browsing network resources—remote files, printers, CD-ROMs. Anything you need access to can be considered a resource. After you find the resource you want, you can use it—such as by printing a document to a network printer or by changing to a server-based database. By using the Network Neighborhood for browsing network resources, you are using the graphical view method or graphical user interface (GUI). You may also browse network resources from the command prompt by using the Net View command. After you specify the server name, a list appears showing the resources available on that specific server. Notice that you must use the correct Universal Naming Convention with the two backslashes (\\Server\Share).

For example:

```
C:\users\default>net view \\instructor
```

results in the following:

```
Shared resources at \\instructor
```

```
Share name    Type        Used as   Comment

.................................................................

cdrom         Disk
MSDOS         Disk
NETLOGON      Disk                  Logon server share
Public        Disk
SQLSETUP      Disk

WGPO          Disk

The command completed successfully.
```

3.3.2   System Roles

Certain predefined roles must be addressed with certain names. The computer that has the resource you are trying to access may be referred to as the *host computer*. While you are trying to access its resources, this computer is also playing the role of a server because it is providing a service: the sharing of its resources. The person trying to access the host computer is in the role of a *client*. Remember, a computer may play the roles of both client and server at the same time. If, for example, you are trying to access a printer on a remote computer while someone is using your shared CD-ROM, you are then both client and server; that is, you are sharing a resource and accessing a remote one.

Anytime a resource—drive, printer, and so forth—is shared, it will appear on the browse list, which is available to everyone on the network. Even if you do not have permission to use the resource, it will still appear on your browse list. The browse list displays all available network resources, not just the network resources that are available to you. There are ways of limiting access to the resource to specific clients (by setting permissions directly on the resource you are sharing), but there is no way to control the browse list itself. Your list is not specific to you; it is the entire list for either your workgroup, domain, or network.

Sometimes the browse list appears incomplete; other times it contains items that you cannot access, even though you have been given the correct permissions. If you do not have enough permissions to access a server, even though it appears in your browse list, you will still be denied access. So why, if you have proper permissions, do you have no access to the server (and why doesn't the server appear on the browse list at all)? Because there is a delay in updating the browse list you are accessing. In effect, the server you attempt to access is either not available anymore (which results in you being denied access to a server you had previously been allowed to access), or the server does not appear in the browse list. Browse-list timing issues are covered later in this section.

3.3.3   The Direct Approach

There is, however, a way around the problem of the browse list delay. This "direct approach" requires you to know the exact name of the network host that has the resource you desire to obtain, but not the resource itself. This workaround is similar to the Net View command but with a graphical interface.

The following steps show how to use the direct approach to access a computer:

1. Click the Start button.

2. Click Find.

3. Click Computer.

4. Type in the name of the server you are trying to find.

5. Click Find Now.

Alternatively, you can go to the Start menu, choose Run, and enter the \\computername.

You should then see a list of resources available on that system.

The direct approach bypasses browsing and resolves the NetBIOS name to an IP address. It is especially helpful when a new resource has been made available but may not have appeared on any browse list, or when you want to see whether a resource to which you are being denied access is really currently available on the network. You can also use the Net Use command at the command prompt to specify the remote resource you are going to access. The Net Use command is usually used with the previously described Net View command; whereas the Net View command only lists that server's shared resources, the Net Use command actually attaches you to the resource.

3.3.4   Browsing Roles

Now that you understand the concept of browsing and what it can do for you, the next stage is to discuss the various browsing processes and the defined roles for browsing. The following browsing roles are available.

- Master Browser—Collects and maintains the master list of available resources in its domain or workgroup as well as the list of names, not resources, in other domains and workgroups. Distributes the browse list to Backup Browsers.

- Backup Browser—Obtains its browse list from the Master Browser and passes this list to requesting clients.

- Domain Master Browser—Fulfills the role of a Master Browser for its domain as well as coordinating and synchronizing the browse list from all other Master Browsers for the domains that reside on remote networks. A Domain Master Browser is required per domain to maintain the list and make the list available to browsers on other domains.

- Potential Browser—A computer that could be a Master, Backup, or Domain Master Browser, if needed, but currently neither fills a role nor holds a browse list.

- Non-Browser—A computer that does not maintain a browse list.

3.3.5   Filling Roles

Now that browsing roles are defined, who can fill them? Windows NT Workstation, Windows NT Server, Windows for Workgroups, and Windows 95 can all perform these browsing roles.

However, only a Windows NT Server acting as a Primary Domain Controller (PDC) may occupy the role of the Domain Master Browser. In a LAN, the Domain Master Browser is also the Master Browser.

Windows NT Workstation and Windows NT Member Servers can become Backup Browsers if there are three Windows NT server–based computers not already filling these roles for the workgroup or domain.

How do you know and control the roles in which your computers are participating? Unfortunately, the only way to discover a computer's browsing role is to look in the Registry. By understanding some default rules and by invoking a little user intervention, however, you can control the browsing environment to a certain extent. The first default to grasp is that Windows NT and Windows 95 are set to auto—meaning either one has the potential to fill a browsing role. The Master Browser is chosen through an election process, which is based on the following criteria:

- A Windows NT–based computer takes precedence over a Windows 95 or Windows for Workgroups computer. Windows 95 will take priority over Windows for Workgroups. This hierarchy is true at any time. Even if a Windows 95 machine has been on for two years, as soon as a Windows NT computer comes online, an election will be held. The Windows NT computer will always win because of its higher priority rating.

- If the two operating systems are equal, the computer that has been turned on the longest wins the election and will become the new Master Browser. The idea here is that the computer that has been on the longest has the most potential to not go down frequently, thus providing a more accurate and current browse list.

- If none of the above criteria fit, the server with a NetBIOS name of lowest alphabetical lettering will win the election. For example, if the contest is between Argyle and Zot, the server named Argyle will become the next Master Browser.

Controlling Your Browser Role

To control the browser role that your computer is playing for a Windows NT Server and Windows NT Workstation, you can change the `IsDomainMaster` Registry setting to a true or yes to force your computer to be the Master Browser. This setting is found in the following Registry subkey:

```
\HKEY_LOCAL_MACHINE\SYSTEM\CurrentControlSet\Services\Browser\Parameters
```

To control your browser role for Windows 95, the File and Print Sharing for Microsoft Networks service is required. Browsing roles can be implemented through the following steps:

1. Right-click Network Neighborhood.

2. Choose Properties.

3. Select the File and Print Sharing for Microsoft Networks service if you have it installed. If it is not installed, you are not currently participating in browsing. You can install the service by clicking the Add button, selecting Microsoft, and then adding File and Print Sharing for Microsoft Networks.

4. Choose Properties.

5. Select Browse Master, which is set to Automatic by default; you can either enable or disable it.

These are the only controls you have for configuring the browser roles of your computers. So you could turn the IsDomainMaster Registry setting off on all but the specific machines that you want to participate in browsing. If one of those machines goes down, however, there goes your browsing. You cannot directly control Backup Browsers, only set them to auto with one set to IsDomainMaster.

Understanding the Cost of Browsing

The first cost of browsing is the bandwidth consumed by network traffic. Aside from that, does being a Browse Master affect a computer's performance? Yes, it affects system performance. This performance degradation may be noticeable on slower systems, such as a 486/66, but not as noticeable on most newer machines, such as a P5/100. Anything the computer does in some way affects its performance, but remember that being a Browse Master means keeping an updated list of network resources. The number of network resources that the Browse Master needs to keep up obviously affects that computer's performance accordingly. The best you can do to minimize this performance degradation is to minimize the number of computers sharing network resources. Doing so keeps the browse list short, thereby relieving the strain on the Master Browser.

3.3.6   Windows NT Browsing Services

A lot is involved with browsing to make it do what it does—most of which happens automatically without any intervention. Sometimes, however, problems develop, and understanding the browsing process can help you find solutions.

The browsing services have three main break points, or sections, in Windows NT:

1.   Collecting information for the browse list

2.   Distributing the browse list itself

3.   Servicing browser client requests for the list

Each of these break points is discussed in the following sections.

3.3.7   Collecting the Browse List

The first important part of being able to browse network servers is the collection of the browse list itself. The Master Browser continually updates its browse list to include the current network servers available. This update process is continual, in that it is constantly having to revise its browse list as servers appear and disappear. This process happens every time a computer that has something to share is turned on and every time one that is sharing resources is turned off. The Master Browser obtains a list of servers in its own domain or workgroup, as well as a list of other domains and workgroups, and updates these servers with network resources to the browse list as changes are made. Much of this process has to do with browser announcements.

When a computer that is running a server service is turned on, it announces itself to the Master Browser, which then adds this new resource to its browse list. This step happens whether or not the computer has resources to share. When a computer is shut down properly, it announces to the Master Browser that it is leaving; again, the Master Browser updates its list accordingly.

Master Browsers also receive DomainAnnouncement packets from other domains and place these packets in their own local browse lists. DomainAnnouncement packets contain the following information:

- The name of the domain.

- The name of the Master Browser for that domain.

- Whether the browser is a Windows NT Server or Windows NT Workstation computer.

- If the browser is a Windows NT Server computer, it is the Primary Domain Controller for that domain.

3.3.8 Distributing the Browse List

The next important part of browsing is the distribution of the previously collected browse list. The extent of this distribution depends largely on the size of the network. A Master Browser broadcasts a message every so often to let the Backup Browsers know the Master Browser is still around. If the Master Browser does not send this message, the network holds an election process to elect a new Master Browser.

The Master Browser holds the list of network resources. The Backup Browser contacts the Master Browser and copies the list from the Master Browser. Therefore, the Backup Browsers are the active components, intermittently contacting the passive Master Browser for the updated list.

Complications often develop with the distribution of this browse list. The following sections discuss some of these difficulties, such as browsing over subnets, announcement period timings, and Domain Master Browser failure, and provide corresponding solutions.

Browsing over Subnets

Within Windows NT, every local subnet, a collection of computers separated by a router, is its own browsing area. This browsing area is complete with its own Master Browser and Backup Browsers. Subnets hold browser elections for their own subnet. Therefore, if you have multiple subnets on your internetwork, it needs a Domain Master Browser to permit browsing over more than just one subnet. Additionally, each subnet needs at least one Windows NT controller to register with the Domain Master Browser to support multiple-subnet browsing.

Generally, broadcasts do not go through a router; the router needs to be enabled to allow passing of broadcasts (137 and 138 UDP are the NetBIOS ports). If a domain has multiple subnets, each Master Browser for each subnet uses a directed datagram called a MasterBrowserAnnouncement. The MasterBrowserAnnouncement tells the Domain Master Browser that the subnet Master Browser is available and what it has on its browse list. These datagrams pass through the routers enabling these updates to occur.

The Domain Master Browser adds all the subnet Master Browser lists to its own browse list, providing a complete browse list of the entire domain, including all subnets. This process occurs, by default, every 15 minutes to ensure regular list updates. The timing of the MasterBrowserAnnouncement is controlled by `HKEY_LOCAL_MACHINE\system\currentcontrolset\services\browser\parameters\MasterPeriodicity` in Windows NT 4. Prior to Windows NT 4, the timing was not adjustable. Windows NT workgroups and Windows for Workgroups are not able to send a MasterBrowserAnnouncement packet and therefore cannot span these multiple subnets or have a complete list—thus the need for Windows NT domain controllers to allow for multiple-subnet browsing.

Announcement Periods

When the Master Browser first comes online it sends out a DomainAnnouncement once a minute for the first five minutes and then only once every 15 minutes. If the domain does not respond by sending out its own DomainAnnouncement for three successive announcement periods, the domain is removed from the Master Browser list. A server, therefore, might appear on your browse list but actually be unavailable, because it remains on the browse list until three full announcement periods have passed. It is therefore possible for a server to appear on a browse list for up to 45 minutes after it is originally unavailable, perhaps because the Primary Domain Controller is turned off or is having physical connectivity problems, such as a bad network card and/or cable. You cannot change these announcement times or removal periods.

Domain Master Browser Failure

In the event of a Domain Master Browser failure, users on the entire network are limited to their own individual subnets, assuming they have a Master Browser for their subnet, of course. If your subnet doesn't have a Master Browser, you are left with no browsing capabilities whatsoever. Without a Domain Master Browser, no complete overall browse list exists of the entire domain, and within three announcement periods all other servers not on the local subnet are removed from the browse list. You then need to either promote a Backup Domain Controller, to perform the role of Domain Master Browser, or bring the downed Domain Master Browser back online before the time limit expires for its three announcements. Remember the Backup Domain Controller does not automatically promote itself, and once a new Domain Master Browser is elected, it will take time to collect the browse list from all the different subnets. There is no way you can force the browse list.

3.3.9 Servicing Client Requests

The final browsing service process is the actual servicing of client requests. Now that a browse list exists and has been distributed, clients have something to access.

The process follows these steps:

1. The client tries to access a domain or workgroup using Explorer. In doing so, it contacts the Master Browser of the domain or workgroup that it is trying to access.

2. The Master Browser gives the client a list of three Backup Browsers.

3. The client then asks for the server from one of the Backup Browsers.

4. The Backup Browser provides the list of servers in the relevant domain or workgroup.

5. The client chooses a server and obtains a list of that server's shared resources.

This process can occasionally cause some conflict if the Master Browser has a resource in its list, but the Backup Browser has not updated itself yet, and the client connects to that Backup Browser and looks for the current list. The resource is not listed in the backup browse list yet, which is another reason why items that are not available may appear on the list or may not be on the list at all.

3.3.10 Browsing in an IP Internetwork

Now that you've learned about browsing itself and know how it works, you are ready to learn about browsing in an IP internetwork, that is, browsing over multiple subnets. This type of browsing is not as easy as it sounds. This topic was partially explained through the process of domain announcement. But domain announcement only allows for Master Browsers to talk to the Domain Master Browser. Browsing in an IP internetwork requires a Windows NT domain controller to be in each subnet. Because putting a domain controller at each subnet may not be feasible, such browsing may be impossible.

The first major obstacle is that browsing relies on broadcast packets, which means they are actually sent to everyone on the network segment. However, routers do not generally forward these broadcast packets, creating a browsing problem for collecting, distributing, and servicing the client request for browse lists. If these packets are not forwarded, you are unable to browse in an internetwork environment without a local domain controller.

If the browse list cannot be distributed properly, you have no browsing capability.

Solutions

There are a few possible solutions to the problem of being able to browse in an IP internetwork, for example, the use of a UDP port 137\138–enabled router and an LMHOSTS file. The following section discusses the usefulness of the IP router.

IP Router

The first way to work around the problem of routers and multiple subnets not being able to browse without a Windows NT controller on each subnet is to have a specific router that can forward these NetBIOS name broadcasts. This approach makes all the broadcasts and network resource requests appear to all client computers as if the broadcasts are all on the same subnet. Master Browsers have their own lists as well as those of the other domains and workgroups, so when a client makes an inquiry for a browse list, the list can be provided for any domain or workgroup.

Having a BOOTP-enabled router, of course, fixes the browsing problem across routers. But this solution may not be perfect for every network layout and size. The reason this UDP port 137/138–enabled router is not the perfect solution is that if you do have the BOOTP-enabled router, all NetBIOS traffic is broadcast over the entire network, rather than limited to each subnet. This adds extremely high overhead to all the nodes of the network, degrading overall performance. The subnets are no longer isolated to their own specific areas, which causes a higher potential for browser election conflicts and excessive network traffic. Therefore, even though the BOOTP-enabled router does fix the problem of routers and multiple subnets, you will need to anticipate other problems, such as excessive traffic.

Directed Traffic

Additional solutions to the problem of browsing an IP internetwork without using a BOOTP-enabled router are available. The following section explains how to use directed IP traffic to service the client's browsing requests.

LMHOSTS File

An LMHOSTS file helps distribute the browsing information and service client requests. You can also use WINS to collect the browse lists and service client requests.

In the LMHOSTS file, the *LM* stands for LAN Manager; *HOSTS* is for the host computer. The job of the LMHOSTS file is to resolve NetBIOS names to the corresponding IP address of remote hosts on different subnets. The purpose is to allow communication between Master Browsers on remote subnets and the Domain Master Browser. This solution sets up direct communication, enabling an updated list to be developed across a subnet. The one thing to remember about an LMHOSTS file is that it is your responsiblity to create and maintain the file.

Using an LMHOSTS file is a workable solution but has some special requirements. For example, the LMHOSTS file must be on each subnet's Master Browser with an entry to the Domain Master Browser. It must also be updated manually any time there are changes to the LMHOSTS list. The LMHOSTS file needs to be placed in the `winntroot\system32\drivers\etc` directory. (There are sample TCP/IP files you can use to reference.) It is just a regular text file that can be created using any text editor. There is no file extension, and Windows NT will look for and reference the file in this location whenever it needs to.

To work across a subnet, the LMHOSTS file needs the following two items:

- The IP address and computer name of the Domain Master Browser
- The domain name preceded by `#PRE` and `#DOM:`

For example:

```
129.62.101.5      server1          #PRE #DOM:try
129.62.101.17     server2          #PRE
129.62.101.25     server3          #PRE
```

The `#PRE` statement preloads the specific line it is on into the NetBIOS name cache as a permanent entry, making it easily available without having to first access the domain.

`#DOM:<domain_name>` supports logon validation over a router, account synchronization, and, in this case, browsing. Every time the computer sends a broadcast to a domain, it also sends the broadcast to every computer that has a `#DOM:` in its LMHOSTS file. These types of broadcasts do go across routers, but are not sent to workgroups. The many difficulties to watch out for are discussed in the following subsections.

Domain Master Browser

For the Domain Master Browser, you need an LMHOSTS file that is set up with entries pointing to each of the remote subnet Master Browsers. You should also have a #DOM: statement in each of the Master Browsers' LMHOSTS files pointing to each of the other subnet Master Browsers. If any of them gets promoted to the Domain Master Browser, you then do not have to change all your LMHOSTS files.

Duplicate Names

If it finds duplicate LMHOSTS entries for a single domain, the Master Browser decides which one relates to the Domain Master Browser by querying each IP address for each entry it has. None of the Master Browsers respond; only the Domain Master Browser does that. Therefore the Master Browser narrows down the list of duplicates and because only the real one responds, the Master Browser communicates with the one that responds and proceeds to exchange browse lists.

LMHOSTS File Placement

The placement of the LMHOSTS file is in the \etc directory of the client. For Windows NT, for example, it is placed in \systemroot\system32\drivers\etc. For Windows 95 and Windows for Workgroups, it is placed in \system_root (c:\windows).

LMHOSTS File Problems

The most common problems you might have with the LMHOSTS file are the following:

- The NetBIOS name is misspelled.

- The IP address is incorrect.

- An entry is not listed for that host.

- There are too many entries for a host where only the first entry is used. For example, if there are multiple entries in the LMHOSTS file for the same host computer, only the first one listed will be used.

- The LMHOSTS file is in the incorrect location and is not being read.

The LMHOSTS file certainly has its place in IP internetwork browsing, but it is certainly not the ultimate solution. Hence the final name resolution method: WINS.

The WINS Solution

WINS helps fix the problem of NetBIOS broadcast difficulties by dynamically registering the IP address and NetBIOS name and keeping track of them in a database. Keeping these computer names in its database greatly enhances the network performance. Whenever they need to find a server, clients access the WINS server rather than broadcast on the network. Accessing the WINS server directly allows for a more direct approach when looking for network resources. In addition, this approach makes updating much easier because you do not have to manually configure anything. Using a WINS server also provides easier browsing capability because you can freely use NetBIOS names in the place of IP address. The following example uses the PING utility with the NetBIOS name, rather than specifying the entire IP address.

```
ping Server2
```

rather than

```
ping 207.0.58.33
```

Domain Browser

If the computer is made a WINS client, the Domain Master Browser periodically queries the WINS server to update its database of all the domains listed in the WINS database, thereby providing a complete list of all the domains and subnets, including remote ones. This list now has only domain names and their IP address, not the names of the Master Browsers of each particular subnet.

Client Access

When a client needs access to a network resource, it calls up the WINS server directly and asks for a list of domain controllers in the domain. WINS provides a list of servers of up to 25 domain controllers, referred to as a *domain group*. The client is then able to quickly access the domain controller it needs without a complete network broadcast.

3.3.11   Practice Problems

1. When users access the Network Neighborhood, they are viewing a list of computers on the network known as

   A. A browse list

   B. A browse table

   C. A resource list

   D. A resource table

2. Browse lists can be distributed on Microsoft and NetWare networks using what protocol?

   A. TCP/IP

   B. NetBIOS

   C. PPP

   D. IPX/SPX

3. The browse list is compiled by

   A. A static resource table

   B. LMHOSTS files

   C. WINS servers

   D. A Master Browser

4. To whom does the Master Browser distribute the browse list?

   A. Primary Domain Controllers

   B. Backup Browsers

   C. Windows-based clients

   D. NT Servers

5. From whom does the client view the browse list?

   A. Primary Domain Controllers

   B. Backup Browsers

   C. Windows-based clients

   D. NT Servers

6. Master and Backup Browsers are determined by

   A. Primary Domain Controllers

   B. WINS servers

   C. Elections

   D. Polling

7. All other factors being equal, which of the following machines on a network is most likely to be the Master Browser?

   A. Windows 95 workstation

   B. Windows NT workstation

   C. Windows NT server

   D. Windows for Workgroups workstation

8. A Windows 95 computer can be configured to maintain or to not maintain browse lists by configuring which of the following?

   A. The File and Printer Sharing service

   B. The Share Level Security tab

   C. The LMHOSTS file

   D. The Network Neighborhood properties

9. Normal setup would be for a Windows 95 machine to be a Master Browser under what circumstances?

   A. Always

   B. Never

   C. When elected

   D. When polled

10. What would be one reason to prevent a Windows 95 machine from being a Master Browser or Backup Browser?

    A. When performance load is critical

    B. When connected to a NetWare server

    C. When user-level security is config-ured

    D. When you have failed to register the machine with the local polling server

11. To have Windows 95 automatically determine whether the computer is needed as a browse server, which option should you select?

    A. Enabled: May Be Master

    B. Enabled: Must Be Master

    C. Master: Enabled

    D. Master: May Be Enabled

12. To prevent the computer from maintaining browse lists for the network, which option should you select?

    A. Enabled: May Not Be Master

    B. Enabled: Must Not Be Master

    C. Master: Disabled

    D. Master: May Not Be Enabled

13. Selecting the Enabled: May Not Be Master option has what effect on browsing the network?

    A. Stops all LMANNOUNCE messages, effectively stopping browsing

    B. Prevents the computer from browsing the network resources

    C. Requires the reenabling of the service before browsing can take place

    D. Does not prevent the computer from browsing the network resources

14. To prevent the computer from using the browse service altogether, what option should you select?

    A. NOT

    B. DISABLED

    C. INVALID

    D. LMANNOUNCE NO

15. To give the computer a higher weighting for the browse elections, which option should you select?

    A. Enabled: May Be Master

    B. Enabled: Must Be Master

    C. Enabled: Preferred Master

    D. Master: Enabled

3.3.12 Practice Problems: Answers and Explanations

1. **A** When users access the Network Neighborhood, they are viewing a list of computers on the network known as a *browse list*.

2. **D** Microsoft and NetWare networks can use IPX/SPX to distribute browse lists throughout a domain.

3. **D** The Master Browser of the domain compiles the browse list.

4. **B** When the Master Browser has com-piled the browse list, it distributes the list to the Backup Browsers.

5. **B** When a client requires access to the browse list, it obtains it from a Backup Browser so that the Master Browser does not become overloaded with requests from all the computers.

6. **C** The decision of which computers are Master and Backup Browsers is determined through browse elections.

7. **C** Windows NT computers are favored over Windows 95 computers to be brows-ers.

8. **A** A Windows 95 computer can be configured to maintain or to not maintain browse lists by configuring the File and Printer Sharing service.

9. **C**   Normally, you let the browser elections automatically determine which computers are the browsers.

10. **A**   If you do not want the potential performance load on the Windows 95 computer that can result from browsing, you can configure the computer to never be a browser.

11. **A**   To have Windows 95 automatically determine whether the computer is needed as a browse server, select Enabled: May Be Master.

12. **A**   To prevent the computer from maintaining browse lists for the network, select Enabled: May Not Be Master.

13. **D**   Selecting the Enabled: May Not Be Master option does not prevent the computer from browsing the network resources.

14. **B**   Select the Disabled option to prevent the computer from using the browse service.

15. **C**   To give the computer a higher weighting for the browse elections, select Enabled: Preferred Master.

3.3.13   Keywords

browse list   A dynamic list of resources available across the network

browsing   The ability to see other resources available across the network

client computer   A computer that can access the resource from a host

election   The process of determining roles each machine will play in the browsing process

host computer   The computer that has the resource you are trying to access

3.4   Practice Exam

1. Which utility can you use to transfer a file to a remote host using the connection-oriented services of TCP/IP?

A.   TFTP

B.   HTML

C.   FTP

D.   Telnet

2. Which remote execution utility encrypts user names and passwords before transmission?

A.   REXEC

B.   RSH

C.   Telnet

D.   No remote execution utility encrypts user names and passwords.

3. Which of the following statements about REXEC are incorrect?

A.   REXEC can start processes on Windows NT computers.

B.   REXEC does not require a user name or password.

C.   REXEC can establish terminal sessions on a remote host.

D.   REXEC does not encrypt passwords and user names during authentication.

4. Given a remote host system running TCP/IP and having an SMB server service, which of the following provides the most transparent network connectivity for file transfer?

A.   Using an NFS client on a Windows NT computer

B.   Using Microsoft networking functions on a Windows NT computer

C.   Using FTP to copy files from the remote host to your local computer

D.   Using Telnet to establish a remote terminal session with the remote host

5. Which of the following statements about Telnet are incorrect?

A. Telnet can be used to remotely administer Windows NT computers.

B. Telnet encrypts user names and passwords for enhanced security.

C. Telnet can be used to provide terminal emulation when connecting to remote host systems.

D. Telnet can be used to view HTML documents with graphical images.

6. A user on a Windows NT computer wishes to run an interactive text editor on a remote host computer. Which utilities would be suitable for use?

A. Telnet

B. FTP

C. REXEC

D. RSH

E. HTTP

7. Your network includes a number of NT Servers, Workstations, and TCP/IP host systems. To establish a secure terminal session to a host system from a Windows NT client, which of the following utilities would be adequate?

A. Telnet

B. FTP

C. TFTP

D. You need a third-party utility.

8. You have a client computer using TCP/IP on a local subnet, and you want to transfer a file to a remote system overseas. Which of the following utilities would provide the most reliable file transfer?

A. Telnet

B. TFTP

C. TCP

D. FTP

9. In a network that has a mixture of Windows NT and remote host systems, you want to administer remote host systems from a Windows NT computer by running remote system jobs. Which of the following utilities would allow you to execute a job on a remote system without requiring a logon password?

A. TFTP

B. REXEC

C. RSH

D. Telnet

10. Which of the following statements about FTP are incorrect?

A. FTP encrypts user names and passwords.

B. FTP does not encrypt user names and passwords, but uses MD5 and CHAP to encrypt data transfer.

C. FTP does not perform any encryption whatsoever.

D. FTP is connection oriented.

11. Your network provides a Web server to the Internet through a firewall. Which of the following protocols would usually *not* be available to a client on the other side of your firewall?

A. HTTP

B. FTP

C. TFTP

D. Telnet

12. HTML documents are transferred using the HTTP protocol. Of the following statements, which accurately describes the HTTP protocol?

A. HTTP uses the nonconnection-oriented communication features of TCP/IP for data transfer.

B. HTTP requires a user name and password for all HTML documents.

C. The HTTP protocol uses the connection-oriented communication features of TCP/IP for data transfer.

D. HTTP can be used only for text files.

13. Where can you enable a log that will record all the communications between the modem and the system?

A. In the Telephony API Advanced options

B. In the RAS Administration tool under Advanced options

C. In the Modem Advanced Properties

D. In the Port Settings Advanced dialog box

14. Can the Telephony API be set to turn off call waiting?

A. Yes

B. No

C. Only by the anonymous account

D. Only by the IUSR_computername account

15. What types of security does the RAS server accept?

A. Clear text

B. Kerberos

C. Shiva

D. Microsoft

16. How do you create a shortcut to a phonebook entry?

A. From the RAS administrator

B. From the Dial-Up Networking icon

C. From the RAS Administrator

D. Using drag and drop

17. What do you have to change in order to use a different DNS for a phonebook entry?

A. Change the Dial-Up Networking properties

B. Change the TCP/IP properties

C. Change the settings in RAS Administrator

D. Dial-Up Networking will always use the default

18. What condition must be met before you can select a frame size of 1,006 or 1,500 bytes?

A. User must use PPP

B. User must use PPTP

C. User must use SLIP

D. User must use CSLIP

19. If your dial-in server requires you to log on and the logon cannot be scripted, what can you do?

A. Use NT logon

B. Bring up a terminal window

C. Use Client Services for NetWare

D. You will not be able to dial in

20. How can the Dial-Up Networking Monitor be displayed?

A. As an icon on the Taskbar (beside the clock)

B. As a regular icon on the Taskbar

C. As a window

D. As an animated GIF

21. What does Autodial do for you?

A. Allows you to dial users from the User Manager

B. Allows you to connect to your ISP using Windows Messaging

C. Reconnects network resources when accessed

D. Will automatically dial at a given time

22. Which events can cause the Dial-Up Networking Monitor to make a sound?

    A. On connection

    B. On errors

    C. When the program starts

    D. When the program terminates

23. From where can you grant a user dial-in permissions?

    A. From the command prompt

    B. From the User Manager

    C. From the RAS Administrator

    D. From Server Manager

24. Where can you get the IP address for a client?

    A. From the client

    B. From the DHCP server

    C. From a scope of addresses on the RAS server

    D. From a WINS server

25. What is the purpose of PPTP?

    A. New form of the PPP protocol

    B. Allows tuned connections

    C. Allows secured connections across the Internet

    D. Allows the user to dial in using more than one line

26. How does PPTP show up in the Remote Access Admin?

    A. RPN

    B. VPN

    C. SPN

    D. DPN

27. What enables users to search for availability of network resources without knowing the exact location of the resources?

    A. Browsing through Network Neighborhood

    B. The Net Use command

    C. The Net View command

    D. The Net Search command

28. If a server name doesn't appear on the browse list, what are some possible causes?

    A. The server is on a different domain.

    B. The Master Browser hasn't updated the Backup Browser.

    C. The Master Browser hasn't updated the server.

    D. The Master Browser is currently processing other requests.

29. You are running a Windows NT 4.0 server that is currently the Primary Domain Controller, and you have a multiple domain network. What browser role/roles does the server have?

    A. Backup Browser

    B. Master Browser

    C. Potential Browser

    D. Domain Master Browser

30. Which one of these situations is true regarding Master Browser to Backup Browser synchronization?

    A. The Master Browser copies the updates to the Backup Browser.

    B. The Backup Browser copies the updates to the Master Browser.

    C. The Master Browser copies the updates from the Backup Browser.

    D. The Backup Browser copies the updates from the Master Browser.

3

31. If I have a domain set up with two Windows 95 computers, three Windows NT Workstation computers, three Windows NT Server computers, and four Windows for Workgroup computers, which is the third Backup Browser for this domain?

    A. Windows 95

    B. Windows for Workgroups

    C. Windows NT Workstation

    D. No computer can fill this role

32. Which of the following is in charge of continually updating the browse list and managing the database of network servers on domains and workgroups?

    A. Backup Browser

    B. Master Browser

    C. Potential Browser

    D. Browser Browser

33. Which of these statements is not true about the DomainAnnouncement packet?

    A. It has the name of a domain.

    B. It has the name of the Master Browser for that domain.

    C. It specifies whether the Master Browser is a Windows NT Server or Workstation.

    D. If it is a Windows NT Server, it specifies the version number of the server.

34. You have a network with five different subnets, each with its own Master Browser. The network administrator wants to be able to see resources of each subnet at the same time. Which process allows for this?

    A. Directed datagram

    B. Directed telegram

    C. Replication

    D. Synchronization

35. If a domain announcement is sent out to a domain and the domain does not respond, how long is it before the remote domain is removed from the browse list?

    A. Four announcement periods

    B. Three announcement periods

    C. Two announcement periods

    D. Five announcement periods

36. You have a network with three subnets: subnet A, subnet B, and subnet C. What happens if the Domain Master Browser on subnet A goes down?

    A. Browsing is restricted to each subnet.

    B. Subnet B can see C but not A.

    C. Subnet C can see B but not A.

    D. All subnets continue browsing normally.

37. How is it possible to browse across routers without the use of WINS, DNS, HOSTS, or LMHOSTS?

    A. You can browse using Network Neighborhood.

    B. You can use an IP-enabled router.

    C. You can use a NetBIOS-enabled router.

    D. You can manually update the ARP cache file.

38. The LMHOSTS file is mainly used on a network with non-WINS clients specifically for the job of _____.

    A. Resolving NetBIOS names to MAC-level address

    B. Resolving a NetBIOS name to an IP address

    C. Resolving an IP address to Internet names

    D. Routing BOOTP information

39. What does the #PRE statement in an LMHOSTS file do?

    A. Prepares a name to load into memory

    B. Preloads an entry into cache

    C. Permanently caches a preloaded file

    D. Identifies comment lines

40. When should you put the other Master Browsers' addresses into the LMHOSTS file as well as the Domain Master Browser?

    A. If the Domain Master Browser is busy, you have to change your LMHOSTS file to access the new Domain Master Browser.

    B. If the Domain Master Browser goes down, you do not have to change your LMHOSTS file to access the new Domain Master Browser.

    C. If your LMHOSTS file is unavailable, you have to update your Domain Master Browser list.

    D. When your server has more free space than others.

41. WINS can take the place of an LMHOSTS file over a network by _____ updating across routers.

    A. Dynamically

    B. Statically

    C. Manually

    D. Not

42. Which two additional Windows NT network services initiate a broadcast in a domain, but not across routers?

    A. Logging in and passwords; PDC to PDC replication

    B. Directory replication and authentication

    C. Logging in and passwords; PDC to BDC replication

    D. Remote execution and file transfer utility usage

3.4.1 Answers and Explanations: Practice Exam

1. **C** FTP is used to transfer a file to a remote host using the connection-oriented services of TCP/IP.

2. **D** None of the remote execution utilities encrypt user names or passwords.

3. **A, B, C** REXEC does not encrypt passwords and user names during authentication. All other statements are false.

4. **B** Using Microsoft networking functions on a Windows NT computer provides the most transparent network connectivity of the choices listed.

5. **A, B, D** Telnet can be used to provide terminal emulation when connecting to remote host systems. All other statements given are false.

6. **A, D** Both Telnet and RSH enable a user to run an interactive text editor on a remote host computer.

7. **D** None of the utilities included with NT would allow for a secure terminal session.

8. **D** FTP would provide the most reliable file transfer of the choices listed.

9. **C** The RSH utility will allow you to execute a job on a remote system without requiring a password.

10. **A, B** FTP does not perform encryption, and it is connection oriented.

11. **D** Telnet will not be available through a firewall.

12. **C** HTTP is connection oriented and used for data transfer.

13. **C** The Modem Advanced Properties enable logging.

14. **A** The Telephony API can be set to turn off call waiting.

15. **A, D** Clear text and Microsoft represent two types of authentication security that a RAS server accepts.

16. **B** Shortcuts to a phonebook entry can be created from the Dial-Up Networking icon.

17. **A** Changing the Dial-Up Networking properties enables you to use a different DNS for a phonebook entry.

18. **C** You must use SLIP before you can select a frame size of 1,006 or 1,500 bytes.

19. **B** If your dial-in server requires you to log on and the logon cannot be scripted, you must bring up a terminal window.

20. **A, B, C** The Dial-Up Networking monitor can be displayed as an icon on the Taskbar, as a regular icon, or as a window.

21. **C** Autodial reconnects network resources when accessed.

22. **A, B** The Dial-Up Networking Monitor will make a sound on connection and when errors occur.

23. **B, C** User dial-in permission can be configured from the User Manager or from the RAS Administrator.

24. **A, B, C** An IP address can come from the client, a DHCP server, or the scope of addresses on a RAS server.

25. **C** PPTP allows secured connections across the Internet.

26. **B** PPTP shows up in the Remote Access Administrator as VPN.

27. **A** Browsing through the Network Neighborhood allows users to search for available resources without specifying their exact location.

28. **B** The most likely cause of the server name not appearing on the browse list is that the Master Browser has not updated the Backup Browser.

29. **B, D** The Primary Domain Controller can be a Master Browser or Domain Master Browser.

30. **D** The Backup Browser copies the updates from the master.

31. **C** A Windows NT Workstation is the most likely choice for the third Backup Browser in the situation given.

32. **B** The Master Browser is in charge of continually updating the browse list.

33. **D** The DomainAnnouncement packet carries the name of a domain, the name of the Master Browser, and whether the Master Browser is a server or workstation.

34. **A** A directed datagram enables you to see resources for each subnet at the same time.

35. **B** A remote domain is removed from the browse list after not responding to an initial announcement after three announcement periods (which occur within 45 minutes).

36. **A** If a domain's Master Browser goes down, browsing is restricted to each subnet.

37. **C** You can use a NetBIOS-enabled router to browse across routers.

38. **B** The LMHOSTS file resolves IP address to NetBIOS names.

39. **B** The #PRE statement in the LMHOSTS file preloads an entry into cache.

40. **B** Other Master Browsers' domains should be placed in the LMHOSTS file to access new Domain Master Browsers in case your Domain Master Browser goes down.

41. **A** WINS updates dynamically, whereas LMHOSTS is static.

42. **C** Broadcasts can be initiated by users logging in, as well as by PDC to BDC replication.

## CHAPTER 4

Monitoring and Optimization

This chapter helps you prepare for the exam by covering the following objective:

- Given a scenario, identify which tool to use to monitor TCP/IP traffic.

4.1 Utilities Used to Monitor TCP/IP Traffic

Optimization changes are made primarily through the Registry Editor (`Regedt32.exe`), while two other tools are used primarily for monitoring TCP/IP traffic:

- Performance Monitor
- Network Monitor

There are a number of other utilities that do not perform actual monitoring but can be used to gather configuration and statistical information. Most of these utilities are discussed in other sections, but you must know what they offer when compared to Performance Monitor and Network Monitor, and when you would use each one. For that purpose, a short description of each is also included in this chapter.

4.1.1 Performance Monitor

The Performance Monitor is NT's all-around tool for monitoring a network using statistical measurements called *counters*. It has the capability to collect data on both hardware and software components, called *objects*, and its primary purpose is to establish a baseline from which everything can be judged. It offers the ability to check/monitor/identify the following:

- The demand for resources
- Bottlenecks in performance
- The behavior of individual processes

- The performance of remote systems
- The generation of alerts to exception conditions
- The exportation of data for analysis

Every object has a number of counters, and you should be familiar with the ones for the Paging File object—%Usage and %Usage Peak—which will determine whether a paging file is reaching its maximum size.

> To get numerical statistics, use the Report (columnar) view. To see how counters change over a period of time, use the log feature. To spot abnormalities that occur in data over a period of time, use the Chart view.

To monitor a number of servers and be alerted if a counter exceeds a specified number, create one Performance Monitor alert for each server on your workstation. Enter your user name in the Net Name field on the Alert Options dialog box (below the Send Network Message check box) and you will be alerted when the alert conditions arise. Only one name can be placed here; that name can be of a user or group, but cannot be multiple users or groups.

If you are monitoring a number of performance counters and that monitoring is slowing down other operations on your workstation, the best remedy is to increase the monitoring interval or perform the monitoring from a separate station on the network.

To tune or optimize Windows NT, you will need to be able to look at the performance of the server on many different levels.

> There are two important pieces of knowledge to remember: You *must* install the Network Monitor Agent to be able to see several of the network performance counters, and SNMP service *must* be installed in order to gather TCP/IP statistics.

4.1.2   Network Monitor

Network Monitor is a Windows tool that enables you to see network traffic that is sent or received by a Windows NT computer. Network Monitor is included with Windows NT 4.0, but must be installed to be active.

To install Network Monitor, select Control Panel | Network, and then add the Network Monitor Tools and Agent from the Services tab. The version of Network Monitor that comes with Windows NT 4.0 is a simple version; it captures traffic only for the local machines (incoming and outgoing traffic).

Microsoft's System Management Server, a network management product, comes with a more complete version of Network Monitor that enables you to capture packets on the local machine for the entire local network segment. Both versions (the NT and SMS versions) allow you to capture the packets that are flowing into and out of your computer. The full version that comes with SMS will also allow you extra functionality such as the ability to capture all packets on the local network or on remote networks, to edit those packets, and to derive statistics about protocols and users on the network.

There are two pieces to the Network Monitor—the Agent that will capture the data, and the Monitor Tool, which can be used to view the data. You also can filter out traffic that isn't important to the troubleshooting process.

The Network Monitor can be used to diagnose more complex connectivity issues by allowing you to see the actual packets that are flowing on the network, verifying which steps are being used to resolve names or which port numbers are being used to connect.

To hammer home exam fodder at the risk of redundancy:

Filters allow you to limit what you are viewing and to keep the data from being overwhelming. The most commonly used filters are INCLUDE and EXCLUDE, which capture or avoid capturing (respectively) specific data. The Network Monitor included with Windows NT Server can monitor only the specific system on which it is installed, unlike the Network Monitor in SMS, which can monitor other systems on the network.

4

4.1.3   Other Utilities

You can use a number of tools to help troubleshoot and isolate the source of TCP/IP problems. Each tool gives you a different view of the process used to resolve an IP address to a hardware address, and then route the IP packet to the appropriate destination. As a general rule of thumb, however, the following items apply to the tools listed in this section:

- If TCP/IP cannot communicate from a Microsoft host to a remote host system, the utilities discussed in this chapter will not work correctly.

- If the systems are on different subnets and cannot communicate, remember that TCP/IP requires routing to communicate between subnets.

- If the systems were previously able to communicate but can no longer do so, suspect either your router(s) or changes in software configuration.

- Utilities that require user names and passwords on the remote host need a user account on the remote system. If you have an account on a Windows NT system, the remote host system does not know or care. Trust relationships are not the same as achieving connectivity.

- On Windows NT computers, never forget to consult the Event Viewer. Messages that are out of the ordinary often provide valuable clues about the cause of the problem.

ARP

After the name has been resolved to an IP address, you computer must resolve the IP address to a MAC address. This is handled by the Address Resolution Protocol (ARP).

ARP, as a utility, can be used to see the entries in the address resolution table, which maps network card addresses (MAC addresses) to IP addresses. You can check whether the IP addresses you believe should be in the table are there and whether they are mapped to the correct computers. You do not usually know the MAC addresses of the hosts on your network. However, if you cannot contact a host, or if a connection is made to an unexpected host, you can check this table with the arp command to begin isolating which host is actually assigned an IP address.

The ARP utility enables you to view the addresses that have been resolved with the following syntax options:

```
C:\>arp /?Displays and modifies the IP-to-physical address
translation tables used by address resolution protocol (ARP).

ARP -s inet_addr eth_addr [if_addr]
ARP -d inet_addr [if_addr]
ARP -a [inet_addr] [-N if_addr]


    -a          Displays current ARP entries by interrogating the
                current protocol data. If inet_addr is specified,
                the IP and physical addresses for only the specified
                computer are displayed. If more than one network
                interface uses ARP, entries for each ARP table are
                displayed.
    -g          Same as -a.
    inet_addr   Specifies an Internet address.
    -N if_addr  Displays the ARP entries for the network interface
                specified by if_addr.
    -d          Deletes the host specified by inet_addr.
    -s          Adds the host and associates the Internet address
                inet_addr with the physical address eth_addr. The
                physical address is given as 6 hexadecimal bytes
                separated by hyphens. The entry is permanent.
    eth_addr    Specifies a physical address.
    if_addr     If present, this specifies the Internet address of the
                interface whose address translation table should be
                modified. If not present, the first applicable
                interface will be used.
```

Event Log

The Event Log in Windows NT is used to track events and errors. The System Event Log in NT is where all critical system messages are stored, and not just those related to TCP/IP.

IPCONFIG

One of the key areas that causes problems with TCP/IP is configuration. Windows NT provides a utility that will allow you to view and verify the configuration of a workstation. The following listing provides a summary of the usage of IPCONFIG.

```
C:\>ipconfig /?Win dows NT IP Configurationusage: ipconfig
[/? ¦ /all ¦ /release [adapter] ¦ /renew [adapter]]
      /?       Display this help message.
      /all     Display full configuration information.
      /release Release the IP address for the specified adapter.
      /renew   Renew the IP address for the specified adapter.
```

The default is to display only the IP address, subnet mask, and default gateway for each adapter bound to TCP/IP.

If no adapter name is specified for /release and /renew, the IP address leases for all adapters bound to TCP/IP will be released or renewed.

NBTSTAT

NBTSTAT is a command-line utility that enables you to check the resolution of NetBIOS names to TCP/IP addresses. With NBTSTAT, you can check the status of current NetBIOS sessions. You also can add entries to the NetBIOS name cache from the LMHOSTS file or check your registered NetBIOS name and the NetBIOS scope assigned to your computer, if any.

> **Whereas NETSTAT deals with all the connections that your system has with other computers, NBTSTAT deals with only the NetBIOS connections.**

NBTSTAT also allows you to verify that name resolution is taking place by providing a method of viewing the name cache. A number of parameters can be used with the utility, as shown in the following code list.

```
C:\>nbtstat /?
Displays protocol statistics and current TCP/IP connections using NBT
(NetBIOS over TCP/IP).
NBTSTAT [-a RemoteName] [-A IP address] [-c] [-n]
        [-r] [-R] [-s] [-S] [interval] ]
   -a   (adapter status) Lists the remote machine's name table given its
                         name
   -A   (Adapter status) Lists the remote machine's name table given its
                         IP address.
   -c   (cache)          Lists the remote name cache including the IP
                         addresses
   -n   (names)          Lists local NetBIOS names.
   -r   (resolved)       Lists names resolved by broadcast and via WINS
   -R   (Reload)         Purges and reloads the remote cache name table
   -S   (Sessions)       Lists sessions table with the destination IP
                         addresses
   -s   (sessions)       Lists sessions table converting destination IP
                         addresses to host names via the hosts file.

   RemoteName   Remote host machine name.
   IP address   Dotted decimal representation of the IP address.
```

```
    interval        Redisplays selected statistics, pausing interval seconds
                    between each display. Press Ctrl+C to stop redisplaying
                    statistics.
```

NETSTAT

NETSTAT is a command-line utility that enables you to check the status of current IP connections. Executing NETSTAT without switches displays protocol statistics and current TCP/IP connections.

After you have determined that your base-level communications are working, you will need to verify the services on your system. This involves looking at the services that are listening for incoming traffic and/or verifying that you are creating a session with a remote station. The netstat command will allow you to do this.

A number of parameters can be used with the utility, as shown in the following code list.

```
    C:\>netstat /?

    Displays protocol statistics and current TCP/IP network connections.

    NETSTAT [-a] [-e] [-n] [-s] [-p proto] [-r] [interval]
      -a              Displays all connections and listening ports.
                      (Server-side connections are normally not shown.)
      -e              Displays Ethernet statistics. This may be combined
                      with the -s option.
      -n              Displays addresses and port numbers in numerical form.
      -p proto        Shows connections for the protocol specified by proto;
                      proto may be tcp or udp. If used with the -s option
                      to display per-protocol statistics, proto may be tcp,
                      udp, or ip.
      -r              Displays the contents of the routing table.
      -s              Displays per-protocol statistics. By default,
                      statistics are shown for TCP, UDP and IP; the -p
                      option may be used to specify a subset of the default.
    interval          Redisplays selected statistics, pausing interval seconds
                      between each display. Press CTRL+C to stop redisplaying
                      statistics. If omitted, netstat will print the current
                      configuration information once.
```

NSLOOKUP

NSLOOKUP is a command-line utility that enables you to verify entries on a DNS server. You can use NSLOOKUP in two modes: interactive and noninteractive. In interactive mode, you start a session with the DNS server in which you can make several requests. In noninteractive mode, you specify a command that makes a single query of the DNS server. If you want to make another query, you must type another noninteractive command.

> One of the key issues in using TCP/IP is the capability to resolve a host name to an IP address—an action usually performed by a DNS server.

A number of parameters can be used with the utility, as shown in the following code list:

```
Usage:   nslookup [-opt ...]
# interactive mode using default server
nslookup [-opt ...] - server
# interactive mode using 'server'
nslookup [-opt ...] host
# just look up 'host' using default server
nslookup [-opt ...] host server
# just look up 'host' using 'server'
```

PING

The ping command is one of the most useful commands in the TCP/IP protocol. It sends a series of packets to another system, which in turn sends back a response. This utility can be extremely useful in troubleshooting problems with remote hosts.

The PING utility is used as a command-line program, and accepts the following parameters:

```
Usage: ping [-t] [-a] [-n count] [-l size] [-f] [-i TTL] [-v TOS]
            [-r count] [-s count] [[-j host-list] ¦ [-k host-list]]
            [-w timeout] destination-list
Options:
    -t              Pings the specified host until interrupted
    -a              Resolves addresses to host names
    -n count        Number of echo requests to send
    -l size         Sends buffer size
    -f              Sets Don't Fragment flag in packet
    -i TTL          Time to Live
    -v TOS          Type of Service
    -r count        Records route for count hops
    -s count        Time stamp for count hops
    -j host-list    Loose source route along host-list
    -k host-list    Strict source route along host-list
    -w timeout      Time-out in milliseconds to wait for each reply
```

The ping command indicates whether the host can be reached, and how long it took for the host to send a return packet. On a local area network, the time is indicated as less than 10 milliseconds; across wide area network links, this value can be much greater.

ROUTE

ROUTE is a command-line utility that enables you to see and add entries to the local routing table. It is sometimes necessary to check how a system will route packets on the network. Normally, your system will simply send all packets to the default gateway, but in cases where you are having problems communicating with a group of computers, the ROUTE command might provide an answer.

A number of parameters can be used with the utility, as shown in the following code list.

```
C:\>route
Manipulates network routing tables.
ROUTE [-f] [command [destination] [MASK netmask] [gateway]
[METRIC metric]]
   -f          Clears the routing tables of all gateway entries.
               If this is used in conjunction with one of the commands,
               the tables are cleared prior to running the command.
   -p          When used with the ADD command, this parameter makes a route
               persistent across boots of the system. By default, routes are
               not preserved when the system is restarted. When used with
               the PRINT command, this parameter displays the list of
               registered persistent routes. Ignored for all other commands,
               which always affect the appropriate persistent routes.

   command     Specifies one of four commands
                  PRINT     Prints a route
                  ADD       Adds a route
                  DELETE    Deletes a route
                  CHANGE    Modifies an existing route

   destination Specifies the host.

   MASK        If the MASK keyword is present, the next parameter is
               interpreted as the netmask parameter.

   netmask     If provided, this parameter specifies a subnet mask value to
               be associated with this route entry.  If not specified, it
               defaults to 255.255.255.255.

   gateway     Specifies gateway.

   METRIC      Specifies the metric/cost for the destination.
```

All symbolic names used for destination are looked up in the network database file NETWORKS. The symbolic names for gateway are looked up in the host name database file HOSTS.

If the command is PRINT or DELETE, wildcards may be used for the destination and gateway, or the gateway argument may be omitted.

SNMP

The SNMP protocol enables TCP/IP to export information to troubleshooting tools such as Performance Monitor or to other third-party tools. By itself, SNMP does not report any troubleshooting information. If you are using tools that depend on SNMP, however, you cannot see all the information available from these tools until you install SNMP. To install SNMP, select Control Panel | Network, and then add SNMP from the Services tab.

The SNMP service is an additional component of Windows NT TCP/IP software. It includes the four supported MIBs; each is a dynamic-link library and can be loaded and unloaded as needed. It provides SNMP agent services to any TCP/IP host running SNMP management software. It also performs the following:

- Reports specific happenings, such as traps, to the management systems

- Responds to requests for information from multiple hosts

- Can be set up on any system running Windows NT and TCP/IP

- Sets up special counters in Performance Monitor that can be used to monitor the TCP/IP performance related to SNMP

- Uses host names and IP addresses to recognize which hosts it receives, and requests information

The SNMP service can be installed for the following reasons:

- You want to monitor TCP/IP with Performance Monitor.

- You want to monitor a Windows NT–based system with a third-party application.

- You want to set up your computer as an SNMP agent.

TRACERT

TRACERT is a command-line utility that enables you to verify the route to a remote host. Execute `tracert` *hostname*, where *hostname* is the computer name or IP address of the computer whose route you want to trace. TRACERT will return the different IP addresses the packet was routed through to reach the final destination. The results also include the number of hops needed to reach the destination. Execute TRACERT without any options to see a help file that describes all the TRACERT switches.

The TRACERT utility determines the intermediary steps involved in communicating with another IP host. It provides a road map of all the routing an IP packet takes to get from host A to host B.

A number of parameters can be used with the utility, as shown in the following code list.

```
Usage: tracert [-d] [-h maximum_hops] [-j host-list] [-w timeout]
target_name
Options:
    -d                 Does not resolve addresses to host names
    -h maximum_hops    Maximum number of hops to search for target
    -j host-list       Loose source route along host-list
    -w timeout         Wait time-out milliseconds for each reply
```

As with the `ping` command, `tracert` returns the amount of time required for each routing hop.

4.2 Exercises

4.2.1 Excercise: Exploring Performance Monitor Counters

After you have installed SNMP, you might want to look at the Performance Monitor utility and notice the TCP/IP objects available for monitoring. To do this, perform the following steps:

1. Select Start | Programs | Administrative Tools and select Performance Monitor.

2. Click the Edit menu and click Add to Chart.

3. Look at the list of available TCP/IP objects.

A sample exercise monitoring SNMP using one of the TCP/IP related objects follows:

1. Follow the steps in the previous exercise.

2. Select the ICMP object from the list.

3. Click Messages/sec in the counter box.

4. Set Scale to 1 and click Add.

5. Select another object IP.

6. From the Counter list, click Datagrams sent/sec.

7. Set Scale to 1 and click Add.

8. Select Done.

9. Make sure you are using the Chart view.

10. Change Vertical Maximum to 10 and click OK.

11. Go to a command prompt and ping another computer.

12. Go back to Performance Monitor and notice what happened.

13. PING sends three echo requests and receives three echo replies for a total of six IP datagrams.

4.2.2 Practice Problems

1. You are using Performance Monitor, but very few TCP/IP statistics are available. How can you increase the number of TCP/IP objects and counters to monitor?

   A. Install a promiscuous mode adapter card.

   B. Configure the correct default gateway in Performance Monitor.

   C. Bind TCP/IP to the Monitor service.

   D. Install the SNMP service.

2. TCP/IP is not working. You recall that when Windows NT first booted, the message A Dependency Service Failed to Start appeared. What is a possible cause of the problem?

   A. The SNMP service is not installed.

   B. The network card is not configured correctly.

   C. The secondary WINS server is down.

   D. The PDC of your domain is down.

3. On an NT computer, where does TCP/IP display its error messages?

   A. In the TCP/IP log file

   B. In the SNMP log file

   C. In the System Log

   D. In the TCP.ERR file

4. Referring to question #3, what tool is used to view these errors?

   A. Network Monitor

   B. Performance Monitor

   C. Event Viewer

   D. ARP

5. To see the majority of networking performance counters in Performance Monitor, what must be installed?

   A. NetBEUI

   B. Network Monitor Agent

   C. Network Monitor Server

   D. TCP/IP

6. Which protocol handles the IP address to MAC address resolution?

    A. WINS

    B. ARP

    C. DHCP

    D. NBTSTAT

7. Executing NETSTAT with what parameter will display all connections and listening ports, even those ports not currently involved in a connection?

    A. -a

    B. -s

    C. -p

    D. -?

8. Optimization changes are made primarily through:

    A. Performance Monitor

    B. Network Monitor

    C. ARP

    D. Regedt32.exe

9. Performance Monitor uses statistical measurements called:

    A. counters

    B. baselines

    C. benchmarks

    D. objects

10. In addition to gathering information, which utility can also be used to release an IP address?

    A. Performance Monitor

    B. IPCONFIG

    C. PING

    D. ARP

4.2.3 Practice Problems: Answers and Explanations

1. **D** The SNMP service must be installed in order to collect TCP/IP statistics.

2. **B** If the network card is not properly configured, the message A Dependency Service Failed to Start will most likely appear.

3. **C** TCP/IP displays its error messages in the System Log.

4. **C** The Event Viewer is used to view the System Log.

5. **B** The Network Monitor Agent must be installed to be able to see most of the network performance counters.

6. **B** ARP—the Address Resolution Protocol—resolves IP addresses to MAC addresses.

7. **A** NETSTAT -a will display all connections and listening ports, even those ports not currently involved in a connection.

8. **D** Optimization changes are made primarily through the Registry Editor (Regedt32.exe).

9. **A** Performance Monitor uses statistical measurements called counters.

10. **B** In addition to gathering information, IPCONFIG can also be used to release an IP address.

4.2.4 Keywords

ARP Address Resolution Protocol

baseline A starting point

counters Statistical measurements on objects used by Performance Monitor

objects Hardware and software components monitored with Performance Monitor

SNMP Simple Network Management Protocol

4

## CHAPTER 5

Troubleshooting

This chapter helps you prepare for the exam by covering the following objectives:

- Diagnose and resolve IP addressing problems.

- Use Microsoft TCP/IP utilities to diagnose configuration problems.

- Identify which Microsoft TCP/IP utility to use to diagnose IP configuration problems.

- Diagnose and resolve name resolution problems.

5.1 Diagnosing and Resolving IP Addressing Problems

Three main parameters specify how TCP/IP is configured: the IP address, the subnet mask, and the default gateway, which is the address of the router. These parameters are configured through the Protocols tab of the Network Properties dialog box. Although you may receive an IP address from a Dynamic Host Configuration Protocol (DHCP) server, for the moment this discussion focuses on parameters that are manually configured. DHCP-related issues are discussed later in the chapter in the section "DHCP Client Configuration Problems."

If these three TCP/IP parameters are not configured correctly, you cannot connect with TCP/IP. An incorrect configuration can result from typos; if you type the wrong IP address, subnet mask, or default gateway, you may not connect properly—or you many not be able to connect at all. To illustrate, if you dial the wrong number when making a telephone call, you can't reach the party you're calling. If you read the wrong phone number out of the phone book, you won't ever make a correct call, even if you dial the number you think is correct time and time again.

Regardless of whether the TCP/IP configuration parameters are wrong because of a typo or a mistaken number, the incorrect parameters affect communications. Different types of problems occur when either of these parameters has a configuration error.

5.1.2 IP Address Configuration Problems

An incorrect TCP/IP address will almost always cause problems. However, if you configure an IP address that is on the correct subnet but uses the wrong host ID and is not a duplicate, the client may be able to communicate just fine. On the other hand, if the correct IP address has been entered in a static file or database that resolves host names to IP addresses, such as an LMHOSTS file or a domain name server (DNS) database file, some communication problems can occur. Typically, therefore, an incorrect IP address does cause problems.

Each TCP/IP parameter reacts differently if configured incorrectly. The following sections examine the effects that each TCP/IP parameter can have on IP communications.

IP Address

A TCP/IP address has two and sometimes three components that uniquely identify the computer the address is assigned to. At the very least, the IP address specifies the network address and host address of the computer. Also, if you are *subnetting* (using part of the host address to specify a subnet address), the third part of the address specifies the subnet address of the host.

You're likely to encounter the following problems with IP addresses:

- If the incorrect host (for example, 143.168.3.9) sends a message to a local client (for example, 133.168.3.20), the TCP/IP configuration of the sending host indicates this is a remote address because it doesn't match the network address of the host initiating the communication. The packet won't ever reach the local client, because the address 133.168.3.20 is interpreted as a remote address.

- If a local client (133.168.3.6) sends a message to the incorrect host (143.168.3.9), the message never reaches its intended destination. The message is either routed (if the local client sends the message to the IP address as written) or it stays on the local subnet (if the local client sends it to what should have been the address, 133.168.3.9).

  - If the message is routed, the incorrect client does not receive the message because it is on the same segment of the network as the local client.

  - If the message is not routed, the message still does not reach the incorrect client because the IP address for the destination host (133.168.3.9) does not match the address as configured on the incorrect client (143.168.3.9).

Figure 5.1 gives an example of an incorrect IP address. In this case, a class A address is used, 33.x.x.x. The subnet mask (255.255.0.0) indicates the second octet is also being used to create subnets. In this case, even though the client has the same network address as the other clients on the same subnet, the client has a different subnet number because the address was typed incorrectly. The incorrect address specifies the wrong subnet ID. The client 33.5.8.4 is on subnet 5, whereas the other clients on the subnet have the address 33.4.x.x. If the client 33.5.8.4. tries to contact other clients on the same subnet, the message is routed because the subnet ID doesn't match the subnet number of the source host. If the client 33.5.8.4 tries to send a message to a remote host, the message is routed; however, the message isn't returned to the client, because the router doesn't handle subnet 5, only subnet 4.

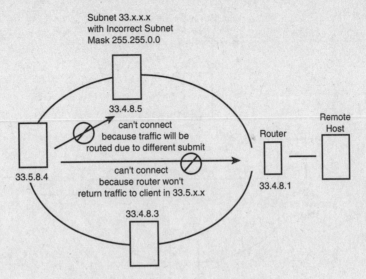

Figure 5.1. An incorrect subnet address.

If a local client tries to send a message to 33.5.8.4, the message doesn't reach the client. If the local client uses the address as configured, the message is routed, which isn't the correct solution, because the destination host is local. If the local client sends the message to what should have been the IP address, 33.5.8.4 doesn't receive the message, because the IP address isn't configured correctly.

The final component of an IP address that can cause communication problems is the host address. An incorrect host address may not always cause a problem, however. In Figure 5.2, a local client has the wrong IP address, but only the host address portion of the address is wrong. The network address and subnet match the rest of the clients on the subnet. In this case, if a client sends a message to the client with the incorrect address, the message still reaches the client. However, if someone tries to contact the client with what should have been the address, he doesn't contact the client. In fact, he could contact another host that ended up with the address that was supposed to be given to the original host. If the original host ends up with the same IP address as another host through the configuration error, the first client to boot works, but the second client to boot may note the address conflict and not load the TCP/IP stack at all. In this case, the second client to boot isn't able to make any TCP/IP communications.

Another problem occurs when the correct address was registered in static files, such as an LMHOSTS file or a DNS database, but an incorrect address is entered elsewhere. In this case, no one can communicate with this client by name because the name resolution for this host always returns the correct address, which can't be used to contact the host, because the address has been typed incorrectly. Basically, the problems you encounter with an incorrect host address are intermittent. However, if the host was configured to be a WINS client, the host name is registered along with the incorrect address. Another WINS client trying to connect with this computer receives an accurate mapping for the host name.

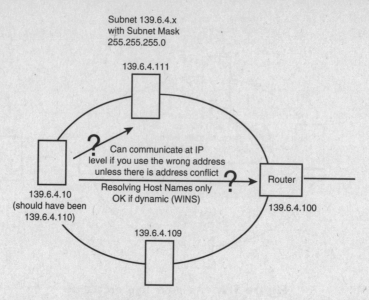

Figure 5.2.   Incorrect host address.

Subnet Mask

The subnet mask states which portion of the IP address specifies the network address and which portion of the address specifies the host address. The subnet mask also can be used to take part of what would have been the host address and use it to further divide the network into subnets. If the subnet mask is not configured correctly, your clients may not be able to communicate at all, or you may see partial communication problems.

Figure 5.3 shows a subnet on a TCP/IP network. The network uses a class B network address of 138.13.*x*.*x*. However, the third octet is used in this case for subnetting, so all the clients in the figure should be on subnet 4, as indicated by the common addresses 138.13.4.*x*. Unfortunately, the subnet mask entered for one client is 255.255.0.0. When this client tries to communicate with other hosts on the same subnet, it should be able to contact them because the subnet mask indicates they are on the same subnet, which is correct.

If the client tries to contact a host on another subnet, however, such as 138.13.3.*x*, the client fails. In this case, the subnet mask still interprets the destination host to be on the same subnet, and the message is never routed. Because the destination host is on another subnet, the message never reaches the intended destination. The subnet mask is used to determine routing for outgoing communications, so the client with the incorrect subnet mask can receive incoming messages. However, when the client tries to return communications, the message isn't routed if the source host is on the same network but on a different subnet. Consequently, the client really can establish communications with only one side of the conversation. Contact with hosts outside the local network still works because those contacts are routed.

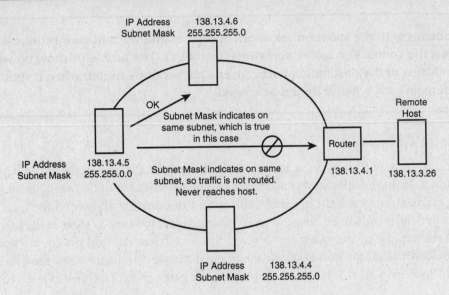

Figure 5.3.   Incorrect subnet mask—missing third octet.

Figure 5.4 shows a subnet mask that masks too many bits. In this case, the subnet mask is
`255.255.255.0`. However, the network designers had intended the subnet mask to be
`255.255.240.0`, with four bits of the third octet used for the subnet and four bits as part of the
host address. If the incorrect client tries to send a message to a local host and the third octet is the
same, the message is not routed and thus reaches the local client. However, if the local client has
an address that differs in the last four bits of the third octet, the message is routed and never
reaches its destination. If the incorrect client tries to send a message to another client on another
subnet, the message is routed because the third octet is different. The whole problem can be
summed up by the incorrect subnet mask in the third octet.

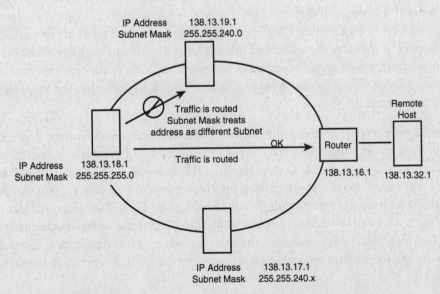

Figure 5.4.   Incorrect subnet mask—incorrect third octet.

> Problems with the subnet mask might appear as intermittent connections. Some-
> times the connection works, sometimes it doesn't. The problems show up when the
> IP address of the destination host causes a packet to be routed when it shouldn't or
> to remain local when it should be routed.

Default Gateway

The default gateway address is the address of the router, the gateway to the world beyond the local subnet. If the default gateway address is wrong, the client with the wrong default gateway address can contact local hosts but is not able to communicate at all beyond the local subnet. It is also possible for the incorrect client to receive a message. However, as soon as the incorrect client attempts to respond to the incoming message, the default gateway address doesn't work and the message doesn't reach the host that sent the original message. In many cases, the default gateway will not show up in an IPCONFIG /all response if the gateway has not been entered correctly.

5.1.3   DHCP Client Configuration Problems

All the TCP/IP parameters mentioned previously can cause communication problems if they are not configured correctly. Using a DHCP server can greatly reduce these configuration problems. If the DHCP scope is set up properly, without any typos or other configuration errors, DHCP clients shouldn't have any configuration problems. Although you can't completely eliminate human error, using DHCP should reduce the points of potential errors to just the DHCP servers, rather than every client on the network.

Even when no configuration problems occur with DHCP addresses, DHCP clients can get a duplicate IP address from a DHCP server. If you have multiple DHCP servers in your environment, you should have scopes on each DCHP server for different subnets. Usually you have scopes with a larger number of addresses for the local subnet where the DHCP server is located and smaller scopes for other subnets. Creating multiple scopes on one server provides backup for giving clients IP addresses. If the server on the local scope is busy or down, the client can still receive an address from a remote DHCP server. When the router forwards this DCHP request to another subnet, it includes the address of the subnet it came from so that the remote DHCP server knows from which scope of addresses to lease an address to the remote client. Using this type of redundancy, however, can cause problems if you don't configure the scopes on all the DHCP servers correctly.

The most important part of the configuration is to make sure you don't have duplicate addresses in the different scopes. On one server, for example, you could have a scope in the range 131.107.2.100 to 131.107.2.170. On the remote DHCP server, you could have a scope of 131.107.2.171 to 131.107.2.200. By setting up the scopes without overlap, you should not have any problems with clients receiving duplicate IP addresses. DHCP servers do not communicate with each other, so one server does not know anything about the addresses the other server has leased. Therefore, you must ensure that the servers never give out duplicate information by making sure the scopes for one subnet on all the different DHCP servers have unique IP addresses.

Another common problem with having multiple scopes on one server is entering the configuration parameters correctly. For example, if you enter the default gateway as 131.107.3.1 (instead of 131.107.2.1) for the scope 131.107.2.100 to 131.107.2.170, the clients receiving these addresses will not be able to communicate beyond the local subnet, because they have the wrong router address. With one scope on a DCHP server, you are usually quite sure of what all the configuration parameters should be. With multiple scopes on one server, however, you can easily get confused about which scope you are editing and what the parameters should be for that scope. To avoid this type of problem, check each scope's parameters very carefully to make sure the parameters match the address of the scope, not the subnet where the DHCP server is located.

Also, if the client doesn't receive an address because the server is down or doesn't respond in a timely manner, the client is not able to contact anyone. Without an IP address, the IP stack does not initialize, and the client can't communicate at all with TCP/IP.

5.1.4   Exercises

Exercise 1: Examine Your Windows 95 TCP/IP Configuration

To examine your TCP/IP configuration information on a Windows 95 system, implement the following steps:

1. Choose Run from the Start menu.

2. Type WINIPCFG.

3. Select the More Info >> button.

4. Note the Host and Adapter information that appears.

Exercise 2: Examine Your Windows NT TCP/IP Configuration

To examine your TCP/IP configuration information on a Windows NT Workstation or Server system that is manually configured, perform the following steps:

1. Right-click Network Neighborhood and choose Properties.

2. Select the Protocols tab.

3. Highlight TCP/IP and choose Properties.

4. Note the configuration information that appears.

5.1.5   Practice Problems

1. Three main parameters that specify how TCP/IP is configured are

   A. The IP address

   B. The TCP address

   C. The subnet mask

   D. The default gateway

2. Which of the following is the address of the router?

   A. The IP address

   B. The TCP address

   C. The subnet mask

   D. The default gateway

3. The three parameters discussed in question 1 are configured through which tab of the Network Properties dialog box?

    A. Services

    B. Adapters

    C. Protocols

    D. Address

4. Which of the following specifies the network address and host address of the computer?

    A. The IP address

    B. The TCP address

    C. The subnet mask

    D. The default gateway

5. What can cause a problem with communication with a client by name but not by IP address?

    A. The IP address

    B. Static files such as an LMHOSTS file or a DNS database

    C. Subnet mask

    D. The default gateway

6. The subnet mask specifies what two components of the IP address?

    A. The network address

    B. The default gateway

    C. The host address

    D. The IP address

7. What can greatly reduce TCP/IP configuration problems?

    A. WINS Server

    B. WINS Proxy

    C. DHCP Server

    D. PDC

8. Addresses available on a DHCP server are called

    A. Pools

    B. Scopes

    C. Ranges

    D. Notes

9. The most important part of a multiple DHCP configuration is to make sure you don't have which of the following in the different scopes?

    A. Duplicate addresses

    B. Duplicate pools

    C. Duplicate subnets

    D. Duplicate default gateways

10. In the absence of configuration problems with DHCP addresses, but using multiple DHCP servers in your environment, the scopes on each DCHP server should be

    A. Unique to that subnet only

    B. For different subnets

    C. For no more than two subnets

    D. For no subnets

5.1.6   Practice Problems: Answers and Explanations

1. **A, C, D**   The three main parameters that specify how TCP/IP is configured are the IP address, the subnet mask, and the default gateway.

2. **D**   The default gateway is the address of the router.

3. **C**   These parameters are configured through the Protocols tab of the Network Properties dialog box.

4. **A**   The IP address specifies the network address and host address of the computer.

5. **B**   Static files, such as an LMHOSTS file or a DNS database, can cause this problem.

6. **A, C** The subnet mask specifies what portion of the IP address specifies the network address and what portion of the address specifies the host address.

7. **C** Using a DHCP server can greatly reduce TCP/IP configuration problems.

8. **C** Scopes are ranges of available addresses on a DHCP server.

9. **A** The most important part of the configuration is to make sure you don't have duplicate addresses in the different scopes.

10. **B** Even when no configuration problems occur with DHCP addresses, DHCP clients can get a duplicate IP address from a DHCP server. If you have multiple DHCP servers in your environment, you should have scopes on each DCHP server for different subnets.

5.1.7 Keywords

default gateway The router to use if the packet is not intended for the subnet

DHCP client A client that obtains TCP/IP configuration information from a DHCP server

DHCP server Dynamic Host Configuration Protocol server that issues TCP/IP configuration information

scope A range of available addresses on a DHCP server

subnet Division of a network into smaller networks

5.2 Microsoft Configuration Utilities

If you configure the TCP/IP address and other TCP/IP parameters manually, you can always verify the configuration through the Network Properties dialog box. However, if the client receives an address from a DHCP server, the only information available in the Network Properties dialog box is that the client is receiving the address from DHCP. Because the configuration information for a DHCP client is received dynamically, you must use a utility that can read the current configuration to verify the settings.

You can use the command-line utility IPCONFIG to see how the local host is configured, regardless of whether the parameters come from manual configuration or from a DHCP server. Running IPCONFIG from a command prompt displays the basic configuration parameters: the IP address, the subnet mask, and the default gateway. You can see additional information by using IPCONFIG with the /all switch.

Executing IPCONFIG /all in a command prompt not only shows the standard parameters but also displays information such as the WINS server address and the DNS server address.

> A Windows NT version of IPCONFIG, called IP Configuration, is included with the Windows NT Resource Kit and is installed under the Internet Utils program group. IP Configuration reports the same information as the IPCONFIG command-line utility. IP Configuration can also be used to release and renew DCHP addresses, as described in the following section.

5.2.1   Using IPCONFIG to Resolve DHCP Address Problems

When a DHCP client gets an IP that is not configured correctly or if the client doesn't get an IP address at all, you can use IPCONFIG to resolve these problems. If the client gets incorrect IP parameters, it should be apparent from the results of IPCONFIG /all. You should be able to see that some of the parameters don't match the IP address or that some parameters are completely blank. For example, you could have the wrong default gateway (in which case the entry would not appear), or the client might not be configured to be a WINS client.

When a DHCP client fails to receive an address, the results of IPCONFIG /all are different. In this case, the client has an IP address of 0.0.0.0—an invalid address—and the DHCP server is 255.255.255.255—a broadcast address.

To fix this problem, you can release the incorrect address with IPCONFIG /release and then try to obtain a new IP address with IPCONFIG /renew. The IPCONFIG /renew command sends out a new request for a DHCP address. If a DHCP server is available, the server responds with the lease of an IP address.

In many cases, the DHCP client will acquire the same address after releasing and renewing. That the client receives the same address indicates the same DHCP server responded to the renewal request and gave out the address that had just been released back into the pool of available addresses. If you need to renew an address because the parameters of the scope are incorrect, you must fix the parameters in the DHCP configuration before releasing and renewing the address. Otherwise, the client could receive the same address again with the same incorrect parameters.

> Occasionally, a DHCP client will not acquire an address regardless of how many times you release and renew the address. One way to try to fix the problem is to manually assign the client a static IP address. After the client is configured with this address, which you can verify by using IPCONFIG, switch back to DHCP.

5.2.2   Exercises

Exercise 1: Examine Your Windows NT TCP/IP Configuration

To examine your TCP/IP configuration information on a Windows NT Workstation or Server system that is configured through DHCP, perform the following steps:

1. From the Start menu, select Programs | Command Prompt.

2. Type in **IPCONFIG**.

3. Note the information that appears. Now type **IPCONFIG /ALL**.

4. Note the information that appears.

Exercise 2: Examine Your NT Configuration with the Resource Kit

To examine your TCP/IP configuration information if the Windows NT Resource Kit CD has been installed on your system, perform the following steps:

1. From the Start menu, Choose Programs | Resource Kit 4.0.

2. Choose Internet Utils and then IP Configuration.

3. Select the More Info >> button.

4. Note the Host and Adapter information that appears.

5.2.3   Practice Problems

1. How can you see the address of the DHCP server from which a client received its IP address?

   A. Using Advanced properties of TCP/IP

   B. Using IPCONFIG /all

   C. Using DHCPINFO

   D. Pinging DHCP

2. If you configure the TCP/IP address and other TCP/IP parameters manually, you can always verify the configuration through the which of the following?

   A. Network Properties dialog box

   B. Server Services dialog box

   C. DHCPINFO command-line utility

   D. Advanced properties tab of TCP/IP Info

3. If the client receives an address from a DHCP server, the only information available in the Network Properties dialog box is

   A. The IP address

   B. The subnet address

   C. That the client is receiving its address from DHCP

   D. The default gateway

4. Because the configuration information for a DHCP client is received dynamically, you must use which utility to read the current configuration to verify the settings?

   A. Ping

   B. TRACERT

   C. ARP

   D. IPCONFIG

5. The command-line utility IPCONFIG can be used to see which two of the following items?

   A. Configuration of the local host

   B. Whether the parameters come from manual configuration or from a DHCP server

   C. Ping request status

   D. Protocol statistics

5.2.4   Practice Problems: Answers and Explanations

1. **B** IPCONFIG /ALL is the command-line utility used to obtain this information.

2. **A** If you configure the TCP/IP address and other TCP/IP parameters manually, you can always verify the configuration through the Network Properties dialog box.

3. **C** If the client receives an address from a DHCP server, the only information available in the Network Properties dialog box is that the client is receiving its address from DHCP.

4. **D** Because the configuration information for a DHCP client is received dynamically, you must use a utility that can read the current configuration to verify the settings.

5. **A, B** You can use the command-line utility IPCONFIG to see how the local host is configured and whether the parameters come from manual configuration or from a DHCP server.

5.2.5 Keywords

IPCONFIG Command-line utility to view IP configuration information

5.3 Microsoft IP Configuration Troubleshooting Utilities

A number of tools come with TCP/IP when the protocol is installed on a Windows NT computer. After you have resolved any problems caused by the Windows NT network configuration, you can focus on using the TCP/IP tools to solve IP problems. Some tools can be used to verify the configuration parameters. Other tools can be used to test the connectivity capabilities of TCP/IP as configured.

5.3.1 Using Ping to Test an IP Configuration

Ping is a command-line tool included with every Microsoft TCP/IP client (any DOS or Windows client with the TCP/IP protocol installed). You can use Ping to send a test packet to the specified address and then, if things are working properly, the packet is returned. Figure 5.5 shows the results of a successful ping command. Note that four successful responses are returned. Unsuccessful pings can result in different messages, depending on the type of problem Ping encounters while trying to send and receive the test packet.

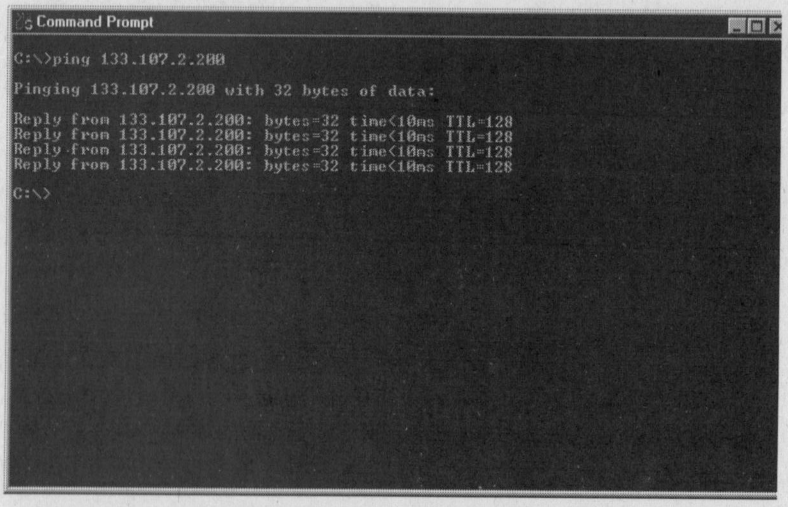

```
Command Prompt                                                    _ □ x

C:\>ping 133.107.2.200

Pinging 133.107.2.200 with 32 bytes of data:

Reply from 133.107.2.200: bytes=32 time<10ms TTL=128
Reply from 133.107.2.200: bytes=32 time<10ms TTL=128
Reply from 133.107.2.200: bytes=32 time<10ms TTL=128
Reply from 133.107.2.200: bytes=32 time<10ms TTL=128

C:\>
```

Figure 5.5. The results of a successful ping command.

Although Ping is a simple tool to use (from the command prompt simply type ping with the IP address or host name you want to ping), choosing what to ping is the key to using it for successful troubleshooting. The remainder of this section covers which IP addresses or hosts you should ping to troubleshoot TCP/IP connectivity problems.

Troubleshooting IP Protocol Installation by Pinging the Loopback Address

The first step in troubleshooting many problems is to verify that TCP/IP is installed correctly on the client. You can look at the configuration through the Network Properties dialog box or with IPCONFIG, but to actually test the working status of the protocol stack you should try to ping the loopback address. The loopback address is 127.0.0.1. When you ping this address, a packet is not sent on the network. The ping command simply sends a packet down through the layers of the IP architecture and then up the layers again. If TCP/IP is installed correctly, you should receive an immediate successful response. If IP is not installed correctly, the response fails.

To correct problems of this type, you should verify the NT network configuration and the protocol installation. You can check the following items:

- Make sure TCP/IP is listed on the installed protocols.

- Make sure the network adapter card is configured correctly.

- Make sure TCP/IP shows up in the bindings for the adapter card and that the bindings are not disabled for TCP/IP.

- Check the System Log for any errors indicating that the network services didn't start.

If you try the preceding steps, including rebooting the system, and have no success, you may have to remove TCP/IP and install it again. Sometimes NT gets hung up somewhere and thinks things are really installed when they are not. Removing the protocol and then installing it again can often resolve this halfway state.

Troubleshooting Client Address Configuration by Pinging the Local Address

Another step in verifying the TCP/IP configuration, after you have verified that TCP/IP is installed correctly, is to ping the address of the local host. Simply ping the IP address that you think is configured for the client. You should receive an immediate successful reply if the client address is configured as specified in the ping command. You can also ping the name of the local host, but problems with name resolution are discussed later in this chapter's section "Name Resolution Problems." For the moment, you are concerned with raw TCP/IP connectivity—the capability to communicate with another IP host by using its IP address.

Correcting a failure at this level involves checking the way the client address was configured. Was the address typed in correctly? Did the client receive the IP address from the DHCP server that you expected? Also, does the client have a connection on the network? Pinging the local host address does not cause a packet to be sent on the network, so if you have lost network connectivity, this ping won't indicate a network failure.

Troubleshooting Router Problems by Pinging the Default Gateway

If you can communicate with hosts on the same subnet but cannot establish communications with hosts beyond the subnet, the problem may be with the router or the way its address is configured. To communicate beyond the subnet, a router must be enabled with an address that matches the subnet address for the clients on the local subnet. The router also has other ports configured with different addresses so it can send packets out to the network at large. Pinging the default gateway address tests the address you have configured for the router and also tests the router itself.

If the default gateway ping fails, there are several possible sources for the error:

- The router has failed or is down. In this case, you cannot make connections outside the subnet until the router is brought up again. However, you should be able to communicate with hosts on the same subnet.

- The client has lost a physical connection with the router or with the network. You can test a network connection at a hardware level and also through the software by trying to establish a session with a server with another protocol, such as NetBEUI. If you only have TCP/IP on your network, you can temporarily install NetBEUI on the client and on another computer on the same subnet. Test connectivity by connecting to a file share on the other computer. Remember, the computer should be on the same subnet because NetBEUI packets don't usually route.

- The IP address on the router may be configured incorrectly. The router address must match the client's default gateway address so that packets can move outside the subnet.

- The client has the wrong router address. Of course, if you ping the correct router address and it works, you also want to make sure the default gateway address configured on the client matches the address you successfully pinged.

- The wrong subnet mask is configured. If the subnet mask is wrong, packets destined for a remote subnet may not be routed!

You should also ping each IP address used by the different ports on your router. The local interface for your subnet may be working, but other interfaces on the router, which actually connect the router to the other subnets on the network, could have some type of problem.

Pinging a Remote Host

As a final test in using Ping, you can ping the IP address of a remote host, a computer on another subnet, or even the IP address of a Web server or FTP server on the Internet. If you can successfully ping a remote host, your problem doesn't lie with the IP configuration; you are probably having trouble resolving host names.

If pinging the remote host fails, your problems may be with the router, the subnet mask, or the local IP configuration. However, if you have followed the earlier steps of pinging the loopback, local host address, and the default gateway address, you have already eliminated many of the problems that could cause this ping to fail.

When a remote host ping fails after you have tried the other ping options, the failure may be due to other routers beyond the default gateway used for your subnet. If you know the physical layout of your network, you can ping other router addresses along the path to the remote host to see where the trouble lies. Remember to ping the addresses on both sides of the router: the address that receives the packet and the address that forwards the packet on. You can also use the ROUTE command, as described in the following section, to find the path used to contact the remote host.

Another possibility is that a physical path to the remote host no longer exists because of a router crash, a disruption in the physical network, or a crash on the remote host.

Many troubleshooters prefer to simply try this last step when using Ping to troubleshoot IP configuration and connectivity. If you can successfully ping a remote host, then the other layers of TCP/IP must be working correctly. For a packet to reach a remote host, IP must be installed correctly, the local client address must be configured properly, and the packet must be routed. If a ping to the remote host works, then you can look to other sources (usually name resolution) for your connection problems. If the ping fails, you can try each preceding step until you find the layer where the problem is located. Then you can resolve the problem at that layer. You can either start by pinging the loopback address and working up through the architecture, or you can ping the remote host. Of course, if pinging the remote host works, you can stop. If not, you can work back through the architecture until you find a layer where Ping succeeds. The problem must therefore be at the next layer.

5.3.2 Exercises

Excercise 1: Correcting a Network Configuration Error

Use this exercise to see the effects that an improperly configured network card has on other networking services and protocols. Before starting, make sure you have installed Windows NT Server with a computer that has a network adapter card and that TCP/IP has been installed.

1. Clear the System Log in Event Viewer.

2. From the desktop, right-click Network Neighborhood and choose Properties from the resulting menu.

3. From the Network Properties dialog box, select the Adapters tab.

4. Select your adapter card from the list and choose Properties.

5. Note the correct setting as it is and change the IRQ of your adapter card to an incorrect setting.

6. Close this dialog box and choose to reboot your computer when prompted.

7. When your computer reboots, note the message received after the Logon prompt appears. The message should say A Dependency Service Failed to Start.

8. Log on and open Event Viewer.

9. Note the error message generated from the adapter card. Note the other error messages generated after the adapter card error.

10. Clear the System Log in Event Viewer.

11. From the command prompt, type ping 127.0.0.1. This ping fails because TCP/IP doesn't start if the adapter doesn't start.

12. From the Network Properties dialog box, return the IRQ of your adapter card to its proper setting and reboot.

13. Log on and check the System Log. There should be no adapter card errors or errors from networking services.

14. From the command prompt, type ping 127.0.0.1. This ping succeeds because TCP/IP is started now.

Exercise 2: Using Ping to Test an IP Configuration

This exercise uses Ping to verify a TCP/IP installation and configuration. You should have installed Windows NT Server and TCP/IP.

1. From the desktop, right-click Network Neighborhood and choose Properties from the menu that appears.

2. From the Bindings tab, expand all the networking services.

3. Select TCP/IP and choose Disable.

4. Repeat step 3 until you have disabled TCP/IP for all the listed networking services.

5. Close the dialog box and choose to reboot your computer when prompted.

6. When the computer reboots, log in.

7. From a command prompt, type ping 127.0.0.1. This ping works because TCP/IP is installed.

8. From a command prompt, type ping x.x.x.x, where x.x.x.x is your default gateway address. This ping fails because you have disabled TCP/IP from all the networking services. There isn't a way for TCP/IP packets to be sent on the network.

9. From the Bindings tab in Network Properties, enable TCP/IP for all the networking services.

10. Close the dialog box and when prompted, choose to reboot your computer.

11. When the computer reboots, log in.

12. From a command prompt, ping your default gateway. The ping works this time because a path now exists by which TCP/IP communications can reach the network.

5.3.3 Practice Problems

1. Which command-line tool is included with every Microsoft TCP/IP client?

   A. DHCP

   B. WINS

   C. PING

   D. WINIPCFG

2. The first step in troubleshooting many problems is to verify the following:

   A. The subnet mask is valid.

   B. TCP/IP is installed correctly on the client.

   C. The WINS server is running.

   D. The BDC is operable.

3. The loopback address is

   A. `127.0.0.1`

   B. `255.0.0.0`

   C. `255.255.0.0`

   D. `255.255.255.0`

4. The default subnet mask for a class C network is

   A. `127.0.0.1`

   B. `255.0.0.0`

   C. `255.255.0.0`

   D. `255.255.255.0`

5. The default subnet mask for a class A network is

   A. `127.0.0.1`

   B. `255.0.0.0`

   C. `255.255.0.0`

   D. `255.255.255.0`

6. The default subnet mask for a class B network is

   A. `127.0.0.1`

   B. `255.0.0.0`

   C. `255.255.0.0`

   D. `255.255.255.0`

7. When you ping the loopback address, a packet is sent

   A. On the network

   B. Down through the layers of the IP architecture and then up the layers again

   C. Across the wire

   D. Through the loopback dongle

8. When using the loopback address, if TCP/IP is installed correctly, you should receive a response:

   A. Immediately

   B. Only if it fails

   C. After the next host comes on line

   D. Within two minutes

9. After you have verified that TCP/IP is installed correctly, what is the next step in verifying the TCP/IP configuration?

   A. Ping the broadcast address.

   B. Ping the Microsoft Web site.

   C. Ping a distant router.

   D. Ping the address of the local host.

10. If you can communicate with hosts on the same subnet but cannot establish communications with hosts beyond the subnet, the problem may be with:

    A. The router or the way its address is configured

    B. The subnet mask

    C. The IP address

    D. The WINS server

11. If the default gateway ping fails, possible sources for the error include which of the following? (Select all correct answers.)

    A. The router has failed or is down.

    B. The client has lost a physical connection with the router or with the network.

    C. The IP address on the client may be configured incorrectly.

    D. The client has the wrong router address.

    E. The wrong subnet mask is configured.

5.3.4 Practice Problems: Answers and Explanations

1. **C** Ping is a command-line tool included with every Microsoft TCP/IP client.

2. **B** The first step in troubleshooting many problems is to verify that TCP/IP installed correctly on the client.

3. **A** The loopback address is `127.0.0.1`.

4. **D**   The default subnet mask for a class C network is 255.255.255.0.

5. **B**   The default subnet mask for a class A network is 255.0.0.0.

6. **C**   The default subnet mask for a class B network is 255.255.0.0.

7. **B**   When you ping the loopback address, Ping simply sends a packet down through the layers of the IP architecture and then up the layers again.

8. **A**   If TCP/IP is installed correctly, you should receive an immediate successful response.

9. **D**   After you have verified that TCP/IP is installed correctly, the next step in verifying the TCP/IP configuration is to ping the address of the local host.

10. **A**   If you can communicate with hosts on the same subnet but cannot establish communications with hosts beyond the subnet, the problem may be with the router or the way its address is configured.

11. **A, B, D, E**   If the default gateway ping fails, there are several possible sources for the error: the router has failed or is down, the client has lost a physical connection with the router or with the network, the IP address on the router may be configured incorrectly, the client has the wrong router address, or the wrong subnet mask is configured.

5.4   Diagnosing and Resolving Name Resolution Problems

Name resolution problems are easily identified as such with the PING utility. If you can ping a host using its IP address, but cannot ping it by its host name, then you have a resolution problem. If you cannot ping the host at all, then the problem lies elsewhere.

Problems that can occur with name resolution and their solutions fit into the following five categories:

- The entry is misspelled. Examine the HOSTS or LMHOSTS file to verify that the host name is correctly spelled. If you are using the HOSTS file on a system prior to NT 4.0, capitalization is important, as this file is case sensitive; LMHOSTS is not case sensitive (regardless of NT version number).

- Comment characters prevent the entry from being read. Verify that a pound sign is neither at the beginning of the line nor anywhere on the line prior to the host name.

- The file has duplicate entries. Because the files are read in linear fashion, with any duplication only the first entry is read and all others are ignored. Verify that all host names are unique.

- A host other than the one you want is contacted. Verify that the IP address entered in the file(s) is valid and corresponds to the host name.

- The wrong file is used. HOSTS and LMHOSTS are not as interchangeable as you might think. HOSTS maps IP addresses to host names, whereas LMHOSTS maps NetBIOS names to IP addresses.

In addition to the PING utility, the all-purpose TCP/IP troubleshooting tool, two other useful name resolution utilities are

- NBTSTAT

- Hostname

5.4.1   NBTSTAT

The NBTSTAT utility (NetBIOS over TCP/IP) displays protocol statistics and current TCP/IP connections. It is useful for troubleshooting NetBIOS name resolution problems, and various parameters and options can be used with it:

- `-a` (adapter status)—lists the remote machine's name table given its name

- `-A` (Adapter status)—lists the remote machine's name table given its IP address

- `-c` (cache)—lists the remote name cache including the IP addresses

- `-n` (names)—lists local NetBIOS names

- `-r` (resolved)—lists names resolved by broadcast and via WINS

- `-R` (Reload)—purges and reloads the remote cache name table

- `-s` (sessions)—lists sessions table converting destination IP addresses to host names via the LMHOSTS file

- `-S` (Sessions)—lists sessions table with the destination IP addresses

5.4.2   Hostname

The `hostname.exe` utility, located in `\systemroot\System32`, returns the name of the local host. You cannot use this utility to change the name. The host name is changed from the Network Control Panel applet.

If you have configured TCP/IP correctly and the protocol is installed and working, then the problem with connectivity is probably associated with errors in resolving host names. When you test connectivity with TCP/IP addresses, you are testing a lower level of connectivity than users generally use. When users want to connect to a network resource, such as mapping a drive to a server or connecting to a Web site, they usually refer to that server or Web site by its name rather than by its TCP/IP address. In fact, users do not usually know the IP address of a particular server.

The name used to establish a connection must be resolved down to an IP address so that the networking software can make a connection. Once you've tested the IP connectivity, the next logical step is to check the resolution of a name down to its IP address. If a name cannot be resolved to its IP address or if it is resolved to the wrong address, users will not be able to connect to the network resource with that name, even if you can connect to it using an IP address.

Two types of computer names are used when communicating on the network. A NetBIOS name is assigned to a Microsoft computer, such as a Windows NT server or a Windows 95 client. A host name is assigned to non-Microsoft computers, such as a UNIX server. (Host names can also be assigned to a Windows NT server running Internet Information Server. For example, the name `www.microsoft.com` refers to a Web server on the Microsoft Web site. This server is running on Windows NT.) In general, when using Microsoft networking, such as connecting to a server for file sharing, print sharing, or applications, you refer to that computer by its NetBIOS name. When executing a TCP/IP-specific command, such as FTP, or using a Web browser, you refer to that computer by its host name.

A NetBIOS name is resolved to a TCP/IP address in several ways. Figure 5.6 shows how NetBIOS names are resolved. The TCP/IP client initiating a session first looks in its local name cache. If the client cannot find the name in a local cache, the client queries a WINS server if configured to be a WINS client. If the WINS server cannot resolve the name, the client tries a broadcast that reaches only as far as the local subnet. (Routers, by default, are not configured to forward broadcasts.) If the client cannot find the name through a broadcast, it looks for any LMHOSTS or HOSTS files if it has been configured to do so. Finally, if the client cannot resolve a name in any other way, it queries a DNS server if configured to be a DNS client. However, if the client specifies a name longer than 15 characters (the maximum length of a NetBIOS name), the client first queries DNS before trying a HOSTS file or WINS.

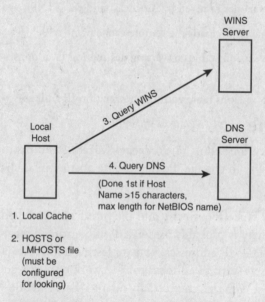

Figure 5.6. Resolving NetBIOS names.

Host names are resolved in a similar manner. The client, however, checks sources that are used solely to resolve host names before trying sources that are used to resolve NetBIOS names. In resolving host names, the client first tries the local host name, then the HOSTS file, and then the DNS server, if configured to be a DNS client. These two sources resolve only host names. If the client cannot resolve the name, it checks the WINS server, if configured as a WINS client; tries a broadcast; and then looks in the LMHOSTS file. The last three methods to resolve a name are used to resolve NetBIOS names, but a host name might be listed in these sources.

Several tools for testing name resolution are discussed in the following sections.

5.4.3   Testing Name Resolution with PING

Just as you can use PING to verify the TCP/IP configuration, you can also use PING to verify host name resolution. If you can successfully ping a host name, then you have verified TCP/IP communication from the network interface layer of the TCP/IP architecture to the transport layer. When you ping a host name, a successful reply shows the IP address of the host. This test shows that the name has been successfully resolved to an IP address and that you can communicate with that host.

5.4.4   Testing NetBIOS Name Resolution by Establishing a Session

The ultimate test of connectivity is to establish a session with another host. If you can establish a session through mapping a drive or by executing a Net Use command (which is the command-line equivalent of mapping a drive), you have made a NetBIOS connection. If you can FTP, Telnet, or establish a Web session with another host, you have made a Sockets connection. NetBIOS connections and Sockets connections are the two main types of connections made by a TCP/IP client.

After the drive has been mapped with Net Use, you can switch to the new drive letter, view files and directories, and do any other things that are specified in the permissions of the share mapped to the drive letter. To get more information about the syntax of the Net Use command, type net help use in a command prompt.

A common problem in making NetBIOS connections is that the wrong NetBIOS name is used. Verify that the destination host has the same name that you are using to make the connection.

Another potential problem with the name configuration occurs when NetBIOS scope IDs are used. Only NetBIOS hosts with the same scope ID can communicate with each other. The scope ID is configured through the advanced TCP/IP parameters. Incorrect share permissions can prevent you from establishing a NetBIOS session. When you try to connect a drive to a share where you have no access, you receive an Access Denied message. This message indicates that you can connect to the server, but your rights did not allow you to make a connection to this specific share. This type of failure has nothing to do with TCP/IP connectivity. Remember that if the administrator adds your account to a group that has access and you want to try again, you must log out and log in again to receive a new access token with the updated permissions.

To resolve NetBIOS connectivity problems, you must know what sources are used to resolve NetBIOS names. The first place a client looks to resolve a NetBIOS name is the local cache. You can view the contents of the NetBIOS cache with the NBTSTAT command. You should verify that no incorrect entry is in the cache that maps the NetBIOS name to an incorrect IP address. If you find an incorrect entry, however, you can remove the entry and try to make another connection.

The next place to attempt NetBIOS name resolution is in a query to a WINS server. The client must be configured to be a WINS client. You can verify the address of the WINS server through the Advanced properties of TCP/IP or by using IPCONFIG /all. You can view the contents of the WINS database by using WINS Manager on the WINS server (or any computer where the management tools are installed). Verify that the host name is in the database and, if so, make sure it is mapped to the correct IP address.

If the WINS server is configured to do a DNS lookup, you have another way to get NetBIOS resolution. The WINS server queries DNS if the WINS server cannot resolve the name from its own database. You can view the contents of the DNS database files by using DNS Manager on the DNS server or by using the NSLOOKUP utility from any client.

The client next tries a broadcast to resolve NetBIOS names, although you cannot configure what the client finds through the broadcast. The next place the client looks for NetBIOS name resolution is the LMHOSTS file. You can configure the contents of this file. The client must be configured for LMHOSTS lookup in the advanced TCP/IP configuration. Also, the LMHOSTS file must be located in the correct directory path. On an NT computer, the LMHOSTS file must be in the path *winnt root*\system32\drivers\etc.

Next, verify the entries in the LMHOSTS file. The correct host name and IP address must be entered in this file. If you have multiple entries in the file for a host name, only the first entry is used. If you added another entry for a host in the file, you must delete it so that it will not be used.

Domain names are another source of potential problems with LMHOSTS files in a non-WINS environment. The domain name must be registered with the IP address of the Primary Domain Controller (PDC) and #DOM (a switch that registers the server as a domain controller) on the same line. This entry is necessary to log on to the domain as well as to see the domain in a browse list.

Another problem with LMHOSTS files doesn't prevent connectivity, but it can greatly delay it. If you have #INCLUDE statements at the top of the LMHOSTS file, the files specified by #INCLUDE are included first before any other entries lower in the LMHOSTS file are searched. You can speed connections to hosts entered in the LMHOSTS file by moving the #INCLUDE entries to the bottom of the LMHOSTS file.

5.4.5   Testing TCP Name Resolution by Establishing a Session

Typical TCP/IP connections from a Microsoft client, such as FTP or Telnet, use Windows Sockets. To test connectivity at this level, try establishing an FTP or Telnet session or try to connect to a Web server. When you successfully connect to a Web server, you see the site's Web page and you can navigate through the page. When the connection fails, you receive a message on your Internet browser that the connection failed.

To resolve problems with a Windows Sockets connection, you must understand how a client resolves TCP host names. The first place a client looks to resolve a host name is the local host name. You can see what TCP/IP thinks is the local host name by executing the Hostname command. Verify that the local host is what you expect it to be. You can modify the host name in the DNS tab of the TCP/IP properties.

The next place the client looks is in a HOSTS file. This file must be located in the path *winnt root*\system32\drivers\etc. Verify that any entry in the file for the host is correct, with the correct host name and IP address. If multiple entries for the same host name are in the file, only the first name is used. The HOSTS file can also have links to HOSTS files on other servers. If links are specified in the local HOSTS file, you should make sure entries in the other HOSTS files are also correct.

The final place a client can use host name resolution is a DNS server. The client must be configured to use DNS on the DNS tab in the TCP/IP properties dialog box. The DNS server must have a zone file corresponding to the domain name specified in the host name, or it must be able to query another DNS server that can resolve the name.

5.4.6 Exercise

Exercise 1: Using NBTSTAT to View the Local NetBIOS Name Cache and Add Entries to the Cache from an LMHOSTS File

This exercise examines the contents of the local NetBIOS name cache and loads entries into the cache from an LMHOSTS file. You should have installed TCP/IP and have another Windows client with TCP/IP installed and file sharing enabled.

1. Use Notepad to open the file \WINNT\SYSTEM32\DRIVERS\ETC\LMHOSTS.SAM.

2. Add an entry to the bottom of the file for the other Windows client, specifying the NetBIOS name and the IP address of the Windows client. Make sure that no comment (#) appears in front of this line.

3. Save the file in the same directory as LMHOSTS (without an extension).

4. From a command prompt on your NT computer, type nbtstat -c. This command displays the local cache.

5. From a command prompt, type nbstat -R. This command purges the cache and loads the contents of the LMHOSTS file into the local cache.

6. From a command prompt, type nbtstat -c to display the new contents of the local cache.

7. Using Windows NT Explorer, map a network drive to the other Windows client. The local cache was used to resolve the NetBIOS name for this connection.

8. From a command prompt, type nbtstat /? to see all the switches available with the NBTSTAT command.

5.4.7 Practice Problems

The next three questions refer to the following HOSTS file:

```
127.0.0.1      localhost
192.200.2.4    karen Kristin #Evan
192.200.2.5    Spencer Sales
192.200.2.6    #Lorraine Buis
192.200.2.7    Sales
```

1. Kristin, in finance, is having trouble connecting to the host called Lorraine. When she pings 192.200.2.6, the result is successful, but when she pings Lorraine, the error message says the host is not found. What is causing this problem?

   A. Invalid IP address

   B. Duplicate entry

   C. Comment character in the wrong position

   D. Improper spelling of host name

2. Evan, in accounting, needs to get into 192.200.2.7. He can ping the IP address, but if he tries to ping sales, the results tell him that 192.200.2.5 is responding. What is causing this problem?

   A. Invalid IP address

   B. Duplicate entry

   C. Comment character in the wrong position

   D. Improper spelling of host name

3. Spencer, in sales, needs to connect to the host Karen and has the preceding host file on his NT 3.51 machine. He can ping the IP address successfully, but if he attempts to ping Karen, the host is not found. What is causing this problem?

   A. Invalid IP address

   B. Duplicate entry

   C. Comment character in the wrong position

   D. Improper spelling of host name

4. Which utility is useful for troubleshooting NetBIOS name resolution problems?

   A. NBTSTAT

   B. NETSTAT

   C. PING

   D. Hostname

5. Which utility is useful for finding the local host name?

   A. NBTSTAT

   B. NETSTAT

   C. PING

   D. Hostname

6. Which utility is an all-purpose tool for troubleshooting TCP/IP problems?

   A. NBTSTAT

   B. NETSTAT

   C. PING

   D. Hostname

7. HOSTS file entries are limited to how many characters?

   A. 8

   B. 255

   C. 500

   D. Unlimited

8. The number of entries in the HOSTS file is limited to

   A. 8

   B. 255

   C. 500

   D. Unlimited

9. Which of the following files are case sensitive on NT 3.5 systems?

   A. HOSTS

   B. LMHOSTS

   C. ARP

   D. FQDN

10. Which of the following files is used for NetBIOS name resolution?

    A. HOSTS

    B. LMHOSTS

    C. ARP

    D. FQDN

11. Which address is the loopback address?

    A. `0.0.0.1`

    B. `127.0.0.0`

    C. `127.0.0.1`

    D. `255.255.255.255`

5.4.8 Practice Problems: Answers and Explanations

1. **C** The comment character is preceding the host name and thus preventing the name from being recognized.

2. **B** The sales entry is duplicated on two lines and thus the second entry is never activated.

3. **D** Prior to NT 4.0, the HOSTS file was case sensitive. This file has the entry karen, but he is trying to reach Karen—two different entries.

4. **A**   NBSTAT is used for troubleshooting NetBIOS name resolution problems.

5. **D**   Hostname is used to find the name of the local host.

6. **C**   PING is the all-around utility used for troubleshooting TCP/IP problems.

7. **B**   HOSTS file lines are limited to 255 characters.

8. **D**   The HOSTS file can have an unlimited number of lines.

9. **A**   The HOSTS file, prior to NT 4.0, was case sensitive and remains so on non-NT systems.

10. **B**   LMHOSTS is the static file used for NetBIOS name resolution.

11. **C**   `127.0.0.1` is known as the loopback address.

5.5   Other Symptoms of TCP/IP Configuration Problems

The material in this section is not part of the exam; nevertheless this information is useful for troubleshooting in the real world. You can refer to this section for additional troubleshooting help with your network.

Other symptoms can indicate problems with TCP/IP connectivity or its configuration.

5.5.1   Default Gateway Does Not Belong to Configured Interfaces

When you configure TCP/IP manually, you can receive the message `The Default Gateway does not belong to configured interfaces`. You get this message when the address of the default gateway cannot logically belong to the same subnet as the host IP address. This condition can happen because the subnet mask is wrong, the default gateway address is wrong, or the local host address is wrong.

5.5.2   The TCP/IP Host Does Not Respond

If a remote TCP/IP host does not respond, you can check the status of the connection with the `NETSTAT -a` command. This command shows all the connections established with TCP. Successful connections should have zero bytes in the send and receive queues. If bytes are in the queues, then the problem is with the connection. If the connection appears to be hung but no bytes are in the queues, there's probably a delay in the connection.

5.5.3   The Client Connects to the Wrong Host

You've checked everything in the IP configuration on the host and the client, yet the client connects to the wrong host. (This situation can happen when you establish a session using an IP address rather than a host name, such as when using Telnet.) This symptom can occur when duplicate IP addresses are on the network. You have to find the computer with the duplicate address and modify the address so it is unique. With duplicate addresses, connections are inconsistent—clients sometimes connect to one host, sometimes to another.

5

5.5.4   Error 53 Is Returned When Trying to Make a NetBIOS Session

You are trying to establish a NetBIOS session, such as mapping a drive by using the Net Use command, but Error 53 is returned. This error happens because the computer name cannot be found on the network. In other words, TCP/IP can't find a computer name to resolve to an IP address. You can use the normal NetBIOS host resolution troubleshooting to resolve this problem. If the host names are correct, it's possible you are using NetBIOS scopes. If NetBIOS scopes are configured (nonblank), only hosts with the same scope ID can communicate with each other.

5.5.5   An FTP Server Does Not Seem to Work

FTP must be installed correctly before any clients can make connections to the server. Just as you can ping the loopback address to test a TCP/IP installation, you can also FTP the loopback address on the FTP server to test the FTP installation.

5.5.6   Exercise

Exercise 1: Using NETSTAT to Examine TCP/IP Connections

You can perform this exercise to see the information returned by the NETSTAT command. You should have installed TCP/IP and have access to other TCP/IP servers, such as Internet access.

1.   Connect to another TCP/IP server through a Web browser or by mapping a network drive.

2.   From a command prompt, type netstat. This command displays the statistics about your current connections.

3.   From a command prompt, type netstat -a. Note that this command also displays any listening ports.

4.   From a command prompt, type netstat -r. Note that this command also displays the route table in addition to the connection information.

5.   From a command prompt, type netstat /? to display all the switches available for the NETSTAT command.

5.5.7   Practice Problems

1.   Which of the following steps should you perform to verify that your router is configured correctly?

   A.   Ping a remote host.

   B.   Ping 127.0.0.1.

   C.   Execute the ROUTE command.

   D.   Execute IPCONFIG /all.

2.   Your IP address is 136.193.5.1, your subnet mask is 255.255.240.0, and you are trying to ping a host with the command ping 136.193.2.23. The ping doesn't work. What could cause the ping to fail?

   A.   The default gateway is not configured correctly.

   B.   The subnet mask interprets the IP address as being on another subnet and the packet is routed.

   C.   The subnet mask interprets the address as being on the local subnet and the packet is not routed.

   D.   You must ping the local host first.

3. TCP/IP is not working. You recall that when Windows NT first booted, the message A Dependency Service Failed to Start appeared. What is a possible cause of the problem?

   A. The SNMP service is not installed.

   B. The network card is not configured correctly.

   C. The secondary WINS server is down.

   D. The PDC of your domain is down.

4. You can ping a remote host's IP address, but you cannot connect to a share on that host. What is a possible cause of this problem?

   A. The share must be configured to enable anonymous connections.

   B. The Host Name Resolution Protocol must be installed.

   C. The LMHOSTS file does not have an entry for this server.

   D. The client has not been configured to use DHCP.

5. You made a mistake in configuring an IP address and typed the client's address as 96.82.49.208 rather than 196.82.49.208. What is the most likely result of this configuration error?

   A. The client can communicate only with hosts having the network address 96.x.x.x.

   B. The client cannot communicate with hosts beyond the local subnet.

   C. The client cannot communicate with hosts on the local subnet.

   D. The client cannot communicate with any hosts.

6. You are using NWLink and TCP/IP. How can you reduce the time that is needed to establish a TCP/IP session with another host?

   A. Move TCP/IP to the top of the bindings for the Workstation service.

   B. Configure the default gateway address to point to a faster router.

   C. Decrease the TTL for WINS registrations.

   D. Use SNMP to tune the TCP/IP cache size.

7. A DHCP client has failed to lease an IP address. What is the best way to have the client try again to get a lease?

   A. Issue a REQUEST command to the DHCP server.

   B. Reserve an address for the client on the DHCP server.

   C. Use IPCONFIG /release, then IPCONFIG /renew.

   D. Reboot the client.

8. What is the effect if you do not configure a router address on a TCP/IP client?

   A. You cannot communicate with any other TCP/IP hosts.

   B. You can communicate only with hosts connected to the default gateway.

   C. You can communicate only with hosts on the local subnet.

   D. TCP/IP doesn't initialize.

9. You have several entries for a host name in an LMHOSTS file. Which entry is used to resolve the host name to an IP address?

   A. The entry with the most current time stamp

   B. The first entry in the file

   C. The last entry in the file

   D. The entry with the largest IP address

5

10. A DHCP client has been configured to use the wrong DNS server. How can you correct the problem?

    A. Change the scope options on DHCP and then renew the lease on the client.

    B. Use `IPCONFIG /update:DNS` to make the change.

    C. Enter the address of the DNS server on the DNS tab of the TCP/IP configuration properties.

    D. Add an entry for the DHCP client on the other DNS server.

11. A TCP/IP client had a drive mapped to an NT server. You have just changed the IP address of the server and rebooted. Now the client can't connect to the new server, even though the server is configured to be a WINS client. What is the most likely cause of this problem?

    A. The WINS server hasn't copied the new registration to all its clients.

    B. The client has the old IP address cached.

    C. The LMHOSTS file on the NT Server needs to be updated.

    D. The DNS server needs to be updated.

12. On an NT computer, where does TCP/IP display its error messages?

    A. In the TCP/IP log file

    B. In the SNMP log file

    C. In the System Log

    D. In the `TCP.ERR` file

13. How can you test the installation of an FTP server?

    A. Ping the FTP loopback address.

    B. Ping another FTP server.

    C. FTP another server.

    D. FTP the loopback address.

5.5.8 Practice Problems: Answers and Explanations

1. **A** Pinging a remote host is a good method of verifying that your router configured correctly.

2. **C** In this case, the subnet mask interprets the address as being on the local subnet, and the packet is not routed.

3. **B** If a dependency service fails to start, the network card is probably not properly configured.

4. **C** The most likely cause of this problem is that the LMHOSTS file does not have any entry for this server.

5. **D** An improper IP address will prevent the client from communicating with any hosts.

6. **A** Moving TCP/IP to the top of the bindings order on the workstation should correct the problem.

7. **C** The IPCONFIG command-line utility can be used to release and renew a lease.

8. **C** If a router is not configured, you can communicate only on your local subnet.

9. **B** The file is read sequentially from the top. As soon as a matching entry is found, the file reading stops, thus only the first entry in the file is found.

10. **A** Changing the scope and then renewing the client lease should solve this problem.

11. **B** The most likely cause is a cached IP address from an old connection.

12. **C** The System Log is where TCP/IP displays its error messages.

13. **D** You can use the FTP loopback address to test the installation of an FTP server.

Practice Exam 1

For information about this exam's duration, the number of questions required to pass, and other details, refer to Appendix B, "About the Exam."

Exam 70–59: Internetworking with Microsoft TCP/IP on Microsoft Windows NT 4.0

1. Kristin Ann's Clothing Co. has seven physical plants, each in a different state. The company plans to open five more within the next year if revenue projections continue to hold true. It has a class C IP address and is using subnets to differentiate each plant. Assuming that Kristin Ann's wishes to have the capability of putting as many hosts at each site as possible, which subnet mask should it use?

   A. 255
   B. 254
   C. 252
   D. 248
   E. 240

2. In reference to question 1, how many hosts would this subnet mask allow for at each site?

   A. 62
   B. 30
   C. 14
   D. 6
   E. 2

3. D. S. Widgets is a startup company with no mentionable network at present. It has tremendous growth potential, however, and wants to plan now for future growth. The company is currently considering which networking protocols to standardize its operations on. Of the following, which should it consider to be unroutable?

   A. TCP/IP
   B. NetBEUI
   C. IPX/SPX
   D. NWLink IPX/SPX-compatible transport protocol

4. Custom Cabinet Creations has a network ID of 192 and needs a minimum of six subnets, yet it never anticipates needing more than 20 hosts at any subnet. Which of the following subnets should be recommended for this situation?

   A. 192
   B. 224
   C. 240
   D. 248
   E. 252

5. Which of the following services require a daemon that is not provided with Windows NT?

   A. rexec
   B. ftp
   C. lpq
   D. lpr

6. Bill wants to gather detailed host information for remote management of his network. Which of the following protocols will he need to install?

    A. ICMP
    B. LPD
    C. ARP
    D. SNMP

7. Pistols are drawn as two of your administrators begin arguing over what DHCP reservations are assigned to. To ease the tension, you correctly answer the question as

    A. Computer
    B. Network adapter card
    C. Domain
    D. Workgroup

8. Which of the following command-line utilities compacts a DHCP database?

    A. Compress
    B. Compact
    C. Pack
    D. JetPack

9. The default subnet mask assigned to an IP address of 100.100.100.200 is

    A. 0.0.0.0
    B. 255.0.0.0
    C. 255.255.0.0
    D. 255.255.255.0

10. Evan's Worldwide Tractors and Trailers has more than 20 plants around the world manufacturing parts. The tractor and trailer market is on the decline, and Evan's does not anticipate opening more plants in the near future. It has a class B IP address and uses subnets to differentiate each plant. Assuming that Evan's wants to be able to put as many hosts at each site as possible, and not open new plants, what subnet mask should the company use?

    A. 255
    B. 254
    C. 252
    D. 248
    E. 240

11. In reference to question 10, how many hosts would this subnet mask allow for at each site?

    A. 254
    B. 510
    C. 1,022
    D. 2,046
    E. 4,094

12. Which of the following services is used to map IP addresses to NetBIOS names?

    A. WINS
    B. DHCP
    C. DNS
    D. TCP

13. Which of the following are examples of NetBIOS names?

    A. www.microsoft.com
    B. ComputerOne
    C. 192.14.2.15
    D. \\ComputerOne

14. The protocol responsible for providing message addressing and routing is

    A. TCP
    B. IP
    C. UDP
    D. SNMP

15. A substitute for TCP that performs the same function only on a connectionless basis is

    A. PPP
    B. IP
    C. UDP
    D. SNMP

16. AN IP address of 222.1.1.2 would have a default subnet mask of
    A. 0.0.0.0
    B. 255.0.0.0
    C. 255.255.0.0
    D. 255.255.255.0

17. Which of the following are not valid IP addresses for a host you are adding to a network?
    A. 200.200.256.1
    B. 127.0.0.1
    C. 191.0.0.1
    D. 1.2.3.4

18. What is the role of a WINS proxy?
    A. WINS proxy is a secondary WINS server.
    B. A WINS proxy is any WINS server configured to provide name registration, renewal, release, and resolution services to non-WINS clients.
    C. A WINS proxy is any WINS client configured to provide name resolution services to non-WINS clients.
    D. A WINS proxy is a WINS server located on a different subnet from a WINS client.

19. Your network has client computers that are not WINS clients, and you have added a WINS proxy. Which services are not provided by the WINS proxy?
    A. Name registration
    B. Name resolution
    C. Name renewal
    D. Name release

20. Your Windows NT network has both a primary and a secondary WINS server. Which statement is accurate?
    A. If the primary WINS server is unavailable, the secondary WINS server can provide the same services to WINS clients.

B. If the primary WINS server is unavailable, a WINS proxy agent provides name services.
C. If the primary WINS server is unavailable and the secondary WINS server is also unavailable, a workstation automatically becomes a WINS proxy and provides name services.
D. None of the above.

21. When does name renewal occur?
    A. Name renewal occurs when a WINS client is shut down in an orderly fashion.
    B. Name renewal occurs when the name registration's time to live expires.
    C. Name renewal occurs automatically before the name registration's time to live expires.
    D. Name renewal occurs only when initiated by a WINS proxy.

22. When does name registration occur?
    A. Name registration occurs whenever a WINS client sends a request to a WINS server to obtain the IP address of a NetBIOS host.
    B. Name registration occurs when a non-WINS client starts and sends a broadcast to a WINS proxy.
    C. Name registration occurs when a WINS client starts and sends a name registration request to a WINS server.
    D. Name registration occurs when a WINS client sends a name registration request to a WINS server and then the WINS server sends a negative acknowledgment because the name is already registered.

23. In architectural models, how many layers are in the OSI model?
    A. 7
    B. 5
    C. 4
    D. 3
    E. 2

24. In architectural models, how many layers are in the TCP/IP model?

A. 7

B. 5

C. 4

D. 3

E. 2

25. By default, what is the network ID for the address 121.212.112.122?

A. 121.0.0.0

B. 121.212.0.0

C. 121.212.112.0

D. 0.0.0.122

26. By default, what is the network ID for the address 198.81.91.119?

A. 198.0.0.0

B. 198.81.0.0

C. 198.81.91.0

D. 0.0.0.119

27. By default, what is the host ID for the address 179.79.234.234?

A. 179.0.0.0

B. 0.0.234.234

C. 0.79.234.234

D. 0.0.0.234

28. A company is assigned the network ID 150.134.0.0 by InterNIC. The company wants to have 15 subnets and up to 1,000 hosts per subnet. How many bits are needed for the custom subnet mask?

A. 4

B. 5

C. 6

D. 7

29. In question 28, what should the company use for the subnet mask?

A. 255.255.0.0

B. 255.255.5.0

C. 255.255.31.0

D. 255.255.248.0

30. An organization is assigned the network ID 114.0.0.0 by InterNIC. The organization currently has five subnets with about 100,000 hosts per subnet. The vice president wants to divide the subnets into 25 new subnets to make each subnet more manageable. How many bits are used for the custom subnet mask?

A. 4

B. 5

C. 6

D. 7

31. In question 30, what should the organization use for the subnet mask?

A. 252.0.0.0

B. 255.0.0.0

C. 255.252.0.0

D. 255.255.252.0

32. How do you create a shortcut to a phonebook entry?

A. From the RAS administrator

B. From the Dial-Up Networking icon

C. From the Internet Service Manager

D. Using drag and drop

33. What do you have to change to use a different DNS for a phonebook entry?

A. The Dial-Up Networking properties.

B. The TCP/IP properties.

C. The settings in the RAS administrator.

D. Dial-Up Networking always uses the default.

34. If your dial-in server requires you to log on and this procedure cannot be scripted, what can you do?

    A. Use Windows NT logon.

    B. Bring up a terminal window.

    C. Use Client Services for NetWare.

    D. You will not be able to dial in.

35. What does autodial do for you?

    A. Enables you to dial users from User Manager

    B. Enables you to use Windows Messaging to connect to your ISP

    C. Reconnects network resources when accessed

    D. Automatically dials at a given time

36. What events can cause the Dial-Up Networking Monitor to make a sound?

    A. Connections

    B. Errors

    C. When the program starts

    D. When the program terminates

37. Where can you grant a user dial-in permissions?

    A. From the command prompt

    B. From User Manager

    C. From the RAS administrator

    D. From Server Manager

38. A DHCP client has been configured to use the wrong DNS server. How can you correct the problem?

    A. Change the scope options on DHCP and then renew the lease on the client.

    B. Use IPCONFIG /update:DNS to make the change.

    C. Enter the address of the DNS server in the advanced properties of TCP/IP.

    D. Add an entry for the DHCP client on the other DNS server.

39. A TCP/IP client had a drive mapped to a Windows NT Server. You have just changed the IP address of the server and rebooted. Now the client can't connect to the new server, even though the server is configured to be a WINS client. What is the most likely cause of this problem?

    A. The WINS server hasn't copied the new registration to all its clients.

    B. The client has the old IP address cached.

    C. The LMHOSTS file on the Windows NT Server needs to be updated.

    D. The DNS server needs to be updated.

40. On a Windows NT computer, where does TCP/IP display its error messages?

    A. In the TCP/IP log file

    B. In the SNMP log file

    C. In the System Log

    D. In the TCP.ERR file

41. How can you test the installation of an FTP server?

    A. Ping the FTP loopback address.

    B. Ping another FTP server.

    C. FTP another server.

    D. FTP the loopback address.

42. In a network that has a mixture of Windows NT and remote host systems, you want to administer remote host systems from a Windows NT computer by running remote system jobs. Which of the following utilities enables you to execute a job on a remote system without requiring a logon password?

    A. TFTP

    B. REXEC

    C. RSH

    D. Telnet

43. Your network provides a Web server to the Internet through a typical firewall. Which of the following protocols would usually NOT be available to a client on the other side of your firewall?

    A. HTTP

    B. FTP

    C. TFTP

    D. Telnet

44. HTML documents are transferred using the HTTP protocol. Which of the following statements, accurately describes the HTTP protocol?

    A. HTTP uses the non-connection-oriented communication features of TCP/IP for data transfer.

    B. HTTP requires a user name and password for all HTML documents.

    C. The HTTP protocol uses the connection-oriented communication features of TCP/IP for data transfer.

    D. HTTP can be used only for text files.

45. Which parameters are required when using the LPR command on a Windows NT computer to send a print job to a remote host?

    A. The remote host name

    B. User name and password for the remote system

    C. The remote printer name

    D. The name of the file to be printed

    E. The remote system's SMB server name

46. Which of the following describes the functions that are added when you create an LPR printer on a Windows NT computer and share the newly created printer?

    A. Remote host systems can print to the LPR printer, and Windows NT client computers can print to the LPR printer, but only by using the LPR command.

    B. Remote host systems can print to the LPR printer, and Windows NT computers can print to the LPR printer using Windows NT printing, but other Windows NT computers cannot print to the LPR printer.

    C. Remote host systems can print to the LPR printer, Windows NT computers can print to the LPR printer using Windows NT printing, and other Windows NT computers can print to the LPR printer.

    D. Remote host systems cannot print to the LPR printer, Windows NT computers can print to the LPR printer using Windows NT printing, and other Windows NT computers can print to the LPR printer.

47. What is the purpose of the Domain Suffix Search Order?

    A. When you look for a host name, entries here can be used to complete the FQDN.

    B. When you look for a NetBIOS name, entries here can be used as the NetBIOS scope ID.

    C. Allows your computer to be in more than one domain at a time.

    D. Tells your systems which Windows NT domains to search when looking for a logon server.

48. Which of the following best describes the order in which you should configure the DNS server?

    A. Install the server, create the zone, enter all the records, create the reverse lookup zone, and add the WINS records

    B. Install the server, create the reverse lookup zone, add the zone information, add the WINS lookup records, and add the other hosts

C. Create the DNS server database files using a text editor, install the server, and verify the information

D. Install the DNS server and then transfer the zone from the WINS server

49. What information is contained in an MX record? (Choose all that apply.)

A. A Preference entry.

B. The mail server name.

C. The WWW server name.

D. There is no such record.

50. What is the purpose of the cache file?

A. Stores the names of hosts that your server has resolved

B. Enables you to enter commonly used hosts that will be loaded to the cache

C. Stores the addresses of root-level servers

D. Temporarily builds the DNS server information as the server starts

51. If a domain announcement is sent out to a domain and the domain does not respond, how long is it before the remote domain is removed from the browse list?

A. Four announcement periods

B. Three announcement periods

C. Two announcement periods

D. Five announcement periods

52. You have a network with three subnets: subnet A, subnet B, and subnet C. What happens if the domain Master Browser on subnet A goes down?

A. Browsing is restricted to each subnet.

B. Subnet B can see C, but not A.

C. Subnet C can see B, but not A.

D. All subnets continue browsing normally.

53. How can you configure a WINS server to automatically replicate its database with any other WINS servers?

A. Specify All Servers as push partners for replication.

B. Turn on the Migrate On/Off switch in WINS Manager.

C. Set the UseSelfFndPnrs parameter in the Registry to 0.

D. Turn off the Replicate Only with Partners switch in WINS Manager.

54. How does a client decide which WINS server to use?

A. The first WINS server that responds to a broadcast

B. The WINS server that WINS an election

C. The initial WINS server configured in TCP/IP

D. The primary WINS server specified in the DHCP scope options

55. What happens to a name registration when the host crashes?

A. The WINS server marks the record as released after it queries the client at half of TTL.

B. The name is marked as released after three renewal periods are missed.

C. The name is scavenged after the registration expires.

D. The name is released after the TTL is over.

56. On which platform can you install a WINS server? (Select all that apply.)

A. On a Windows NT 3.51 member server

B. On a Windows NT 4.0 Workstation running the WINS proxy agent

C. On a Windows NT 4.0 Backup Domain Controller

D. On a Windows NT 4.0 Primary Domain Controller

57. How many WINS servers should be installed?

    A. One primary for each subnet and one secondary for every two subnets

    B. One primary for every 2,000 clients and one secondary for each additional 2,000 clients

    C. One primary and one secondary for every 10,000 clients

    D. One primary and secondary for each domain

58. How do you configure automatic address resolution for DHCP clients?

    A. Specify the Create WINS database option in the DHCP scope

    B. Install a WINS server with an address specified by the DHCP scope

    C. Schedule the active leases to be copied from DCHP Manager to an LMHOSTS file

    D. Locate a DHCP relay agent on the same subnet as the WINS server

Answers and Explanations

1. **E** A subnet mask of 240 is needed to make up to 14 subnets available on a class C network.

2. **C** A subnet mask of 240 on a class C network allows for up to 14 hosts at each subnet.

3. **B** NetBEUI is considered an unroutable protocol.

4. **B** A subnet mask of 224 will make six subnets available with up to 30 hosts at each site.

5. **A** The rexec daemon support is not provided with standard Windows NT 4.0.

6. **D** SNMP—Simple Network Management Protocol—obtains detailed host information for remote management.

7. **B** DHCP reservations are made to Network adapter cards.

8. **D** The Jetpack utility compacts a DHCP database.

9. **B** The default subnet mask for a class A network is 255.0.0.0.

10. **D** A subnet mask of 248 will allow for up to 30 subnets.

11. **D** A subnet mask of 248 on a class B network will allow for up to 2,046 hosts at each subnet.

12. **A** WINS maps IP addresses to NetBIOS names.

13. **B, D** ComputerOne is a NetBIOS name, as is \\ComputerOne. www.microsoft.com is an example of a fully qualified domain name (FQDN); 192.14.2.15 is an example of an IP address.

14. **B** IP is the protocol that provides message addressing and routing.

15. **C** UDP is connectionless, whereas TCP is connection oriented.

16. **D** The default subnet mask for class C networks is 255.255.255.0.

17. **A, B** 200.200.256.1 exceeds the maximum value in the third octet: 127.0.0.1 is the loopback address.

18. **C** A WINS proxy is any WINS client configured to provide name resolution services to non-WINS clients.

19. **A, C, D** Services not provided by the WINS proxy to non-WINS clients include name registration, resolution, renewal, and release.

20. **A** If the primary WINS server is unavailable, the secondary WINS server can provide the same services to WINS clients.

21. **C** Name renewal occurs automatically before the name registration's time to live expires.

22. **C** Name registration occurs when a WINS client starts and sends a name registration request to a WINS server.

23. **A** The OSI model has seven layers.

24. **C** The TCP/IP model has four layers.

25. **A**   The default network ID for address 121.212.112.122 is 121.0.0.0.

26. **C**   The default network ID for address 198.81.91.119, by default, is 198.81.91.0.

27. **B**   The default host ID for address 179.79.234.234 is 0.0.234.234.

28. **B**   Fifteen subnets are required, which converts to binary 1111. Four bits don't have enough subnets because 0000 and 1111 can't be used. Therefore, 5 bits are needed, which allows for 30 subnets. C and D also allow for enough subnets, but more is not always better. Because this is a class B network, using 6 bits barely allows for 1,000 hosts per subnet (1,022), leaving very little room for growth. Using 7 bits allows for only 510 hosts per subnet.

29. **D**   This subnet mask uses the 5 higher-order bits in the third octet to specify the subnet, as calculated in question 28. A is the default subnet mask, which allows for only one network ID. C is binary 11111. Remember when converting the required number of bits to a decimal number, you must fill in the lower-order bits with zeroes. The correct binary subnet mask is 11111000, which is decimal 248.

30. **C**   Although B is certainly a correct answer because it allows for 30 subnets, there is very little room for growth in the number of subnets. Because you have a class A network ID, 524,286 host IDs are possible within each of the 30 subnets. A better approach is to sacrifice one of the host address bits to allow for 62 subnets. This solution still allows for 262,142 hosts on each subnet, 160 percent more than the original needs.

31. **C**   The subnet mask 255.252.0.0 is correct for a class A network that allows 62 subnets. A puts the 252 one octet too soon. D puts the octet too late, making it a class B subnet mask. B is the default subnet mask for a class A network.

32. **B**   You can create a shortcut to a phonebook entry from the Dial-Up Networking icon.

33. **A**   To use a different DNS for a phonebook entry, you must change the Dial-Up Networking properties.

34. **B**   If your dial-in server requires you to log on and this procedure cannot be scripted, you can bring up a terminal window.

35. **C**   Autodial reconnects network resources when accessed.

36. **A, B**   Events that can cause the Dial-Up Networking Monitor to make a sound include on connection and on errors.

37. **B, C**   You can grant a user dial-in permissions from User Manager or from the RAS administrator.

38. **A**   You can correct the problem by changing the scope options on DHCP and then renewing the lease on the client.

39. **B**   The most likely cause of the problem is that the client has the old IP address cached.

40. **C**   On a Windows NT computer, TCP/IP displays its error messages in the System Log.

41. **D**   You can FTP the loopback address to test the installation of an FTP server.

42. **C**   RSH enables you to execute a job on a remote system without requiring a logon password.

43. **D**   Telnet would usually *not* be available to a client on the other side of a firewall.

44. **C**   The HTTP protocol uses the connection-oriented communication features of TCP/IP for data transfer.

45. **A, C, D**   The LPR command on a Windows NT computer needs the remote host name, the remote printer name, and the name of the file to be printed.

46. **C**   Remote host systems can print to the LPR printer, Windows NT computers can print to the LPR printer using Windows NT printing, and other Windows NT computers can print to the LPR printer.

47. **A**   The Domain Suffix Search Order is used when you look for a host name. Entries here can be used to complete the FQDN.

48. **B** Configure the DNS server as follows: Install the server, create the reverse lookup zone, add the zone information, add the WINS lookup records, and add the other hosts.

49. **A, B** An MX record contains a Preference entry and the mail server name.

50. **C** The purpose of the cache file is to store the addresses of root-level servers.

51. **B** If a domain announcement is sent out to a domain and the domain does not respond, three announcement periods and 45 minutes pass before the remote domain is removed from the browse list.

52. **A** Browsing is restricted to each subnet.

53. **D** A WINS server can automatically replicate with any other WINS server. However, WINS is configured by default to replicate only with specified partners. You must turn off this parameter to enable the automatic replication.

54. **D** A WINS client communicates only with WINS servers for which the client is configured. You can configure these WINS servers in one of two ways. You can manually specify a WINS server with the primary WINS server address in TCP/IP. Or you can specify the primary WINS server address through the scope options of DHCP for clients that receive their TCP/IP addresses from DHCP.

55. **D** After a client registers its NetBIOS name with a WINS server, it is the client's responsibility to renew that registration. The WINS server does not initiate any registration renewals with clients. The registration is released if not renewed by the time the TTL expires. However, the entry is not scavenged until the Extinction Interval and the Extinction Timeout have expired.

56. **A, C, D** You can install a WINS server on any Windows NT Server platform.

57. **C** You should have one primary and one secondary WINS server for every 10,000 WINS clients. Although the secondary server is not required, it can serve as a backup if the primary WINS server goes down.

58. **B** Resolving addresses for DHCP clients needs to be automated because DHCP clients can end up with a different TCP/IP address every time they reboot. Installing a WINS server, which is configured as part of the DHCP scope options, is the only practical way to resolve NetBIOS names in this environment.

Practice Exam 2

For information about this exam's duration, the number of questions required to pass, and other details, refer to Appendix B, "About the Exam."

Exam 70–59: Internetworking with Microsoft TCP/IP on Microsoft Windows NT 4.0

1. Where can you enable a log that will record all the communications between the modem and the system?
    - A. In the Telephony API Advanced options
    - B. In the RAS Administration tool under Advanced options
    - C. In the Modem Advanced properties
    - D. In the Port Settings Advanced dialog box

2. What types of security does the RAS server accept?
    - A. Clear text
    - B. Kerberos
    - C. Shiva
    - D. Microsoft

3. You are an Internet administrator in a small foam packaging firm. You've set up IIS to run an Internet site. What is the name of the new user created by IIS during installation? (Computername is the computer name on which IIS is installed.)
    - A. IISR_computername
    - B. anon_computername
    - C. IWAM_computername
    - D. IUSR_computername

4. You are using Performance Monitor but very few TCP/IP statistics are available. How can you increase the number of TCP/IP objects and counters to monitor?
    - A. Install a Promiscuous mode adapter card.
    - B. Configure the correct default gateway in Performance Monitor.
    - C. Bind TCP/IP to the Monitor service.
    - D. Install the SNMP service.

5. TCP/IP is not working. You recall that when Windows NT first booted, the message A Dependency Service Failed to Start appeared. What is a possible cause of the problem?
    - A. The SNMP service is not installed.
    - B. The network card is not configured correctly.
    - C. The secondary WINS server is down.
    - D. The PDC of your domain is down.

6. You can ping a remote host's IP address, but you cannot connect to a share on that host. What is a possible cause of this problem?

   A. The share must be configured to enable anonymous connections.

   B. The Host Name Resolution Protocol must be installed.

   C. The LMHOSTS file does not have any entry for this server.

   D. The client has not been configured to use DHCP.

7. You made a mistake in configuring an IP address and typed the client's address as 96.82.49.208 rather than as 196.82.49.208. What is the most likely result of this configuration error?

   A. The client can communicate only with hosts having the network address 96.x.x.x.

   B. The client cannot communicate with hosts beyond the local subnet.

   C. The client cannot communicate with hosts on the local subnet.

   D. The client cannot communicate with any hosts.

8. You are using NWLink and TCP/IP. How can you reduce the time that is needed to establish a TCP/IP session with another host?

   A. Move TCP/IP to the top of the bindings for the Workstation service.

   B. Configure the default gateway address to point to a faster router.

   C. Decrease the TTL for WINS registrations.

   D. Use SNMP to tune the TCP/IP cache size.

9. A DHCP client has failed to lease an IP address. What is the best way to have the client try again to get a lease?

   A. Issue a REQUEST command to the DHCP server.

   B. Reserve an address for the client on the DHCP server.

   C. Use IPCONFIG /release and IPCONFIG /renew.

   D. Reboot the client.

10. What happens if you do not configure a router address on a TCP/IP client?

   A. You cannot communicate with any other TCP/IP hosts.

   B. You can communicate only with hosts connected to the default gateway.

   C. You can communicate only with hosts on the local subnet.

   D. TCP/IP doesn't initialize.

11. For SNMP agents and management systems to communicate with each other, they need to be set up with the same _____ name.

   A. Public

   B. Unity

   C. Group

   D. Community

12. If you are having problems with SNMP, where in Windows NT should you look?

   A. Event Viewer in Windows NT Administrative tools

   B. Performance Monitor

   C. The SNMP log

   D. Windows NT diagnostics

13. Which agent services are enabled by default when setting up the Windows NT SNMP agent?

   A. Internet

   B. Physical

C. End to End

D. Application

14. Which SNMP operation is instituted by the agent instead of the management system?

A. Walk

B. Set

C. Trap

D. Get

15. The message sent by an SNMP agent to warn an SNMP management system of an error or specific event is known as a _____.

A. Net

B. Trap

C. Get

D. Warning event

16. What is the name of the utility found in the Windows NT Resource Kit that you can use to check whether the SNMP service is configured correctly and working with the SNMP management system?

A. SNMPCHECK

B. SNMPSTAT

C. SNMPUTIL

D. SNMPMANG

17. What is the object identifier for a MIB II?

A. iso.org.dod.internet.management. mib2

B. iso.org.dod.internet.management. mibii

C. 1.3.6.2.2

D. 2.2.6.3.1

18. The MIB architecture can be extended to enable developers to create their own MIB libraries by using _____.

A. Extension agents

B. Extendor agents

C. Additional dynamic link libraries

D. Cover agents

19. Why would you install the SNMP service?

A. You want to monitor TCP/IP with Performance Monitor.

B. You want to remotely manage a proxyagent.

C. You want to monitor a Windows NT–based system with a third-party application.

D. You want to set up your computer as an SNMP agent.

20. Which utility can you use to transfer a file to a remote host using the connection-oriented services of TCP/IP?

A. TFTP

B. HTML

C. FTP

D. Telnet

21. Given a remote host system running TCP/IP and having an SMB server service, which of the following methods provides the most transparent network connectivity for file transfer?

A. Using an NFS client on a Windows NT computer

B. Using Microsoft networking functions on a Windows NT computer

C. Using FTP to copy files from the remote host to your local computer

D. Using Telnet to establish a remote terminal session with the remote host

22. Which of the following statements about Telnet are incorrect?

A. Telnet can be used to remotely administer Windows NT computers.

B. Telnet encrypts user names and passwords for enhanced security.

C. Telnet can be used to provide terminal emulation when connecting to remote host systems.

D. Telnet can be used to view HTML documents with graphical images.

23. A user on a Windows NT computer wishes to run an interactive text editor on a remote host computer. Which utilities would be suitable?

    A. Telnet
    B. FTP
    C. REXEC
    D. RSH
    E. HTTP

24. A user at a Windows NT computer running the TCP/IP protocol wishes to send a print job to an LPR printer on a remote host system. Which methods enable the user to send the print job to the remote host?

    A. Using the LPD command-line utility from the Windows NT system, specifying the host name, printer name, and filename
    B. Using the LPR command-line utility from the Windows NT system, specifying the host name, printer name, and filename
    C. Creating an LPR printer via Control Panel | Printers and specifying the host name and printer name required for the creation of an LPR port
    D. Creating an LPR printer via Control Panel | Printers and specifying the host name and printer name required for the creation of an LPD server on the Windows NT computer

25. Your organization currently uses a UNIX server for DNS. The server is fully configured using BIND files. In which two ways can you configure your Microsoft DNS server so you will not need to reenter any information?

    A. Set up Microsoft DNS as the primary and transfer the zone to the UNIX system.
    B. Set up Microsoft DNS as the secondary and transfer the zone from the UNIX system.

    C. Configure the Microsoft DNS server as an IP forwarder.
    D. Configure the Microsoft DNS server as a caching only server.

26. What is the default subnet mask for an IP address of 199.1.2.3?

    A. 255.255.255.0
    B. 255.255.0.0
    C. 255.0.0.0
    D. 127.0.0.1

27. You have a computer called WEBSERVER with a TCP/IP address of 148.53.66.45 running Microsoft Internet Information Server. This system provides the HTTP and FTP services for your organization on the Internet. Which of the following sets of entries are correct for your database file?

    A. www IN A 148.53.66.45
       ftp IN A 148.53.66.45
    B. www IN A 148.53.66.45
       ftp IN A 148.53.66.45
       webserver CNAME www
    C. webserver IN A 148.53.66.45
       www CNAME webserver
       ftp CNAME webserver
    D. 45.66.53.148 IN PTR webserver

28. Which of the following is *not* part of a Fully Qualified Domain Name? (Choose all that apply.)

    A. Type of organization
    B. Host name
    C. Company name
    D. CPU type

29. Your organization uses a firewall; inside the firewall, you have five subnets. You intended to provide a DNS server on each subnet, but want them to query the main DNS server that sits outside the firewall. What configuration should you choose for

the DNS servers that you will put on each subnet?

A. Configure the DNS server outside the firewall to use a WINS server on each local subnet. Then configure the DNS servers on the local subnets to use WINS resolution.

B. Set up the DNS servers on the local subnets as IP forwarders to the DNS server outside the firewall.

C. Create a primary zone on each DNS server inside the firewall and configure the DNS server outside the firewall to transfer each zone.

D. This is not possible.

30. When you are configuring your DNS server, where do you configure the length of time that an entry will be cached on your server?

A. Set the TTL in the DNS Manager properties on your server.

B. Set the TTL in the cache file on the remote server.

C. Set the TTL in the Registry under HKEY_LOCAL_MACHINE\ SYSTEM\CurrentControlSet\Services\ TCPIP\Parameters.

D. Set the TTL in the remote server in the SOA record.

31. What are the benefits of DNS? (Select all that apply.)

A. It allows a distributed database that can be administered by a number of administrators.

B. It allows host names that specify where a host is located.

C. It allows WINS clients to register with the WINS server.

D. It allows queries to other servers to resolve host names.

32. With what non-Microsoft DNS platforms is Microsoft DNS compatible?

A. Only UNIX DNS servers that are based on BIND

B. Only UNIX DNS servers that are based on the DNS RFCs

C. UNIX DNS servers that are either BIND-based or RFC-based

D. Only other Microsoft DNS servers

33. In the DNS name www.microsoft.com, what does "microsoft" represent?

A. The last name of the host

B. The domain in which the host is located

C. The IP address of the building in which the host is located

D. The directory in which the host name file is located

34. If you do not specify the host name and domain in the TCP/IP configuration before installing DNS, what happens during the DNS installation?

A. An NS record is not created on the server.

B. DNS doesn't install.

C. Default values are used to create NS and SOA records.

D. You cannot create any zones on the server.

35. How do you create a Primary DNS server?

A. Install DNS on a Primary Domain Controller

B. Use the server properties to configure the DNS server to be a primary server

C. During DNS installation, specify that it is to be a primary server

D. Create a primary zone

36. Where can a secondary server receive a copy of the zone file?

    A. Only from the primary server for the zone

    B. From any server that has a copy of the zone file

    C. Only from the master server for the zone

    D. Only from the top-level DNS server for the domain

37. What record must be added to a zone file to alias a host to another name?

    A. An A record

    B. An SOA record

    C. A CNAME record

    D. A PTR record

38. Who is in charge of continually updating the browse list and managing the database of network resources of domains and workgroups?

    A. Backup Browser

    B. Master Browser

    C. Potential Browser

    D. Browser Browser

39. Which of these statements is not true about the DomainAnnouncement packet?

    A. It has the name of a domain.

    B. It has the name of the Master Browser for that domain.

    C. It specifies whether the Master Browser is a Windows NT Server or Workstation.

    D. If it is a Windows NT Server, it specifies the version number of the server.

40. You have a network with five different subnets, each with its own Master Browser. The network administrator wants to see resources of each subnet at the same time. Which process allows for this?

    A. Directed datagram

    B. Directed telegram

    C. Replication

    D. Synchronization

41. How does a WINS server gather entries to add to its database?

    A. It examines each packet sent on the network.

    B. It receives a copy of the browse list from the Master Browser on each network segment.

    C. WINS clients send a name registration to the WINS server.

    D. It retrieves a copy of the computer accounts in each domain.

42. Where does a client first look to resolve a NetBIOS name?

    A. In the NetBIOS cache on the WINS server

    B. In the NetBIOS cache on the WINS proxy agent

    C. In the NetBIOS cache on the Primary Domain Controller

    D. In the NetBIOS cache on the client

43. What type of names are registered by WINS clients? (Select all that apply.)

    A. The computer name

    B. The domain name of a domain controller

    C. Share names created on that computer

    D. The names of network services

44. How do you configure automatic backup of the WINS database?

    A. Use the AT command to schedule the backup.

    B. Specify the name of the backup directory in WINS Manager.

    C. Specify the backup interval in WINS Manager.

    D. Install a tape device via Control Panel | SCSI Adapters

45. When does a WINS client try to renew its registration?

   A. After three days

   B. One day before the registration expires

   C. Every 24 hours

   D. When half of the registration life has expired

46. By default, where does the WINS server first write changes to the database?

   A. To the log file

   B. To the database

   C. To the Registry

   D. To the temporary database

47. How do you configure replication to occur at specified intervals?

   A. Configure a WINS server to be a pull partner

   B. Use the AT command to schedule replication

   C. Configure a WINS server to be a push partner

   D. Edit the ReplIntrvl parameter in the Registry

48. Your network has 100 client computers and four servers. Name resolution is handled by broadcast. By implementing a primary and a secondary WINS server to your network and configuring all client computers to use WINS for name resolution, which of the following will not occur?

   A. Broadcast traffic will decrease.

   B. Broadcast traffic will increase.

   C. Non-WINS clients will be able to register their computer names on the WINS server.

   D. Non-WINS clients will be able to resolve name queries from both the primary and secondary WINS servers.

49. Your network has 50 client computers using WINS and two servers acting as primary and secondary WINS servers. You want to add a WINS proxy to your network to provide name services to non-WINS clients. Which of the statements below would satisfy this requirement?

   A. Do nothing; non-WINS clients can use WINS servers directly.

   B. Configure the primary WINS server as a WINS proxy.

   C. Configure the secondary WINS server as a WINS proxy.

   D. Configure one of the WINS client computers as a WINS proxy.

50. Your network has 20 client computers configured as WINS clients using p-node name resolution. If the primary and secondary WINS servers are not available, but a WINS proxy is available, how will names be resolved by clients?

   A. Clients will use broadcast name resolution.

   B. Clients will attempt to resolve names from a WINS proxy.

   C. One of the client computers will be promoted to the primary WINS server.

   D. Clients will be unable to resolve names.

51. Your network has 800 client computers configured as WINS clients using m-node name resolution. The client computers are split onto four subnets of 200 computers. Each subnet has a primary WINS server. You want to decrease broadcast traffic and increase reliability. Your solution is to add a secondary WINS server to each subnet and to change the client configuration from m-node to h-node. This solution:

   A. Accomplishes both of the objectives

   B. Accomplishes the first objective, but not the second

C. Accomplishes the second objective, but not the first

D. Accomplishes neither objective

52. Before a client can receive a DHCP address, what must be configured on the DHCP server?

A. The DHCP relay agent

B. A scope for the client's subnet

C. A scope for the server's subnet

D. A host name

53. What must a router support in order to pass DHCP broadcasts?

A. RFC 1543

B. BOOTP Relay

C. RFC 1544

D. This can't be done.

54. What is the recommended method of providing backup to the DHCP server?

A. Configure two DHCP servers with the same scope

B. Configure a BOOTP server

C. Replicate the database using directory replication

D. Configure two DHCP servers with different sections of the scope

55. What is the effect of an Unlimited lease duration?

A. DHCP configuration options will never be updated.

B. There is no effect.

C. There will be an increase in network traffic.

D. Addresses cannot be shared dynamically.

56. In what environment is it advisable to have a short lease duration?

A. In static environments where addresses don't change often

B. When you have fewer hosts than IP addresses

C. In environments where you have hosts moving and many changes to IP addresses

D. When you have more hosts than IP addresses

57. What portions of the DHCP process are initiated by the server?

A. Lease acquisition.

B. Lease renewal.

C. Lease release.

D. No processes are initiated by the server.

58. An organization is assigned the network ID 114.0.0.0 by InterNIC. The organization currently has five subnets with about 100,000 hosts per subnet. The vice-president wants to divide the subnets into 25 new subnets to make each subnet more manageable. How many bits are used for the custom subnet mask?

A. 4

B. 5

C. 6

D. 7

Answers and Explanations

1. **C** In the Modem Advanced properties you can enable a log that will record all the communications between the modem and the system.

2. **A, D** The RAS server will accept clear text and Microsoft types of security.

3. **D** The name of the anonymous account is always IUSR_ and the name of the host computer.

4. **D** The SNMP service must be installed to increase the number of TCP/IP objects and counters to monitor.

5. **B** A Dependency Service Failed to Start message can indicate that the network card is not configured correctly.

6. **C**   A problem with connecting to shares can be symptomatic of the LMHOSTS file not having an entry for this server.

7. **D**   An incorrect IP address can prevent the client from communicating with any hosts.

8. **A**   Moving TCP/IP to the top of the bindings for the Workstation service can reduce the time that is needed to establish a TCP/IP session with another host.

9. **C**   Use IPCONFIG /release and IPCONFIG /renew.

10. **C**   You can communicate only with hosts on the local subnet.

11. **D**   For SNMP agents and management systems to communicate with each other, they need to be set up with the same community name.

12. **A**   If you are having problems with SNMP, look in Event Viewer in Windows NT Administrative tools.

13. **A, C, D**   SNMP agent services enabled by default when setting up the Windows NT SNMP agent include Internet, End to End, and Application.

14. **C**   The trap SNMP operation is instituted by the agent instead of the management system.

15. **B**   The message sent by an SNMP agent to warn an SNMP management system of an error or specific event is known as a trap.

16. **C**   SNMPUTIL is the utility found in the Windows NT Resource Kit that can be used to check whether the SNMP Service is configured correctly and working with the SNMP management system.

17. **B**   iso.org.dod.internet.management.mibii is the object identifier for a MIB II.

18. **A**   The MIB architecture can be extended to enable developers to create their own MIB libraries by using extension agents.

19. **A, C, D**   The SNMP Service should be installed if you want to monitor TCP/IP with Performance Monitor, monitor a Windows NT–based system with a

third-party application, or set up your computer as an SNMP agent.

20. **C**   You can use FTP to transfer a file to a remote host using the connection-oriented services of TCP/IP.

21. **B**   Using Microsoft networking functions on a Windows NT computer provides the most transparent network connectivity for file transfer.

22. **A, B, D**   The only true statement is that Telnet can be used to provide terminal emulation when connecting to remote host systems. The others are all incorrect.

23. **A, D**   Telnet and RSH can be used to run an interactive text editor on a remote host computer.

24. **B, C**   You can send the print job to the remote host by using the LPR command-line utility from the Windows NT system and specifying the host name, printer name, and filename or by creating an LPR printer via Control Panel | Printers and specifying the host name and printer name required for the creation of an LPR port.

25. **B, C**   Both Setup Microsoft DNS as the Secondary and transfer the zone from the UNIX system and configure the Microsoft DNS server as an IP Forwarder are correct.

26. **A**   The default subnet mask for a class C address is 255.255.255.0.

27. **C**   The correct answer is webserver IN A 148.53.66.45, www CNAME webserver, ftp CNAME webserver.

28. **D**   An FQDN contains the type of organization, host name, and company name.

29. **B**   The correct configuration is to set up the DNS servers on the local subnets as IP forwarders to the DNS server outside the firewall.

30. **D**   Set the TTL in the remote server in the SOA record.

31. **A, B, D**   Although DNS on a Windows NT Server can be configured to query the WINS server for a name resolution, WINS clients do not register themselves directly with the DNS server.

32. **C**   NT DNS is based on the RFCs for DNS, but it is designed to be compatible with DNS servers based on BIND as well.

33. **B**   The path specifies a host named www in a domain microsoft. The domain microsoft is located in the top-level domain com.

34. **A**   The host name and domain values are used to create default records when the server is installed. You may have to create these records later so the DNS server can communicate with its clients and other servers, but you can still install DNS and create zones. If the values aren't specified, only the SOA record is created automatically.

35. **D**   The designation Primary Server means the DNS server is the primary server for a zone file. It can also be the secondary server for another zone file. In other words, the role of a DNS server is determined on a zone-by-zone basis.

36. **B**   A secondary server can receive a copy of the zone file from a primary server or from a secondary server that has a copy of the zone file. The server from which the secondary server receives the copy is its master server. However, there is not the concept of a master server for a zone. There may be five secondary servers in a zone, each receiving a copy of the zone file from another secondary server in the zone. The number of master servers for a zone file is unlimited.

37. **C**   A CNAME record is a Canonical Name record used to create aliases. An A record is used to register the real host name. An SOA record contains the authority information for the zone file. A PTR record exists only in reverse lookup zones; it maps the IP address to a host name, not the host name to an IP address.

38. **B**   The Master Browser is in charge of continually updating the browse list and managing the database of network resources of domains and workgroups.

39. **D**   The DomainAnnouncement packet has the name of a domain, has the name of the Master Browser for that domain, and specifies whether the Master Browser is a Windows NT Server or Workstation.

40. **A**   Directed datagrams allow the network administrator to see resources on each subnet at the same time.

41. **C**   The only time a WINS server automatically collects entries is when a WINS client is configured with that WINS server's address. When the client starts up, it sends a registration request to the WINS server.

42. **D**   A client always tries to resolve a NetBIOS name through its own name cache. If the entry is not found, then the client sends a name resolution request to the WINS server. The WINS server looks in the WINS database for the resolution at that point.

43. **A, B, D**   All networking services register with WINS. A domain controller must also register its domain name with WINS, along with its computer name, so clients of that domain can log on.

44. **B**   You can back up the WINS database only through the WINS Manager. After you specify the path of the backup directory, backups automatically take place every 24 hours. The 24-hour option is the only backup interval that you can set. However, you can do a manual backup through WINS Manager.

45. **D**   A client first tries to renew its registration when half of the time to live has expired. Although the default time to live is six days, the more correct answer is half of the TTL because the default TTL could have been changed.

46. **A**   The WINS database is a transactional database in which changes are first written to a log file and then to the database. This process gives the database a backup source for all its changes.

47. **A**   Only pull partners can have replication occur at specified times. Push replication occurs after a specified number of changes

have been made to the WINS database. The Registry does not have a ReplIntrvl parameter.

48. **B, C, D** Broadcast traffic will increase, non-WINS clients will not be able to register their computer names on the WINS server, and non-WINS clients will not be able to resolve name queries from both the primary and secondary WINS servers.

49. **D** Configure one of the WINS client computers as a WINS proxy to provide name services to non-WINS clients.

50. **D** In the scenario described, if the primary and secondary WINS servers are not available, but a WINS proxy is available, clients will be unable to resolve names.

51. **A** The solution given accomplishes both objectives.

52. **B** Before a client can receive a DHCP address, a scope for the client's subnet must be configured on the DHCP server.

53. **B** A router must support BOOTP Relay to pass DHCP broadcasts.

54. **D** Configuring two DHCP servers with different sections of the scope is the recommended method of providing backup to the DHCP server.

55. **A** With a lease duration of Unlimited, DHCP configuration options will never be updated.

56. **C** A short lease duration should be used in environments where you have hosts moving and many changes to IP addresses.

57. **D** No portions of the DHCP process are initiated by the server.

58. **C** Although B is certainly a correct answer because it allows for 30 subnets, there is very little room for growth in the number of subnets. Because you have a class A network ID, 524,286 host IDs are possible within each of the 30 subnets. A better approach is to sacrifice one of the host address bits to allow for 62 subnets. This solution still allows for 262,142 hosts on each subnet, 160 percent more than the original needs.

Practice Exam 2

Practice Exam 3

For information about this exam's duration, the number of questions required to pass, and other details, refer to Appendix A, "All About the Exam."

Exam 70–59: Internetworking with Microsoft TCP/IP on Microsoft Windows NT 4.0

1. Which of the following are required before two hosts can exchange files using the File Transfer Protocol?
   A. Both hosts must be running TCP/IP.
   B. One host must be running the FTP server service.
   C. The FTP client must have copy privileges on the FTP server share to get or put a file on the FTP server.
   D. The FTP client must have a valid account on the FTP server, or anonymous connections must be allowed on the FTP server.

2. Which of the following is caused by having so many packets in one location that not all of them can be successfully processed or queued at a given time?
   A. Bandwidth
   B. Congestion
   C. Collision
   D. Streaming

3. Which of the following protocols are not considered routable?
   A. TCP/IP
   B. NetBEUI
   C. NWLink
   D. AppleTalk

4. Which of the following services require a daemon not supplied with Windows NT?
   A. REXEC
   B. FTP
   C. LPQ
   D. LPR

5. ICMP operates at which layer of the TCP/IP core architecture model (refer to Figure P3.1 if needed)?
   A. Application
   B. Transport
   C. Internet
   D. Network interface

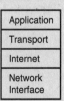

Figure P3.1.

6. If you have a network ID of 192 and need a minimum of six subnets while never employing more than 20 hosts, the best subnet to use is

    A. 192

    B. 224

    C. 240

    D. 248

    E. 252

7. Which of the following is a diagnostic utility used to display NetBIOS over TCP/IP protocol statistics?

    A. NBT

    B. NETSTAT

    C. NBTSTAT

    D. TRACERT

8. A DHCP reservation is assigned to which of the following?

    A. Computer

    B. Network Adapter Card

    C. Domain

    D. Workgroup

9. The protocol responsible for allowing NetBIOS name-to-IP-address mapping is

    A. SNMP

    B. NBT

    C. LPD

    D. ARP

10. The protocol responsible for obtaining detailed host information for remote management is

    A. ICMP

    B. NBT

    C. SNMP

    D. UDP

11. Two potential problems that can occur on a network that uses only b-node name query broadcasts for NetBIOS name resolution include

    A. Broadcasts are unable to use UDP and are dependent upon TCP.

    B. Broadcasts can increase network traffic and lead to congestion.

    C. IP addresses are shared across scopes.

    D. Routers usually are not enabled to forward b-node broadcasts to other networks, so traffic is limited to the local network.

12. Which of the following is a description of the process of buffering sent and received TCP packets long enough to ensure that the reassembly process can occur without delays?

    A. Retransmit timer

    B. Sliding window

    C. SRTT (Smoothed Round Trip Time)

    D. Streaming

    E. Delayed-acknowledgment timer

13. NetBIOS over TCP/IP operates at which layer of the TCP/IP core architecture model (see Figure P3.2 if needed)?

    A. Application

    B. Transport

    C. Internet

    D. Network interface

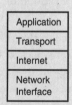

Figure P3.2.

14. What command entered at the command line displays all the information about the IP address for the local host?
    A. IPCONFIG /ALL
    B. ARP
    C. NETSTAT
    D. NBSTAT

15. Steen Realty has 30 offices in Indiana, each with about 100 users and its own subnet. Within the year, both of these numbers are expected to double. You have been assigned the network address of 150.119.0.0 and must assign a subnet to this network to support your number of sites (subnets) and users. You specify a subnet mask of 255.255.240.0. How well does this solution address the problem?
    A. It meets the requirements and is an outstanding solution.
    B. It meets the requirements and is an adequate solution.
    C. It meets the requirements but is not a desirable solution.
    D. It does not meet the requirements, although it will work.
    E. It does not meet the requirements and does not work.

16. The purpose of the application layer of the TCP/IP protocol reference model is
    A. To determine the application required to properly route the packets
    B. To act as an interface between the NetBIOS or Sockets applications and the underlying TCP/IP protocols
    C. To establish the session and connection information between two applications
    D. To encapsulate data and send it to the underlying network layer

17. Which of the following is not a valid type of SNMP transaction that can be performed at an SNMP agent?
    A. get
    B. get-next
    C. put
    D. set
    E. end trap

18. Valid subnet IDs for networks with the ID of 162 needing at least 500 hosts are
    A. 0
    B. 1
    C. 254
    D. 255

19. Leon's House Arrest and Survey-Lance is a national account with three regional sites. Each site has a little over 100 users and its own subnet. Two more offices are opening within the year, and those could have up to 375 users at each site. You have been assigned the network address of 150.50.0.0 and need to assign a subnet mask to support this configuration. You specify a subnet mask of 255.192.0.0. How well does this solution address the problem?
    A. It meets the requirements and is an outstanding solution.
    B. It meets the requirements and is an adequate solution.
    C. It meets the requirements but is not a desirable solution.
    D. It does not meet the requirements, although it will work.
    E. It does not meet the requirements and does not work.

20. With what form of name resolution do hosts on a network use broadcast UDP datagrams to register NetBIOS names and IP addresses?
    A. WINS
    B. DHCP

C. ARP

D. b-node

21. Which utility is used to run commands on a remote UNIX server?

    A. RCP

    B. RSH

    C. REXEC

    D. RRUN

22. A unique physical address assigned to a network card at the time of manufacture is

    A. The destination address

    B. The IP address

    C. The subnet address

    D. The default gateway

23. _____ is a router connected to at least one other (remote) network. If no route is known to reach a destination, it is where IP sends the datagrams.

    A. Bridge

    B. Spool

    C. Multihomed host

    D. Default gateway

24. What command-line utility would be used to compact a DHCP database?

    A. Compress

    B. Compact

    C. JetPack

    D. Pack

25. Differences between FTP and TFTP include

    A. TFTP requires IP addresses, while FTP can also use host names.

    B. FTP uses Telnet while TFTP uses RCP.

    C. TFTP uses UDP and FTP uses TCP.

    D. FTP uses user logon validation while TFTP requires only that the user names be listed in a .rhosts file.

26. Which of the following is a line printing utility that enables a print job to be sent to a UNIX printer?

    A. Daemon

    B. LPD

    C. LPR

    D. LPQ

27. Which of the following items can be monitored using SNMP?

    A. Concentrators

    B. Hubs

    C. LAN Manager servers

    D. Windows 95 dial-up servers

28. Windows Sockets operate at which layer of the TCP/IP core architecture model (see Figure P3.3 if needed)?

    A. Application

    B. Transport

    C. Internet

    D. Network interface

Figure P3.3.

29. Of the following, which network technology offers the highest bandwidth?

    A. RAS

    B. Fast Ethernet

    C. T3

    D. T1

30. What steps can you take to prevent the unauthorized access to an SNMP management information base?

    A. Set the Accepted Community field to blank.

B. Remove the public community name from the Accepted Communities list box.

C. Select the Only Accept SNMP Packets from These Hosts option and enter the host name, IP address, or IPX address of the SNMP managers.

D. Select the Send Authentication Trap check box and specify a community name and trap destination in the SNMP Configuration dialog box.

31. Which of the following is a timer set when two nonsequential packets are received to allow time for the missing packet to arrive before an acknowledgment is sent prematurely?

A. Retransmit timer

B. Sliding window

C. SRTT (Smoothed Round Trip Time)

D. Streaming

E. Delayed-acknowledgment timer

32. The Windows Internet Name Service is used to resolve which of the following?

A. NetBIOS names to IP addresses

B. IP addresses to NetBIOS names

C. Conflicts with multihomed hosts

D. IP addresses to hardware addresses

33. Which of the following is a text file containing DNS-host and domain name–to-IP address mapping?

A. LMHOSTS

B. HOSTS

C. WINS

D. FQDN

34. Which of the following is a diagnostic utility that displays the TCP/IP configuration for each adapter specified and is used to release and renew DHCP IP address leases?

A. HOSTNAME

B. IPCONFIG

C. ARP

D. NBTSTAT

35. Of the following, which network technology offers the highest bandwidth?

A. T3

B. FDDI

C. T1

D. Ethernet

36. Kristin's Magic Land has 24 offices throughout the U.S. Each office has about 100 users and its own subnet. You have heard through the grapevine that at least 12 more offices with as many as 100 users each could open this year. The numbers may be as high as 20 or more offices. You have been assigned the network address of 150.50.0.0 and must assign a subnet mask to meet your needs. You specify a subnet mask of 255.255.254.0. How well does this solution address the problem?

A. It meets the requirements and is an outstanding solution.

B. It meets the requirements and is an adequate solution.

C. It meets the requirements but is not a desirable solution.

D. It does not meet the requirements, although it will work.

E. It does not meet the requirements and does not work.

37. If a minimum of 30 hosts are needed on a network with an ID of 201, valid subnet addresses are

A. 0

B. 1

C. 192

D. 248

38. Applications that can use host names in place of IP addresses include

    A. WWW browser

    B. PING

    C. REXEC

    D. b-node broadcasts

39. A WINS database is used to

    A. Dynamically map IP addresses to network adapter card names

    B. Dynamically map IP addresses to computer names

    C. Dynamically map IP addresses to a user name

    D. Dynamically map IP addresses to subnet masks

40. You have a host with the IP address of 212.42.10.27. The subnet mask is 255.255.255.248. This makes the network ID 212.42.24, and the host ID

    A. 1

    B. 3

    C. 9

    D. 27

    E. 248

41. The following describes a host:

    Ethernet adapter NDISLoop1:
    Description: MS LoopBack Driver
    Physical address: 20-4C-4F-4F-50-20
        DHCP enabled: No
        IP address: 200.20.1.30
        Subnet mask: 255.255.255.0
        Default gateway: 200.0.1.1.

    What is the hardware address of this host?

    A. 200.20.1.30

    B. 255.255.255.0

    C. 200.20.1.1

    D. 20-4C-4F-4F-50-20

42. After installing a new NT Workstation, errors appear on startup saying that a service failed to start. The computer cannot communicate with any other computers on the network. What is the first thing you should do?

    A. Verify that Enable LMHOSTS Lookup is selected in the Advanced Microsoft TCP/IP Configuration dialog box.

    B. Verify that the correct subnet mask is used.

    C. See whether other computers on the network have the same problem. If WINS is used, ensure that the proper IP address is used and that the WINS server is functioning.

    D. Check the Event Viewer to see which services have failed and if related events provide any clues.

43. Which of the following services does not commonly register NetBIOS names using NetBT?

    A. Workstation

    B. Server

    C. Messenger

    D. Client

    E. Master Browser

44. You have a host with an IP address of 12.50.10.27. The host ID is 50.10.27, indicating that the subnet mask must be

    A. 0.0.0.0

    B. 255.0.0.0

    C. 255.255.0.0

    D. 255.255.255.0

45. You find that you can ping a remote host successfully, but you cannot connect to a share on that host in File Manager. You have a primary WINS server configured for the local host. What should you try first?

A. Verify that Enable LMHOSTS Lookup is selected in the Advanced Microsoft TCP/IP Configuration dialog box.

B. Verify that the correct subnet mask is used.

C. See whether other computers on the network have the same problem. If WINS is used, ensure that the proper IP address is used and that the WINS server is functioning.

D. Check the Event Viewer to see which services have failed and if related events provide any clues.

46. Which of the following is a protocol responsible for providing message addressing and routing?

A. TCP

B. IP

C. UDP

D. SNMP

47. Which of the following utilities emulates a command prompt on a remote UNIX server?

A. RCP

B. REXEC

C. RSH

D. RSHELL

48. The following shows a .hosts file:

195.200.19.2   George Mary Accting
195.200.19.3   Mary #Sales
195.200.19.4   Secure Payables #com
195.200.19.5   #Adams

Why can host 195.200.19.3 (named Mary) be contacted by its IP address but not its host name?

A. There are two entries for Mary and the first one is routing to 195.200.19.2.

B. The problem does not exist in the .hosts file.

C. The host must be referred to as Sales or Mary Sales.

D. The pound sign (#) is in the wrong location.

49. Which Microsoft TCP/IP utilities can run on a Windows NT host to copy files from a UNIX host running the proper daemons to the Windows NT host?

A. ARP

B. FTP

C. TFTP

D. RCP

50. Which of the following parameters can be configured manually using the NWLink protocol?

A. IP address

B. Frame type

C. Subnet mask

D. DHCP scope

51. ARP operates at which layer of the TCP/IP core architecture model (see Figure P3.4 if needed)?

A. Application

B. Transport

C. Internet

D. Network interface

Figure P3.4.

52. The maximum number of subnets a network with the ID of 200 can have with a subnet of 248 is
    A. 2
    B. 6
    C. 14
    D. 30
    E. 62

53. Which of the following is a diagnostic utility used to determine whether a destination is receiving packets sent from a source host?
    A. Finger
    B. PING
    C. ARP
    D. TRACERT

54. Which of the following IP addresses are invalid?
    A. 12.54.8.255
    B. 198.107.280.200
    C. 34.54.1.0
    D. 192.2.2.2

55. Suppose you are planning to add 30 subnets over the next year. If you have a network ID of 199 and currently have 100 subnets, which of the following is the best subnet ID to use?
    A. 0
    B. 252
    C. 254
    D. 255

56. If a minimum of 50 hosts are needed on a network with an ID of 201, valid subnet addresses are
    A. 0
    B. 1
    C. 192
    D. 224

57. What is the use of the cache file on a DNS server?
    A. It has records for DNS servers at top-level domains.
    B. It provides initial values to the DNS cache.
    C. It specifies the TTL for cached entries.
    D. It specifies the amount of memory and its location for DNS caching.

58. HOSTS file entries are limited to how many characters?
    A. 8
    B. 255
    C. 500
    D. Unlimited

Answers and Explanations

1. **A, B, D**   To successfully communicate, both hosts must be running TCP/IP, with one confiugured as a server and containing a valid account for the other host.

2. **B**   Congestion is caused by having too many packets to process or queue at any given time.

3. **B**   NetBEUI, while small in overhead, suffers from its inability to be routed (although it can be used with bridged networks).

4. **A**   FTP and LPR\LPQ services are included with Windows NT. To use REXEC, you must purchase utilities from a third party.

5. **C**   ICMP operates at the Internet layer of the TCP/IP model.

6. **B**   A subnet mask of 224 meets the needs for the number of hosts and subnets.

7. **C**   NBTSTAT is used to display NetBIOS over TCP/IP protocol statistics.

8. **B**   DHCP reservations are made at the Network Adapter Card level.

9. **B** NBT is the protocol responsible for allowing NetBIOS name-to-IP-address mapping.

10. **C** SNMP is used to provide host information for remote management.

11. **B, D** b-node broadcasts increase network traffic (which can cause congestion) and are not usually allowed by routers.

12. **B** Sliding windows buffer sent and received TCP packets to prevent delays.

13. **A** The application layer is where NetBIOS over TCP/IP operations are carried out.

14. **A** IPCONFIG /ALL displays all information about the IP address for the host.

15. **E** The solution presented does not meet the requirements given.

16. **B** The application layer acts as an interface between the NetBIOS or Sockets applications and the underlying TCP/IP protocols.

17. **C** SNMP agents can perform get, get-next, set, and send trap transactions.

18. **A, C** Class B networks needing 500 hosts need a subnet mask of 254 or less. 1 is not a valid subnet mask value.

19. **E** Class B networks needing 500 hosts need a subnet mask of 254 or less. 1 is not a valid subnet mask value.

20. **D** b-node broadcasts are used to register NetBIOS names and IP addresses.

21. **C** The REXEC command is used to run commands on a remote UNIX server.

22. **A** The destination address is a unique physical address assigned to a network card at the time of manufacture.

23. **D** The default gateway defines the route for remote network datagrams.

24. **C** The JetPack command is used to compact a DHCP database.

25. **C, D** TFTP uses UDP and user logon validation is much less strict.

26. **C** The LPR command is used to send print jobs to a UNIX printer.

27. **A, B, C** SNMP cannot be used to monitor Windows 95 dial-up servers.

28. **A** Windows Sockets operate at the application layer of the TCP/IP model.

29. **B** Fast Ethernet offers the highest bandwidth of the choices given.

30. **B, C, D** Setting the Accepted Community field to blank does not prevent unauthorized access to the SNMP MIB.

31. **E** A delayed-acknowledgement timer allows times for missing packets to be received before sending an acknowledgement.

32. **A** WINS is used to resolve NetBIOS names to IP addresses.

33. **B** The HOSTS file is a static file of DNS-host and domain-name mappings to IP addresses.

34. **B** The IPCONFIG utility is used to display TCP/IP information, as well as to release and renew DHCP IP address leases.

35. **B** FDDI offers the highest bandwidth of the choices presented.

36. **A** The solution meets the requirements and works as well as any.

37. **A, C** For a class C address to have 30 or more hosts, a mask of 192 or less must be used. A subnet mask of 1 is not valid.

38. **A, B, C** As opposed to the others, b-node broadcasts cannot use host names in place of IP addresses.

39. **B** WINS is used to map IP addresses to computer (NetBIOS) names.

40. **B** The correct host ID is 3.

41. **D** Hardware addresses are unique numbers burned into cards at the time of manufacture.

42. **D** The Event Viewer can be used to show which services have failed to start.

43. **D** Client services do not register NetBIOS names using NetBT.

44. **B** The default subnet mask for a class A network is 255.0.0.0.

45. **C**   The first step is to attempt to isolate the problem and see if it is only happening here.

46. **B**   IP is the protocol that provides message addressing and routing.

47. **C**   The RSH utility emulates a command prompt on a remote UNIX server.

48. **A**   Each entry in the .hosts file must be unique.

49. **B, C, D**   ARP is used for address resolution, and not to copy files.

50. **B**   NWLink can be configured manually as to frame type.

51. **C**   ARP operates at the Internet layer of the TCP/IP model.

52. **D**   A class C network with a subnet value of 248 can have 30 hosts.

53. **B**   The PING utility is used to see if a destination can hear packets from a host.

54. **A, B, C**   Values of 0 or above 254 in any octet are invalid.

55. **D**   A class C network needs a subnet mask of 255 to meet the criteria given.

56. **A, C**   For a class C network to have a minimum of 50 hosts, a subnet mask of 192 or less must be used. 1 is an invalid number.

57. **A**   The cache file holds records for DNS servers at top-level lomains, and thus knows where to forward the address (and data) for further name resolution beneath the top level.

58. **B**   There can be an unlimited number of lines in a HOSTS file, but each line (entry) is limited to 255 characters in length.

Practice Exam 4

For information about this exam's duration, the number of questions required to pass, and other details, refer to Appendix A, "All About the Exam."

Exam 70–59: Internetworking with Microsoft TCP/IP on Microsoft Windows NT 4.0

1. The following shows a HOSTS file:

   195.200.19.2 George #Mary Accting
   195.200.19.3 #Mary #Sales
   195.200.19.4 Secure Payables #com
   195.200.19.5 #Adams

   Why can host 195.200.19.3 (named Mary) be contacted by its IP address but not its host name?

   A. There are two entries for Mary and the first one is routing to 195.200.19.2.

   B. The problem does not exist in the HOSTS file.

   C. The host must be referred to as Sales or Mary Sales.

   D. The pound sign (#) is in the wrong location.

2. An IP address of 191.191.191.191 will have a default subnet mask of

   A. 255.255.255.0

   B. 255.255.0.0

   C. 255.0.0.0

   D. 0.0.0.0

3. From the choices below, select the step that is not required when installing and configuring a printing device using the TCP/IP protocol.

   A. Enter the IP address of the remote controller servicing the print device in the Add LPR Compatible Printer dialog box.

   B. Enter the name of the remote controller servicing the print device in the Add LPR Compatible Printer dialog box.

   C. Enter the IP address of the print device in the Add LPR Compatible Printer dialog box.

   D. Enter the IP address of the print server in the Add LPR Compatible Printer dialog box.

4. Which of the following must be done to allow Microsoft network clients to print to a printing device attached to a UNIX host?

   A. TCP/IP Network Printing Support must be installed on a Windows NT computer on the network.

   B. The UNIX host name or IP address and the printer share name must be specified for the LPR port in the Print To field.

C. Microsoft networking clients on the network must be able to connect to printers on the Windows NT computer.

D. The LPR daemon must be installed on non-NT clients.

5. Bill's Tires and Chains has 22 outlets, each with its own subnet and around 100 users. This year, both of those numbers are expected to double. You have been assigned the network address of 150.50.0.0 and must assign a subnet mask to meet your needs. You specify a subnet mask of 255.255.254.0. How well does this solution address the problem?

A. It meets the requirements and is an outstanding solution.

B. It meets the requirements and is an adequate solution.

C. It meets the requirements but is not a desirable solution.

D. It does not meet the requirements, although it will work.

E. It does not meet the requirements and does not work.

6. The application layer of the TCP/IP protocol sends the application data to the

A. Session layer

B. Presentation layer

C. Network layer

D. Transport layer

7. Where should the HOSTS file be located?

A. In the *systemroot* directory

B. In the *systemroot*\etc directory

C. In the *systemroot*\system32\drivers\etc directory

D. In the *systemroot*\bin directory

8. Which of the following is a constant rate of transmission that is not so high as to cause congestion, but not so low as to cause gaps in the data stream?

A. Retransmit timer

B. Sliding window

C. SRTT (Smoothed Round Trip Time)

D. Streaming

E. Delayed-acknowledgment timer

9. Which of the following is a line printing query utility that displays the status of the UNIX printer and print jobs?

A. Daemon

B. LPD

C. LPR

D. LPQ

10. Eric started a Telnet window and connected to the Telnet server on the host named VAX3, but the Telnet screen says, Welcome to VAX7. What are possible explanations?

A. The HOSTS file might contain an incorrect IP address for the host name VAX3.

B. The DNS database might contain an incorrect IP address for the host name VAX3.

C. The VAX3 server is down and packets are routing to VAX7—either intentionally or erroneously.

D. The server VAX7 erroneously received the same IP address as the server VAX3.

11. What two things do you need for an SNMP agent to report password violations to an SNMP Manager?

A. A public community

B. A predefined end-to-end application

C. A community name

D. A trap destination

12. Which of the following is the process running on UNIX hosts that enables printers to be created for TCP/IP clients?

   A. Daemon

   B. LPD

   C. LPR

   D. LPQ

13. The DLC protocol is used with Windows NT to provide

   A. Access to Macintosh computers

   B. Access to IBM mainframes for terminal emulation

   C. Access to Novell resources

   D. Access to HP JetDirect printers on the network

14. _____ is a timer that is set when a packet is sent. If an acknowledgment for the packet is not received before the timer expires, the packet is resent.

   A. Retransmit timer

   B. Sliding window

   C. SRTT (Smoothed Round Trip Time)

   D. Streaming

   E. Delayed-acknowledgment timer

15. Evan's House of Cards has 26 outlets in the Fort Wayne region—each with about 90 users and each with its own subnets. Those numbers are expected to triple next year. You have been assigned the network address of 150.119.0.0 and must assign a subnet to this network to support your number of sites (subnets) and users. You specify a subnet mask of 255.255.240.0. How well does this solution address the problem?

   A. It meets the requirements and is an outstanding solution.

   B. It meets the requirements and is an adequate solution.

   C. It meets the requirements but is not a desirable solution.

   D. It does not meet the requirements, although it will work.

   E. It does not meet the requirements and does not work.

16. You find that you can only ping hosts on the local network, although other hosts have no communication problems with remote hosts. What should be the first troubleshooting step you try?

   A. Verify that Enable LMHOSTS Lookup is selected in the Advanced Microsoft TCP/IP Configuration dialog box.

   B. Verify that the correct subnet mask is used.

   C. See if other computers on the network have the same problem. If WINS is used, ensure that the proper IP address is used and that the WINS server is functioning.

   D. Check the Event Viewer to see which services have failed and if related events provide any clues.

17. The PING utility can determine whether a host is receiving packets sent from a source by using which of the following?

   A. IP address

   B. Physical address

   C. Host name

   D. Default gateway

18. When does a DHCP client first attempt to renew its IP address lease with a DHCP server?

   A. After one minute

   B. After three minutes

   C. After 50% of the lease duration has expired

   D. After the lease duration has expired

19. You can ping a remote host successfully, but cannot connect to a share of that host in File Manager. You do not use WINS on the network. What is the first thing you should check?

    A. Verify that Enable LMHOSTS Lookup is selected in the Advanced Microsoft TCP/IP Configuration dialog box.

    B. Verify that the correct subnet mask is used.

    C. See if other computers on the network have the same problem. If WINS is used, ensure that the proper IP address is used and that the WINS server is functioning.

    D. Check the Event Viewer to see which services have failed and if related events provide any clues.

20. Which of the following are valid host names for Windows NT computers?

    A. Evan Scott

    B. Evan@Scott

    C. Evan_Scott

    D. EvanScott

21. What are two potential problems that can occur when an LMHOSTS file is being used for NetBIOS name resolution?

    A. LMHOSTS might contain typing mistakes, omissions, or duplicate values because it is manually typed.

    B. LMHOSTS must be manually updated every time a change on the network affects one of the NetBIOS name mappings.

    C. LMHOSTS offers a centralized—versus localized—view of the network and thus there can be duplicate address information across subnets.

    D. LMHOSTS clients can only use DHCP to configure scope availability.

22. A DHCP server eliminates the need to manually configure:

    A. A DHCP scope

    B. A WINS database

    C. An IP address and subnet mask for DHCP clients

    D. An IP address and subnet mask for non-DHCP clients

23. Which of the following are valid subnet IDs for networks with the ID of 192 needing at least six hosts?

    A. 248

    B. 252

    C. 254

    D. 255

24. What print monitor is loaded with TCP/IP and tracks print jobs targeted for TCP/IP print hosts?

    A. IPMON.DLL

    B. LPDMON.DLL

    C. LPRMON.DLL

    D. LOCALMON.DLL

25. Messages that ICMP commonly sends to a source would include

    A. Echo request

    B. Echo reply

    C. Redirect

    D. Handshake

26. Which of the following is essentially a process running in the background on a UNIX host—equivalent to a "service" in NT?

    A. Daemon

    B. LPD

    C. LPR

    D. LPQ

27. Which of the following are SNMP transactions initiated by an SNMP Manager?

    A. get

    B. get-next

    C. set

    D. send trap

28. Which of the following is a packet delivery protocol that is not connection-oriented?

    A. TCP

    B. IP

    C. UDP

    D. SMTP

29. Suppose you're planning to add 30 subnets over the next year. If you have a network ID of 130 and currently have 100 subnets, which of the following is the best subnet ID to use?

    A. 224

    B. 240

    C. 248

    D. 254

    E. 255

30. Benefits of referring to a host by a host name instead of an IP address include which of the following?

    A. The character set is limited to only hex.

    B. The dotted decimal format signifies host and network IDs.

    C. Host names are generally more reliable—staying the same even if the IP address must change.

    D. Host names are easier to remember.

31. In order for Microsoft Network clients to print to a printing device directly attached to the TCP/IP network, which of the following must be true?

    A. The TCP/IP network printing device must have a valid IP address.

    B. The UNIX host name or IP address and the printer share name must be specified for the LPR port.

    C. The printer name of the printer must be the name that the printing device uses to identify itself according to the documentation of the manufacturer.

    D. The TCP/IP network printing device must be configured with a printer name using the LPD.

32. _____ is a line printing query utility that displays the status of the UNIX printer and print jobs.

    A. LPQ

    B. NET PRINTSTAT

    C. SPOOLQUERY

    D. LPSTAT

33. Which of the following are ways in which the duration for a retransmit timer for a packet is determined?

    A. If the host does not participate in a WAN, the duration is decreased to increase the rate of acknowledgments and increase performance.

    B. The SRTT is calculated based on previous round trip times. The value of one second is initially used if the SRTT has not yet been calculated.

    C. The retransmit timer for a packet is initially set to the SRTT.

    D. The retransmit timer is double the previous value for each time the packet is re-sent, up to a maximum of four retransmits.

34. The network ID used to determine whether a destination is local or remote is determined by examining which of the following?

    A. The IP address

    B. The packet header

    C. The ARP information

    D. The subnet mask

35. While browsing in File Manager, you can see only the computers on your local network. What should be the first troubleshooting step you take to remedy the problem?

   A. Verify that Enable LMHOSTS Lookup is selected in the Advanced Microsoft TCP/IP Configuration dialog box.

   B. Verify that the correct subnet mask is used.

   C. See if other computers on the network have the same problem. If WINS is used, ensure that the proper IP address is used and that the WINS server is functioning.

   D. Check the Event Viewer to see which services have failed and if related events provide any clues.

36. The AppleTalk protocol is used with Windows NT to provide

   A. Access to Macintosh computers

   B. Access to IBM mainframes for terminal emulation

   C. Access to Novell resources

   D. Access to HP JetDirect printers on the network

37. Which of the following steps can be taken to reduce the number of retransmitted packets?

   A. Increase the performance of routers by upgrading available memory.

   B. Decrease the size of receive buffers to slow congestion.

   C. Decrease the network traffic by isolating broadcasts at congestion points.

   D. Increase network bandwidth.

38. Spencer's Crafts-n-Stuff is a growing exporter with four offices now running. Each office has 200 users and its own subnet. Two more offices are opening

within the year, and those could have as many as 375 users each. You have been assigned the network address of 150.50.0.0. You specify a subnet mask of 255.224.0.0. How well does this solution address the problem?

   A. It meets the requirements and is an outstanding solution.

   B. It meets the requirements and is an adequate solution.

   C. It meets the requirements but is not a desirable solution.

   D. It does not meet the requirements, although it will work.

   E. It does not meet the requirements and does not work.

39. When the sender and destination are on different networks, what is the first step ARP must perform?

   A. The source host sends the IP message to the router to be forwarded to the correct network.

   B. The source host checks the local ARP cache to see whether there is an IP address for the next router in the string of checkpoints.

   C. The source host sends an ARP broadcast request on the local network to find the default gateway.

   D. ARP IP address resolution is used by the nearest router to get the hardware address of the destination.

   E. The source host checks a local route table to see if it knows the route to the destination host.

40. Of the following, which network technology offers the highest bandwidth?

   A. 56K

   B. Token ring

   C. Fast Ethernet

   D. FDDI

41. DHCP is a Windows NT service used to
    A. Dynamically map NetBIOS names and IP addresses
    B. Dynamically allocate IP addresses to DHCP clients
    C. Dynamically configure PDC to BDC synchronization
    D. Dynamically provide automatic logon validation

42. If the command ping 127.0.0.1 works but you cannot ping any other hosts on the local network, the most likely problem is
    A. The software
    B. The cable or connection
    C. The SRTT setting
    D. The HOSTS file

43. Which of the following statements regarding DHCP servers is false?
    A. If a DHCP server is not available to lease an IP address when a client starts up, the client will use a cached copy of the last granted DHCP lease.
    B. A DHCP server can be installed on either side of a router. It can then lease addresses to other subnets in the event one of the DHCP servers is down.
    C. A DHCP server can lease an IP address to a DHCP client, even if that IP address has previously been leased to another client by the same DHCP server.
    D. A DHCP server can be installed on either side of a router, and can lease addresses to clients in that subnet in the event another DHCP server is down.

44. Suppose you have a network ID of 100, and currently have 100 subnets. If you plan to add 30 more subnets over the next year, which is the best subnet ID to use?

A. 0
B. 248
C. 252
D. 254
E. 255

45. Which of the following statements is true?
    A. An FTP server can be configured to record the user name of every user who attempts to connect.
    B. If anonymous logon to an FTP server is allowed, the password can be set so that it is the same as the guest account password.
    C. The FTP server can override the security on an NTFS volume and prevent users from writing to a volume.
    D. The HOSTS file on the client must contain the name and IP address of the FTP server for anonymous logon.

46. You have a host with the IP address of 212.42.10.27. The subnet mask is 255.255.255.224. This makes the network ID 212.42.10, and the host ID
    A. 1
    B. 3
    C. 9
    D. 27
    E. 224

47. TCP/IP objects do not appear as choices to monitor in Performance Monitor unless what service is installed?
    A. DHCP
    B. DHCP
    C. SNMP
    D. DNS

48. Which of the following items can be monitored using SNMP?

    A. Routers

    B. Gateways

    C. Repeaters

    D. Bridges

49. Johnny's Part Stores, Inc. has a network address of 195.50.50.0. There are now four subnets on the network, and this number will increase within the next two years. You need to assign a subnet mask to support this need, so you specify a subnet mask of 255.255.255.224. How well does this solution address the problem?

    A. It meets the requirements and is an outstanding solution.

    B. It meets the requirements and is an adequate solution.

    C. It meets the requirements but is not a desirable solution.

    D. It does not meet the requirements, although it will work.

    E. It does not meet the requirements and does not work.

50. Suppose you have a network ID of 192 and are currently using six subnets. You may need to add two more in the next three months. Which is the best subnet to use?

    A. 192

    B. 224

    C. 240

    D. 248

    E. 252

51. Which of the following are benefits of installing SNMP service on a Windows NT computer?

    A. The Windows NT Performance Monitor counters for TCP/IP are disabled.

    B. The SNMP agent can report configuration information to an SNMP Manager.

    C. The SNMP agent can send traps to an SNMP Manager, alerting it of unusual events.

    D. Performance Monitor graphs now are capable of displaying 256, rather than 16, colors.

52. A print job can be directed to a UNIX host print device, and its status checked using which two command line utilities?

    A. LPD

    B. LPR

    C. LPQ

    D. LP

53. Users complain that a SQL server database on a remote network is slower since another segment was joined to a single IP router on the network. There are no complaints about resources on the local network. What is the first thing you should check?

    A. Verify that Enable LMHOSTS Lookup is selected in the Advanced Microsoft TCP/IP Configuration dialog box.

    B. Check statistics on router performance. If the ICMP Source Quench counter is above zero, the router is probably congested.

    C. See if other computers on the network have the same problem. If WINS is used, ensure that the proper IP address is used and that the WINS server is functioning.

    D. Check the Event Viewer to see which services have failed and if related events provide any clues.

54. _____ is a packet delivery protocol that is connection oriented.

    A. TCP

    B. IP

    C. UDP

    D. SMTP

55. Wild William's Bird World has a network address of 195.50.50.0. There are now nine subnets on the network and this number will increase within the next two years. You need to assign a subnet mask to support this need, so you specify a subnet mask of 255.255.255.240. How well does this solution address the problem?

   A. It meets the requirements and is an outstanding solution.

   B. It meets the requirements and is an adequate solution.

   C. It meets the requirements but is not a desirable solution.

   D. It does not meet the requirements, although it will work.

   E. It does not meet the requirements and does not work.

56. Different headers that IP adds to the data in a packet before the packet is sent to the network interface layer include

   A. Source TCP port number

   B. Echo request

   C. Acknowledgment number

   D. TCP checksum

57. Which features are not provided directly or indirectly by a WINS server?

   A. Name resolution for WINS clients

   B. Name release for non-WINS clients

   C. Name registration for WINS clients

   D. Name registration for non-WINS clients

   E. Name resolution for non-WINS clients

58. What is the default subnet mask used for a class B network?

   A. 255.0.0.0

   B. 255.255.0.0

   C. 255.255.255.0

   D. 255.255.255.255

Answers and Explanations

1. **D**   The pound sign must follow the DNS name\alias.

2. **B**   Class B networks have a default mask of 255.255.0.0.

3. **D**   Entering the IP address of the print server is not required.

4. **A, B, C**   The LPR daemon does not need to be installed on clients.

5. **A**   The solution presented meets the requirements given and does as well as any solution can.

6. **D**   The application layer sends data to the transport layer.

7. **C**   The HOSTS file belongs in the *systemroot*\system32\drivers\etc directory.

8. **D**   Streaming maintains a constant rate of transmission.

9. **D**   The LPQ utility is used to query the printing service.

10. **A, B, D**   When the VAX3 server is down, it will not route packets erroneously.

11. **C, D**   A trap destination and community name are required.

12. **B**   The LPD UNIX process allows printers to be created for TCP/IP clients.

13. **B, D**   The DLC protocol allows access to HP JetDirect printers on the network and to IBM mainframes for terminal emulation.

14. **A**   The retransmit timer is used to resend packets if an acknowledgment is not heard.

15. **E**   The solution given does not meet the requirements presented and will not work.

16. **B**   Verifying that the correct subnet mask is used should be the first step undertaken.

17. **A, C**   The PING utility can reference a host by IP address or by host name.

18. **C**   A DHCP client attempts to renew its lease when 50% of the lease duration has expired.

Practice Exam 4

19. **A**   Verifying that Enable LMHOSTS Lookup is selected in the Advanced Microsoft TCP/IP Configuration dialog box should be the first step undertaken.

20. **C, D**   Host names should not contain spaces or at (@) characters.

21. **A, B**   Problems will occur when the LMHOST file contains typing mistakes, omissions, or duplicate values. Problems also arise due to the fact that LMHOST must constantly be manually updated.

22. **C**   DHCP servers dynamically assign IP address and subnet mask information for DHCP clients.

23. **A, B**   248 and 252 meet the requirements presented for class C networks.

24. **C**   LPRMON.DLL is loaded with TCP/IP and tracks print jobs targeted for TCP/IP print hosts.

25. **A, B, C**   ICMP does not concern itself with handshakes.

26. **A**   A daemon is to UNIX what a service is to NT.

27. **A, B, C**   The SNMP manager initiates get, get-next, and set transactions. The SNMP client initiates send trap transactions.

28. **C**   UDP is not connection oriented, but is a packet-delivery protocol.

29. **E**   A class B network would need a subnet mask of 255 to meet the specifications given.

30. **C, D**   Host names are easier to remember than IP addresses, and are generally more reliable.

31. **A, C, D**   For Microsoft clients to print in the scenario given, the TCP/IP network printing device must be configured with a printer name using the LPD, it must have a valid IP address, and the printer's name must be the name the printing device uses to identify itself according to the documentation of the manufacturer.

32. **A**   The LPQ utility shows the status of UNIX printers and print jobs.

33. **B, C, D**   The duration for a retransmit timer for a packet is determined by the SRTT and double the previous value.

34. **A, D**   The IP address is used to determine the network ID.

35. **C**   Seeing if other computers on the network have the same problem should be the first step taken.

36. **A**   Access to Macintosh computers is provided by the AppleTalk protocol.

37. **A, C, D**   Decreasing the size of receive buffers will not reduce the number of retransmitted packets.

38. **E**   The solution does not meet the requirements given, and does not work.

39. **E**   When the sender and destination are on different networks, the source host checks a local route table to see if it knows the route to the destination host.

40. **D**   FDDI offers the highest bandwidth of the choices given.

41. **B**   DHCP is used to dynamically allocate IP addresses to DHCP clients.

42. **B**   The most likely cause of this problem is the cable or connection.

43. **A, B**   A DHCP server can lease an IP address to a DHCP client, even if that IP address has previously been leased to another client by the same DHCP server and a DHCP server can be installed on either side of a router. A DHCP server can also lease addresses to clients in that subnet in the event another DHCP server is down.

44. **E**   A class A network would require a subnet mask of 255 to meet the requirements given.

45. **C**   The FTP server can override the security on an NTFS volume and prevent users from writing to a volume.

46. **D**   The host ID is 27 with the values presented.

47. **C**   TCP/IP objects do not appear as choices to monitor in Performance Monitor unless SNMP is installed.

48. **A, B, D**   SNMP can monitor routers, bridges, and gateways.

49. **E**   The solution given does not meet the requirements presented and does not work.

50. **C**   With a class C network, 240 is the subnet mask needed to allow for eight subnets and a maximum number of hosts.

51. **B, C**   The SNMP agent can report configuration information to an SNMP Manager and can send traps to an SNMP Manager alerting it of unusual events.

52. **B, C**   LPR and LPQ are the two utilities used to interact with UNIX host print devices.

53. **B**   Checking statistics on router performance should be one of the first steps you take.

54. **A**   TCP is a connection-oriented packet-delivery protocol.

55. **E**   The solution given does not meet the requirements presented and does not work.

56. **A, C, D**   Headers that IP adds do not include the Echo request.

57. **B, D**   A WINS server does not do name registration or release for non-WINS clients. Since it does not register them, there is no release for it to perform.

58. **B**   A class A address has a default subnet mask of 255.0.0.0, class B is 255.255.0.0, and class C is 255.255.255.0.

All About the Exam

The Microsoft TCP/IP exam—the full name of which is *Internetworking with Microsoft TCP/IP on Microsoft Windows NT 4.0 Exam*—is commonly referred to by its exam number: 70–59. A computer-administered test, like all Microsoft certification exams, it measures your ability to implement and administer TCP/IP on NT Server 4.0.

This exam weighs importantly into two certifications. Upon passing this exam in combination with the core NT Server 4.0 exam (70–67) and the Internet Information Server 3.0 exam (70–77), a candidate becomes a Microsoft Certified Product Specialist (MCPS) with a Web emphasis.

This exam also counts as an elective toward a Microsoft Certified Systems Engineer (MCSE) certification. The MCSE requires passing six exams, and the three for MCPS count, leaving only NT Server in the Enterprise (70–68), a networking exam, and a client exam (Windows NT Workstation, Windows 95, and so on).

Exam 70–59 has 58 questions, and you have 90 minutes to answer them; the minimum passing score is 750. Translated into more meaningful numbers, you can pass with 44 correct answers—and fail with anything less.

The exam has two types of multiple-choice questions: single answer (readily identified by a radio button) and multiple answer with the correct number given. The questions, overall, are extremely verbose and include many exhibits. Choices typically range from A–D; many questions do include an E choice. Most of the questions with E choices are "multiple ranking" questions.

A multiple-ranking question gives a scenario, offers a solution, lists a number of required results, and lists a number of optional desired results. You then must choose how well the solution met the desired results. These questions are very tricky—and difficult. (One word of advice is to mark them the first time through and check them again after you complete the rest of the exam.) Here's an example of a multiple-ranking question:

Situation

Evan is running a predominantly UNIX shop. However, to minimize hardware costs, he wants an NT Server to function as a router. He will install three network cards in the server, and it is currently running only TCP/IP.

Required Result

TCP/IP packets must be routed on the server.

Optional Results

Trap messages should be sent to a UNIX server.

Routing tables should dynamically update themselves.

Proposed Solution

Assign one IP address to the server.

Install SNMP Service on the server and configure trap messages to go to the desired UNIX server.

Enable IP forwarding by checking the Enable IP Forwarding box on the Routing tab of the TCP/IP Properties page.

Which Results were Produced?

- A. The required result and optional results were met.
- B. The required result was met, but only two of the optional results were met.
- C. The required result was met, but only one of the optional results was met.
- D. The required result was met, but not the optional results.
- E. The required result was not met.

In this case, the answer is E—the required result is not met. With an NT Server functioning as a multihomed host (that is, the three network cards), you must assign an IP address to each card. As for the optional results, the SNMP (that is, Simple Network Management Protocol) component is correct, but for routing tables to automatically update, you need to install Routing Internet Protocol (RIP) for IP.

At this point, the tendency is to scoff and point out that RIP for IP is an old solution that has been superseded by the routing enhancements (formerly known as SteelHead) included in Service Pack 3. It is *VERY* important to understand that the exams test you on the core products alone and do not include Service Packs and add-ons in their scenarios. The exam specifically focuses on the NT product that came in the initial box and nothing that has been released since then.

The exam is divided into five objective categories: Planning, Installation and Configuration, Connectivity, Monitoring and Optimization, and Troubleshooting. More information about subobjectives can be found at the Microsoft site: `http://www.microsoft.com/train_cert` .

Although nothing can substitute for real-world, hands-on experience, knowing what to expect on the exam can be very helpful. The information in this book appears in the same five objective sections you need to know to pass the exam. If you really try to understand the concepts presented here, rather than just memorize the words, you will ace the exam without any trouble.

Appendix A

Glossary

In the age of information, buzz words and acronyms seem to grow on trees. Keeping up with all of them can be tiresome and annoying. This glossary covers terms related to TCP/IP and networking.

account—A user ID and disk area (typically the home directory) restricted for the use of a particular person. Usually password protected.

ACK—Acknowledgment—A response from a receiving computer to a sending computer to indicate successful reception of information. TCP requires that packets be acknowledged before it considers the transmission safe.

active open—An action taken by a client to initiate a TCP connection with a server.

address classes—Grouping of IP addresses with each class, defining the maximum number of networks and hosts available. The first octet of the address determines the class.

address mask—A 32-bit binary number used to select bits from an IP address for subnet masking.

address resolution—A translation of an IP address to a corresponding physical address.

agent—The software routine in a Simple Network Management Protocol (SNMP)–managed device that responds to get and set requests and sends trap messages.

alias—A short name that represents a more complicated one. Often used for mail addresses or host domain names.

analog—A form of electronic communication using a continuous electromagnetic wave, such as television or radio. Any continuous wave form, as opposed to digital on/off transmissions.

anchor—A hypertext link in the form of text or a graphic that, when clicked, takes you to the linked file.

annotation—A Mosaic feature that enables you to add a comment to a viewed document.

anonymous FTP—Enables you to download (and sometimes upload) files without requiring a password.

ANSI—American National Standards Institute—The membership organization responsible for defining U.S. standards in the information technology industry.

API—Application Programming Interface—A language and message format that enables a programmer to use functions in another program or in the hardware.

Archie—A search engine that finds filenames on anonymous FTP services.

archive—A repository of files available for access at an Internet site. Also, a collection of files, often a backup of a disk or files saved to tape to allow them to be transferred.

argument—A parameter passed to a subroutine or function.

ARP—Address Resolution Protocol—A protocol in the TCP/IP suite used to resolve an IP address to a physical hardware address.

ARPA—Advanced Research Projects Agency—A government agency that originally funded the research on the ARPANET (became DARPA in the mid-1970s).

ARPANET—The first network of computers funded by the U.S. Department of Defense Advanced Projects Agency. An experimental communications network funded by the government that eventually developed into the Internet.

article—Message submitted to a Usenet newsgroup. Unlike an email message that goes to a specific person or group of persons, a newsgroup message goes to directories (on many machines) that can be read by any number of people.

ASCII—American Standard Code for Information Interchange—A standard character set of data that is limited to letters, numbers, and punctuation.

ATM—Asynchronous Transfer Mode.

attribute—A form of a command-line switch as applied to tags in the HTML language. HTML commands or tags can be more specific when attributes are used. Not all HTML tags use attributes.

au—Extension for audio files.

backbone—Generally very high-speed, T3 telephone lines that connect remote ends of networks and networks to one another; only service providers are connected to the Internet in this way. Can also be the main network segment that connects the network.

bang—A slang term for an exclamation point.

bang address—A type of email address that separates host names in the address with exclamation points. Used for mail sent to the UUCP (UNIX-to-UNIX copy) network, where specifying the exact path of the mail (including all hosts that pass on the message) is necessary. The address is in the form of machine!machine!userID, in which the number of machines listed depends on the connections needed to reach the machine that stores the account userID.

baseband—A network technology that requires all nodes attached to the network to participate in every transmission. Ethernet, for example, is a baseband technology.

best-effort delivery—A characteristic of a network technology that does not ensure link-level reliability. IP and UDP protocols work together to provide best-effort delivery service to applications.

BGP—Border Gateway Protocol

binary—A file or other data that may contain nonprintable characters, including graphics files, programs, and sound files.

BinHex—A program that encodes binary files as ASCII so that they can be sent through email.

BITNET—Because It's Time Network—A non-TCP/IP network for small universities without Internet access.

block—A group of statements enclosed in braces.

bookmarks—Term used by some World Wide Web browsers for marking URLs you access frequently.

Boolean logic—Logic dealing with true/false values. (The operators AND, OR, and NOT are Boolean operators.)

BOOTP—Bootstrap Protocol—A protocol used to configure systems across internetworks.

bounce—An email message you receive that tells you that an email message you sent wasn't delivered. Usually contains an error code and the contents of the message that wasn't delivered.

bps—bits per second—A measurement that expresses the speed at which data is transferred between computers.

bridge—A device that operates at the data link layer of the OSI model and connects one physical section of a network to another, often providing isolation.

broadband—A network technology that multiplexes multiple network carriers into a single cable.

broadcast—A packet destined for all hosts on the network.

brouter—A computer device that works as both a bridge and a router. Some network traffic may be bridged while other traffic is routed.

browser—A utility that lets you look through collections of things. For example, a file browser lets you look through a file system. Applications that let you access the World Wide Web are called browsers.

buffer—A storage area used to hold input or output data.

CERN—The European Laboratory for Particle Physics, where the World Wide Web was first conceived of and implemented.

checksumming—A service performed by UDP that checks to see whether packets were changed during transmission.

child—A subprocess.

CIDR—Classless Interdomain Routing.

client—User of a service. Also often refers to a piece of software that gets information from a server. Additionally, *client* refers to an application that makes a request of a service on a (sometimes) remote computer; the request can be, for example, a function call.

CMIP—Common Management Information Protocol—An OSI network management protocol.

compress—A program that compacts a file so it fits into a smaller space. Also can refer to the technique of reducing the amount of space a file takes up.

concatenate—To join two strings.

connection—A logical path between two protocol modules that provides a reliable delivery service.

connectionless service—A delivery service that treats each packet as a separate entity. Often results in lost packets or packets delivered out of sequence.

context—Many functions return either array values or scalar values depending on the context, that is, whether returning an array or a scalar value is appropriate for the place where the call was made.

CRC—Cyclic Redundancy Check—A computation about a frame of which the result is a small integer. The value is appended to the end of the frame and recalculated when the frame is received. If the results differ from the appended value, the frame has presumably been corrupted and is therefore discarded. CRC is used to detect errors in transmission.

CSMA—Carrier Sense Multiple Access—A simple media access control protocol that enables multiple stations to contend for access to the medium. If no traffic is detected on the medium, the station may send a transmission.

CSMA/CD—Carrier Sense Multiple Access with Collision Detection—A characteristic of network hardware that uses CSMA with a process that detects when two stations transmit simultaneously. If that happens, both back off and retry the transmission after a random time period has elapsed.

cyberspace—Refers to the entire collection of sites accessible electronically. If your computer is attached to the Internet or another large network, it exists in cyberspace.

daemon—A program that runs automatically on a computer to perform a service for the operating system or for clients on the network.

DARPA—Defense Advanced Research Projects Agency, originally ARPA—the government agency that funded the research that developed the ARPANET.

database—A structured way of storing data, often described in terms of a number of tables; each table is made up of a series of records, and each record contains a number of fields.

datagram—A packet of data and delivery information.

debugging—The process of tracking down errors in a program, often aided by examining or outputting extra information designed to help this process.

Glossary

dedicated line—See leased line.

DES—Data Encryption Standard—An algorithm developed by the U.S. government to provide security for data transmitted over a network.

DHCP—Dynamic Host Configuration Protocol—a protocol that provides dynamic address allocation and automatic TCP/IP configuration.

dial-up connection—A connection to the Internet through a modem and telephone line that allows email and running processes to occur on a remote computer.

digest—A form of mailing list where a number of messages are concatenated (linked) and sent out as a single message.

digital—Type of communications used by computers, consisting of individual on and off pulses. Compare to analog.

direct connection—A connection to the Internet through a dedicated line, such as ISDN.

directed broadcast address—An IP address that specifies all hosts on the network.

directory of servers—A service that describes what is available on servers throughout the world.

DNS—See Domain Name System (DNS).

DNS name server—The server(s) that contains information about a portion of the DNS database.

Doc-ID—In a wide area information server (WAIS), an ID that identifies a specific document in a database.

DOD—Department of Defense—A U.S. government agency that originally sponsored the ARPANET research.

domain—Highest subdivision of the Internet, for the most part by country (except in the United States, where it's by type of organization, such as educational, commercial, and government). Usually the last part of a host name; for example, the domain part of ibm.com is .com, which represents the domain of commercial sites in the United States.

Domain Name System (DNS)—The system that translates between Internet IP address and Internet host names.

dot address—See host address.

download—Move a file from a remote computer to your local computer.

EBGP—External Border Gateway Protocol.

effective GID—The group identifier of the current process, which may have been changed from the original GID by various means.

effective UID—The user identifier of the current process, which may have been changed from the original UID by various means.

EIGRP—Enhanced Internet Gateway Routing Protocol.

email—An electronic message delivered from one computer user to another. Short for electronic mail.

email address—An address used to send email to a user on the Internet, consisting of the user name and host name (and any other necessary information, such as a gateway machine). An Internet email address is usually in the form username@hostname.

encryption—The process of scrambling a message so that it can be read only by someone who knows how to unscramble it.

Ethernet—A type of local area network hardware. Many TCP/IP networks are ethernet based.

Eudora—The most widely used email system.

expire—Remove an article from a Usenet newsgroup after a specified interval.

fair queuing—A technique that controls traffic in gateways by restricting every host to an equal share of gateway bandwidth.

FAQ—Frequently Asked Question(s)—Often a question and answer approach to common problems. Most Usenet newsgroups have a FAQ to introduce new readers to popular topics in the newsgroup.

FCS—Frame Check Sequence—A computation about the bits in a frame; the result is appended to the end of the frame and recalculated within the frame it is received. If the results differ from the appended value, the frame has presumably been corrupted and is therefore discarded. It is used to detect errors in transmission.

FDDI—Fiber Distributed Data Interface.

FDM—Frequency Division Multiplexing—A technique of passing signals across a single medium by assigning each signal a unique carrier frequency.

Feed—Send Usenet newsgroups from your site to another site that wants to read them.

FIFO—First-in first-out—A queue in which the first item placed in the queue is the first item processed when the queue is processed.

file—Basic unit of storage of computer data in a file structure; files can normally be binary or text only (ASCII).

Finger—A program that provides information about users on an Internet host; may include a user's personal information, such as project affiliation and schedule.

firewall—A device placed on a network to prevent unauthorized traffic from entering the network.

flame—Communicate in an abusive or absurd manner. Often occurs in newsgroup posts and email messages.

flow control—A mechanism that controls the rate at which hosts may transmit at any time. It is used to avoid congestion on the network, which may exhaust memory buffers.

fushing—When data is output to a text file, it is usually buffered to make processing more efficient. Flushing forces any items in the buffer to be actually written to the file.

forms—Online data-entry sheets supported by some World Wide Web browsers.

FQDN—Fully Qualified Domain Name—A combination of the host name and the domain name.

fragment—A piece that results when a datagram is partitioned into smaller pieces. It is used to facilitate datagrams that are too large for the network technology in use.

frame—A set of packets as transmitted across a medium. Differing frame types have unique characteristics.

frame relay—A type of digital data communications protocol.

freeware—Software that the author makes available at no cost to anyone who wants it (although the author retains rights to the software).

FTP—File Transfer Protocol—A popular Internet communications protocol that allows you to transfer files between hosts on the Internet.

gateway—A device that interfaces two networks that use different protocols.

GIF—Graphics Interchange Format—An image format.

gigabit—Very high-speed (1 billion bits per second) data communications.

gigabyte—A unit of data storage approximately equal to 1 billion bytes of data.

global variables—Variables that can be referred to anywhere within a package.

gopher—Provides menu descriptions of files on Internet servers; used primarily to find Internet information.

Gopher—An application that allows you to access publicly available information on Internet hosts that provide gopher service.

Gopherbook—An application that uses an interface resembling a book to access Gopher servers.

Gopherspace—Connected Gopher services.

GOSIP—Government Open Systems Interconnection Profile—a U.S. government document that defines a specification of a set of OSI protocols that agencies may use.

Greenwich mean time—An international time standard reference, also known as Universal time.

GUI—Graphical User Interface—A computer interface based on graphical symbols rather than text. Windowing environments and Macintosh environments are GUIs.

hacking—Originally referred to playing around with computer systems; now often used to indicate destructive computer activity.

hardware address—The physical address of a host used by networks.

hash lookup—Find the value associated with a specified key in an associative array.

hash table—A method used for implementing associative arrays, which allows the keys to be converted to numbers for internal storage purposes.

HDLC—High Level Data Link Control—A standard data link level protocol.

header—Data inserted at the beginning of a packet that contains control information.

home page—The document that serves as the entry way for all the information contained in a company's WWW service—your World Wide Web browser loads when it starts up.

hop-check—A utility that allows you to find out how many routers are between your host and another Internet host.

host—A server connected to the Internet.

host address—A unique number assigned to identify a host on the Internet (also called an IP address or a dot address). This address is usually represented as four numbers between 1 and 254 and separated by periods, for example, 192.58.107.230.

host ID—The portion of an IP address that identifies the host in a particular network. It is used with network IDs to form a complete IP address.

host name—A unique name for a host that corresponds to the host address.

hosts—Individual computers connected to the Internet.

HOSTS file—A text file that contains mappings of IP addresses to host names.

hot list—A list of your favorite World Wide Web sites that can be accessed quickly by your WWW browser.

html—The extension for HTML files.

HTML—Hypertext Markup Language—The formatting language\protocol used to define various text styles in a hypertext document, including emphasis and bulleted lists.

HTTP—Hypertext Transfer Protocol—The communications protocol used by WWW services to retrieve documents quickly.

hyperlinks—See links.

hypertext—An online document that has words or graphics containing links to other documents. Usually, selecting the link area onscreen (with a mouse or keyboard command) activates these links.

IAB—Internet Architecture Board—An independent group responsible for policies and standards for TCP/IP and the Internet.

IBGP—Internal Border Gateway Protocol.

ICMP—Internet Control Message Protocol—A maintenance protocol that handles error messages to be sent when datagrams are discarded or when systems experience congestion.

IEEE—Institute of Electrical and Electronics Engineers—The professional society for electrical and computer engineers.

IETF—Internet Engineering Task Force—A group of volunteers who help develop Internet standards.

IGMP—Internet Group Management Protocol—A protocol used to carry group membership information in a multicast system.

IGP—Interior Gateway Protocol—A generic term that applies to any routing protocol used within an autonomous system.

index files—Files created by waisindex that make up the WAIS source database.

Internet—The term used to describe all the worldwide interconnected TCP/IP networks.

InterNIC—The NSFNET manager sites on the Internet that provide information about the Internet.

IP—Internet Protocol—The communications protocol used by computers connected to the Internet.

IP address—See host address.

Ipng—Internet Protocol, next generation.

IPv4—Internet Protocol, version 4.

IPv6—Internet Protocol, version 6.

ISDN—A dedicated telephone line connection that transmits digital data at the rate of 56Kbps.

ISO—International Standards Organization—An organization that sets worldwide standards in many different areas.

ISP—Internet service provider.

Java—A programming language developed by Sun Microsystems that is platform independent.

JPEG—Joint Photographic Expert Group—A compression standard.

LAN—Local area network—A network of computers that is usually limited to a small physical area, like a building.

LATA—Local Access and Transport Area.

leased connection—A connection to the Internet through a local phone company that allows your

company to set up, for example, FTP, WWW, and Gopher services on the Internet at a permanent address.

leased line—A dedicated phone line used for network communications.

LIFO—Last-in first-out—A queue in which the last item placed in the queue is the first item processed when the queue is processed.

links—The areas—words or graphics—in an HTML document that cause another document to be loaded when the user clicks them.

list—A series of values separated by commas; lists are often enclosed in parentheses to avoid ambiguity and these parentheses are often necessary.

list context—Same as array.

Listproc—Software that automates the management of electronic mailing lists.

LISTSERV—Software that automates the management of electronic-mailing lists.

LLC—Logical Link Control—A protocol that provides a common interface point to the media access control (MAC) layers.

local host—The computer you are currently using.

local variables—Local variables can be accessed only in the current block and in subroutines called from that block.

logical operators—Boolean operators: that is, those dealing with true/false values.

logon—The process of entering your user ID and password at a prompt to gain access to a service.

MAC—Media Access Control—A protocol that governs the access method a station has to the network.

mail bridge—A gateway that screens mail between two networks to make certain they meet administrative constraints.

mailers—Applications that let you read and send email messages.

mailing list—A service that forwards an email message sent to it to everyone on a list, allowing a group of people to discuss a particular topic.

majordomo—Software that automates the management of electronic mailing lists.

MAN—Metropolitan area network—A physical communications network that operates across a metropolitan area.

match—A string that does fit a specified pattern.

metacharacters—Characters that have a special meaning and so may need to be escaped to turn off that meaning.

MIB—Management Information Base—A database made up of a set of objects that represent various types of information about devices. It is used by SNMP to manage devices.

MIME—Multipurpose Internet Mail Extension—A protocol that describes the format of Internet messages. Also, an extension to Internet mail that supports the inclusion of nontextual data such as video and audio in email.

modem—An electronic device that allows digital computer data to be transmitted via analog phone lines.

moderator—A person who examines all submissions to a newsgroup or mailing list and allows only those that meet certain criteria to be posted. Usually, the moderator makes sure that the topic is pertinent to the group and that the submissions aren't flames.

Mosaic—A graphical interface for the World Wide Web that employs hypertext, images, video clips, and sound.

motd—Message of the day—A message posted on some computer systems to let people know about problems or new developments.

MSS—Maximum Segment Size—The largest amount of data that can be transmitted at one time; negotiated by sender and receiver.

MTU—Maximum Transmission Unit—The largest datagram that can be sent across a given physical network.

multihomed host—A TCP/IP host that is attached to two or more networks, requiring multiple IP addresses.

name resolution—The process of mapping a computer name to an IP address. DNS and DHCP are two ways of resolving names.

Netiquette—Network etiquette conventions used in written communications; usually referring to Usenet newsgroup postings but also applicable to email.

Netnews—A collective way of referring to the Usenet newsgroups.

Netscape—A popular commercial World Wide Web browser.

network—A number of computers physically connected to enable communication with one another.

network ID—The portion of an IP address that identifies the network. It is used with host IDs to form a complete address.

newsgroups—The electronic discussion groups of Usenet.

newsreaders—Applications that let you read (and usually post) articles in Usenet newsgroups.

NFS—Network File System—A file system developed by Sun Microsystems that is now widely used on many different networks.

NIC—Network Information Center—A service that provides administrative information about a network.

NIC—Network Interface Card—An add-on card to allow a machine to access a LAN (most commonly an Ethernet card).

NIS—Network Information Service—A naming service from SunSoft that provides a directory service for network information.

NNTP—Network News Transport Protocol—The communications protocol that is used to send Usenet news on the Internet.

nodes—Individual computers connected to a network.

NSFNET—Network funded by the National Science Foundation, now the backbone of the Internet.

null character—A character with the value 0.

null list—An empty list represented as empty parentheses.

OSF—Open Software Foundation—A nonprofit organization formed by hardware manufacturers who attempt to reduce standard technologies for open systems.

OSI—Open Systems Interconnection—A set of ISO standards that define the framework for implementing protocols in seven layers.

OSPF—Open shortest path first.

packet—The unit of data transmission on the Internet. A packet consists of the data being transferred with additional overhead information, such as the transmitting and receiving addresses.

packet switching—The communications technology that the Internet is based on, where data being sent between computers is transmitted in packets.

parallel—Means of communication in which digital data is sent multiple bits at a time, with each simultaneous bit being sent over a separate line.

parameter—An argument.

pattern—An expression defining a set of strings that match the pattern and a set that do not.

peer-to-peer—Internet services that can be offered and accessed by anyone, without requiring a special server.

Perl—Practical Extraction and Report Language—A language well suited to text-file processing as well as other tasks.

PGP—Pretty Good Privacy—An application that allows you to send and receive encrypted email.

PID—Process identifier—A number indicating the number assigned by the operating system to that process.

PING—A utility that sends out a packet to an Internet host and waits for a response (used to check if a host is up).

pipe—The concept in an operating system where the output of one program is fed into the input of another.

pipeline—A complete Internet service package.

POP—Point of presence—Indicates availability of a local access number to a public data network.

port (hardware)—A physical channel on a computer that allows you to communicate with other devices (printers, modems, disk drives, and so on).

port (network)—An address to which incoming data packets are sent. Special ports can be assigned to send the data directly to a server (FTP, Gopher, WWW, Telnet, or email) or to another specific program.

port ID—The method used by TCP and UD to specify which application is sending or receiving data.

post—To send a message to a Usenet newsgroup.

postmaster—An address to which you can send questions about a site (asking if a user has an account there or if it sells a particular product, for example).

PPP—Point-to-Point Protocol—A driver that enables you to use a network communications protocol over a phone line; used with TCP/IP to enable you to have a dial-in Internet host.

precedence—The order in which operators are evaluated is based on their precedence.

process—In multitasking operating systems such as UNIX, many programs may be run at once, and each one as it is running is called a process.

protocol—The standard that defines how computers on a network communicate with one another.

proxy—A connection through a modem and telephone line to the Internet that enables you to use full-screen programs, such as Mosaic and Netscape, to browse the Internet.

public domain software—Software that is made available by the author to anyone who wants it. (In this case, the author gives up all rights to the software.)

RARP—Reverse Address Resolution Protocol—A protocol that enables a computer to find its IP address by broadcasting a request. It is usually used by diskless workstations at startup to find their logical IP address.

recursion—When a subroutine makes a call to itself.

regular expressions—A way of specifying a pattern so that some strings match the pattern and some strings do not. Parts of the matching pattern can be marked for use in operations such as substitution.

relevance feedback—In WAIS, a score between 0 and 1,000 that represents how closely a document satisfies search criteria.

remote—Pertaining to a host on the network other than the computer you now are using.

remote host—A host on the network other than the computer you currently are using.

repeater—Device that allows you to extend the length of your network by amplifying and repeating the information it receives.

resolver—Client software that enables access to the DNS database.

RFC—Request for Comments—A document submitted to the Internet governing board to propose Internet standards or to document information about the Internet.

RIP—Routing Information Protocol—A router-to-router protocol used to exchange information between routers. RIP supports dynamic routing.

rlogin—A UNIX command that allows you to log on to a remote computer.

RMON—Remote Network Monitor—A device that collects information about network communications.

route—The path that network traffic takes between its source and its destination.

router—Equipment that receives an Internet packet and sends it to the next machine in the destination path.

RPC—Remote Procedure Call—An interface that allows an application to call a routine that executes on another machine in a remote location.

script—An interpreted set of instructions in a text file.

segment—A protocol data unit consisting of part of a stream of bytes being sent between two machines. It also includes information about the current position in the stream and a checksum value.

serial—Means of communication in which digital data is sent one bit at a time over a single physical line.

server—A provider of a service; a computer that runs services. It also often refers to a piece of hardware or software that provides access to information requested from it.

service—An application that processes requests by client applications, for example, storing data or executing an algorithm.

SGML—Standard Generalized Markup Language—A language that describes the structure of a document.

shareware—Software that is made available by the author to anyone who wants it, with a request to send the author a nominal fee if the software is used on a regular basis.

signal—A means of passing information between the operating system and a running process; the process can trap the signal and respond accordingly.

signature—A personal sign-off used in email and newsgroup posts, often contained in a file and automatically appended to the mail or post. Often contains organization affiliation and pertinent personal information.

site—A group of computers under a single administrative control.

SLIP—Serial Line Internet Protocol—A way of running TCP/IP via the phone lines to enable you to have a dial-up Internet host.

SmartList—Software that automates the management of electronic-mailing lists.

smiley face—An ASCII drawing such as :-) (look at it sideways) used to indicate an emotion in a message. Also called emoticon.

SMTP—Simple Mail Transport Protocol—The accepted communications protocol standard for exchange of email between Internet hosts.

SNA—System Network Architecture—A protocol suite developed and used by IBM.

SNMP—Simple Network Management Protocol—A communications protocol used to control and monitor devices on a network.

socket—A means of network communications via special entities.

source—In WAIS, describes a database and how to reach it.

source route—A route identifying the path a datagram must follow that is determined by the source device.

string—A sequence of characters.

subnet—Any lower network that is part of the logical network; identified by the network ID.

subnet mask—A 32-bit value that distinguishes the network ID from the host ID in an IP address.

subscribe—Become a member of a mailing list or newsgroup; also refers to obtaining Internet provider services.

surfing—Jumping from host to host on the Internet to get an idea of what can be found. Also refers to briefly examining a number of different Usenet newsgroups.

syntax—A statement that contains programming code.

T1—A dedicated telephone line connection that transfers data at the rate of 1.544M/sec.

T3—A dedicated telephone line that transfers data at the rate of 45M/sec.

tag—A slang reference for annotations used by HTML, such as <H2>, </H2>.

TCP—Transmission Control Protocol—The network protocol used by hosts on the Internet.

TCP/IP—Transmission Control Protocol/Internet Protocol—A communications protocol that allows computers of any make to communicate when running TCP/IP software.

Telnet—A program that allows remote logon to another computer.

terminal emulation—Running an application that enables you to use your computer to interface with a command-line account on a remote computer as if you were connected to the computer with a terminal.

TFTP—Trivial File Transfer Protocol—A basic, standard protocol used to upload or download files with minimal overhead. TFTP depends on UDP and is often used to initialize diskless workstations, as it has no directory and password capabilities.

thread—All messages in a newsgroup or mailing list pertaining to a particular topic.

TIFF—Tag Image File Format—A graphics format.

TLI—Transport Layer Interface—An AT&T-developed interface that enables applications to interface to both TCP/IP and OSI protocols.

token ring—A network protocol for LAN.

TRACEROUTE—A utility that enables you to find out how many routers are between your host and another Internet host. See also hop-check.

traffic—The information flowing through a network.

transceiver—A device that connects a host interface to a network. It is used to apply signals to the cable and sense collisions.

trap—A block of data that indicates some request failed to authenticate. An SNMP service sends a trap when it receives a request for information with an incorrect community name.

TTL—Time to Live—A measurement of time, usually defined by a number of hops, that a datagram can exist on a network before it is discarded. It prevents endlessly looping packets.

UDP—User Datagram Protocol—A simple protocol that enables an application program on one machine to send a datagram to an application program on another machine. Delivery is not guaranteed, nor is it guaranteed the datagrams will be delivered in proper order.

Universal time—An international time standard reference, also known as Greenwich mean time.

upload—Move a file from your local computer to a remote computer.

URL—Universal Resource Locator—A means of specifying the location of information on the Internet for WWW clients.

Usenet—An online news and bulletin board system accommodating more than 7,000 interest groups.

user name—The ID used to log on to a computer.

UUDecode—A program that lets you construct binary data that was UUEncoded.

UUEncode—A program that enables you to send binary data through email.

Veronica—A tool that helps you find files on Gopher servers.

viewer applications—Software that gives you access to the images, video, and sounds stored on Internet servers.

viewers—Applications that are used to display nontext files, such as graphics, sound, and animation.

virus—A computer program that covertly enters a system by means of a legitimate program, usually doing damage to the system; compare to worm.

VLSM—Variable Length Subnet Masking.

VMS—Virtual Memory System—An operating system used on hosts made by Digital Equipment Corporation.

VRML—Virtual Reality Modeling Language—An experimental language that lets you display 3D objects in Web documents.

WAIS—Wide area information server—A tool that helps you search for documents using keywords or selections of text as search criteria.

WAIS client—An application that formats user-defined search criteria to be used by waisserver; the goal is to find matches between search criteria and data files (of all types).

WAIS sources—Databases created by waisindex that include, for example, a table of all unique words contained in a document.

waisindex—A mechanism that extracts data from raw data files (of most types) to put into databases, called WAIS sources, which allow waisserver to match search criteria to data files quickly.

waisserver—A mechanism that compares search criteria, supplied by a WAIS client, to WAIS sources.

WAN—Wide area network—A network of computers that are geographically dispersed.

Web—Short for World Wide Web (WWW).

Web chat—An application that allows you to carry on live conversations over the World Wide Web.

Web Crawler—A Web search tool.

WHOIS—A service that enables you to look up information about Internet hosts and users.

World Wide Web—WWW or Web—A hypertext-based system that allows browsing of available Internet resources.

worm—A computer program that invades other computers over a network, usually nondestructively; compare to virus.

X.25—A CCITT standard for connecting computers to a network that provides a reliable stream transmission service, which can support remote logons.

X.400—A CCITT standard for message transfer and interpersonal messaging, like electronic mail.

X-modem—A communication protocol that lets you transfer files over a serial line. See also Y-modem and Z-modem.

xbm—X bitmapped—A graphics format.

XDR—External Data Representation—A data format standard developed by Sun Microsystems that defines data types used as parameters and encodes these parameters for transmission.

Y-modem—A communication protocol that enables you to transfer files over a serial line. See also X-modem and Z-modem.

Z-modem—A communication protocol that enables you to transfer files over a serial line.

Glossary

Index

Q-R

REGISTRATION CARD

MCSE Test Prep: TCP/IP

Name _____ Title _____

Company_____ Type of business _____

Address _____

City/State/ZIP _____

Have you used these types of books before? ☐ yes ☐ no

If yes, which ones? _____

_____

How many computer books do you purchase each year? ☐ 1–5 ☐ 6 or more

How did you learn about this book? _____

Where did you purchase this book? _____

Which applications do you currently use? _____

_____

Which computer magazines do you subscribe to? _____

_____

What trade shows do you attend? _____

_____

Comments: _____

_____

_____

Would you like to be placed on our preferred mailing list? ☐ yes ☐ no

☐ **I would like to see my name in print!** You may use my name and quote me in future Que products and promotions. My daytime phone number is: _____

Que Publishing   201 West 103rd Street ◆ Indianapolis, Indiana 46290 USA

Fax to 317-817-7448

Fold Here